# Wasp Studies Afield

PHIL RAU AND NELLIE RAU

*with an introduction by*

*WILLIAM M. WHEELER*

DOVER PUBLICATIONS, INC.
NEW YORK

This Dover edition, first published in 1970, is an unabridged and unaltered republication of the work originally published by Princeton University Press in 1918.

*Standard Book Number: 486-22536-4*
*Library of Congress Catalog Card Number: 75-106487*

Manufactured in the United States of America
Dover Publications, Inc.
180 Varick Street
New York, N.Y. 10014

# PREFACE

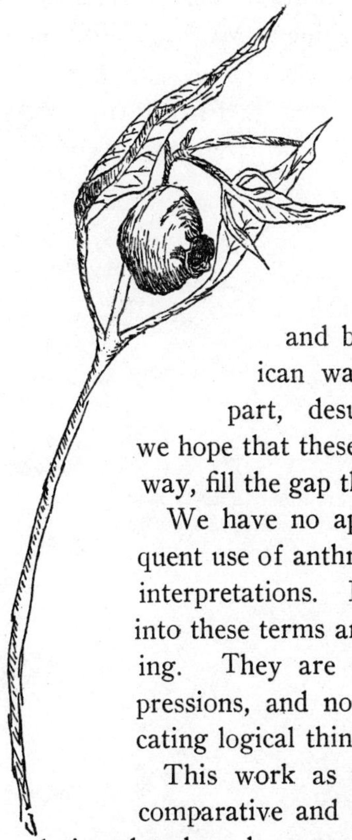

The present volume embodies the results of four years of out-of-door study of some of our most interesting and highly developed insects, in their native haunts, while pursuing their occupations in their own way. Biological and behavior work on the American wasps has been, for the most part, desultory and incomplete, and we hope that these chapters may, in their small way, fill the gap that exists.

We have no apology to make for the frequent use of anthropomorphic ideas, terms and interpretations. However, one must not read into these terms any subtle metaphysical meaning. They are used as apt descriptive expressions, and not for the purpose of predicating logical thinking to these creatures.

This work as a whole is descriptive; the comparative and philosophical, as well as the correlative, data have been reserved for a later volume.

Unless otherwise stated, all of the observations were made at St. Louis or within a radius of thirty miles of that city. The sketches for the illustrations were made in the field and executed in their final form by Dr. Gustave Dahms.

A debt of gratitude is due to Dr. C. H. Turner of Sumner High School of this city for critically reading the manuscript, and to Dr. L. O. Howard and the various specialists connected with the United States Department of Agriculture and the Smithsonian Institution whose names appear in brackets throughout this work we desire to express our thanks for the identification of the various insects. and especially is our gratitude due to Mr. S. A. Rohwer for much taxonomic information.

PHIL RAU,
NELLIE RAU.

SAINT LOUIS, MO.
November 29, 1917.

# CONTENTS

# ILLUSTRATIONS

*"Comparative Psychology is an as yet almost unexplored territory and but little understood, for want of approaching it by the best side, that is to say, by carefully made observations. It is involved either in metaphysical dogmas, * * * or in shallow anthropomorphism which confounds inherited instinct and its automatisms with the plastic judgment of the individual, based upon memory and the association of memories or sensory impressions. * * * Let us be thoroughly imbued with the truth that each species and even each polymorphic animal form has its special psychology, which should be especially studied, and which depends on the one hand, upon the development of its muscles and senses, and on the other, upon that of its brain."*

—FOREL, "The Senses of Insects."

# WASP STUDIES AFIELD

## INTRODUCTION

If any excuse were needed for welcoming another work in addition to the nearly three hundred books and articles that have been published on the habits of the solitary wasps, it would suffice to point to the fact that no other group of insects has so fascinated and baffled the student of animal behavior, the psychologist and the philosopher. When among contemporary generalizers we find an eminent psychologist, William McDougall, claiming for the solitary wasps "a degree of intelligence which (with the doubtful exception of the higher mammals) approaches most nearly to the human," and the illustrious Bergson using the same insects as paradigms of instinct in the sense of "intuition" as contrasted with "intelligence," there is surely need of a renewed presentation of facts already established, of the publication of new observations and of a serious attempt at dispassionate interpretation like that made in the present volume.

The solitary wasps comprise some 10,000 described species scattered over the torrid and temperate regions of the globe and representing a number of more or less closely related natural families of Hymenoptera. To the entomologist these wasps are of unusual interest for several reasons. First, they are in physical structure the most superbly specialized of insects, so that they bear to creatures like the beetles, flies, and grasshoppers, somewhat the same relation that the members of the cat family bear to the rodents, ruminants and insectivores. Even the social Hymenoptera seem to have a less perfected nervous and muscular organization and are certainly less beautifully formed and colored. Second, this unusual physical endowment is correlated, as would be expected, with extraordinary industries, or behavior. Certainly, with the single exception of the social Hymenoptera and the Termites, no insects show such a range of activities as the solitary wasps. Third, they are the lineal descendants of forms which gave rise to the social Hymenoptera. This seems to be so evident that Handlirsch actually derives the bees from the Sphegid, the social wasps from the Eumenid and the ants from the Scoliid wasps, and Roubaud has recently been able to detect in the genera *Synagris* and *Belonogaster* of the Belgian Congo a most interesting series of behavioristic transitions between the solitary and social wasps. And fourth, the ancestry of the solitary species themselves presents an interesting, though more debatable problem, owing to the fact that the group appears fully developed, at least so far as the families Mutillidæ and Scoliidæ are concerned, in the Baltic Amber of lower Tertiary age. Although no species have been found in older geological formations we must suppose, nevertheless, that the group goes back to the Cretaceous and probably even to the Jurassic or Triassic. Hence the evolution of the solitary wasps has extended over a period of at least four to six million years. We are not, therefore, greatly surprised to find that they exhibit such a diversity of habits, especially when we remember that the whole mammalian class, man, of course, included, has had a shorter evolution.

There is another peculiarity of the solitary wasps which is connected with their geological origin and history. The authors of this book repeatedly call attention, especially in their account of the Bembicids (Chapter I), to the fact that these insects are very strongly attached to their nesting sites and stick to them generation after generation. Such a habit has the earmarks of great antiquity and seems to indicate that the present type of nesting site is like the one in which the group originated. This is confirmed by the fact that the group as a whole prefers to nest in dry, sunny, sandy or gravelly soil and is therefore most abundantly represented by species and individuals in the deserts of North Africa, the Southwestern United States, Central Australia, etc., or in similar xerothermal localities of more limited area in other parts of the world (sand-dunes, pine-barrens, dry banks, roads, paths, etc.). Probably, therefore, the group originated during some period of the Mesozoic when there were large tracts of elevated, arid land in the interior of the continents, and this may account for our failure to find any fossil remains of the primitive ancestral forms. In this connection it is interesting to note that the work on the habits of the solitary wasps is mostly confined to particular countries in which the physical conditions are such as I have described. Thus the most important contributions to our knowledge by European observers such as Dufour, Fabre, Picard, Bordage, Roubaud and Ferton, have come from Southern France, Corsica and North Africa or from the tropics, and the more important observations of American investigators, such as Riley, Williston, the Peckhams, Hartman, Hungerford, Williams, Iseley, Barth and the Raus, have been made in the Middle Western and Southwestern States.

The fact that the solitary wasps have so many and such intricate relations with their inorganic and living environment renders their study in the laboratory impossible or, at any rate, very inadequate. A few habits, such as the method of constructing the nest among the mason wasps, can be observed in the laboratory, and sometimes with remarkable results as shown by Bordage's work on *Pison* and *Trypoxylon* in the Island of Reunion, but a knowledge of the complete cycle of behavior of any single species cannot be thus obtained. Field study is therefore indispensable and this demands acute powers of observation, much patience and no little mere physical endurance. Still the limitations of such study are obvious. The finding of the insects and their nests is a matter of chance and frequently only glimpses of their behavior are obtainable so that the whole cycle of behavior has to be pieced together from fragmentary observations and often requires the labor of several observers extending over many seasons. Hence the incompleteness of many accounts in the literature. A good example of this limitation is seen in the present volume in the interesting account of the extraordinary parasitic habits of *Stizus unicinctus*.

Another limitation in field study lies in one's inability to estimate the previous experience of the wasps under observation. Usually the insects are first encountered while engaged in some activity which may or may not have been repeated on some former occasion, such as making the nest or provisioning it, and as they undoubtedly profit by experience and form definite habits, what is evidently an important factor in the performance of the particular activity under observation cannot be taken into consideration. This lacuna is partially bridged in Chapter XII of the present book by a valuable study of individual experience in one of the primitive wasps, *Polistes*.

Even more serious is the limitation to the experimental method in the field. It is, of course, essential for descriptive and other purposes to ascertain by simple observation the course of the normal routine activities of the insect in its natural environment, but it is also of great importance to know what the insect is and is not capable of doing. This can be accomplished only by means of experiment; and experimentation in the field is a rather mild procedure compared with what can be accomplished under the rigorous and indefinitely variable control of the laboratory. Still results of considerable value have been obtained by simple field experimentation as will be apparent to the reader of the ingenious studies of Fabre, the Peckhams and the Raus.

Although the activities of only a few hundred solitary wasps have been carefully observed, we may be sure that every one of the 10,000 described species has its own peculiar behavior. In the non-parasitic forms this appears as a complex cycle, the more important component minor cycles, or phases of which are the digging or construction of the nest, the capture and stinging of the insect or spider prey, oviposition and the sealing of the nest entrance. But the sequence and details of these cycles is subject to great specific and sometimes to considerable individual variation. Thus the sequence of the three first cycles in many species of Sphegids is nest—prey—egg, but in Psammocharids it is commonly prey—nest—egg, and in the Eumenids nest—egg—prey. This is also the sequence in social wasps (*Polistes, Vespa,* etc.). In parasitic species the behavior is, of course, peculiarly modified in adaptation to that of the host.

In their interpretation of wasp behavior the Raus agree essentially with nearly all previous investigators as could be shown by quotations from Marchal, Picard, Bordage, Adlerz, the Peckhams, Hartman and others. Most of the activities can be readily interpreted as chain-reflexes, or "instincts" in the usual biological sense of the term. They are relatively fixed or stereotyped and undoubtedly hereditary and therefore represent the most ancient and most solidified complex of the behavioristic cycle. But there stand out from this complex many activities which are much less mechanized and of such a nature as to demonstrate that the wasps possesss emotions and associative memory, that they exercise discrimination and choice, that they learn by experience and form habits in the restricted sense of the term and that they can modify their behavior adaptively in response to unusual stimuli on the basis of previous experience and therefore behave, to a limited extent, like intelligent beings. Such an interpretation will be accepted by any unbiassed student of the solitary wasps, and those who hold it may be classed as the moderates among behaviorists.

There are, however, three classes of extremists—the mystery-mongers, the simplicists and the humanizers—who fail to take account of all the facts and find support for their opinions in particular aspects of wasp behavior. Fabre may be classed among the mystery-mongers, because when he turned to the interpretation of the wonderful facts he had so carefully observed, his final appeal was always to some mysterious cause. This is best seen in his interpretation of the stinging of the prey as the expression of an inscrutable, intuitive knowledge of the prey's nervous anatomy—a view which Bergson incorporated in his philosophy of instinct. Fabre's treatment of the wasp's homing activities and of her method of finding her prey are similarly attributed to her possession of mysterious senses. This mental attitude was due to preconceptions to which I shall return presently. The simplicists are preoccupied with the reflex or tropistic, i.e., the mechanized behavior. At least one of them, Bethe, is also as much of a mystery-monger as Fabre. Loeb and Bohn have no first hand acquaintance with the wasps and are influenced by their knowledge of the lower invertebrates and insects whose behavior is so highly and consistently mechanized that evidence of its plasticity or modifiability are feeble or difficult to observe. The humanizers, who interpret animals like the wasps as if they were miniature men, are rarely met with at the present time, except among the writers of certain nature books.

The case of Fabre requires some further comment. Acquaintances, who are not entomologists but who read his "Souvenirs" with delight, frequently ask whether I regard him as a reliable chronicler of the habits of insects. I usually reply that, in my opinion, Fabre, Latreille and Réaumur are the three greatest entomologists, but that we must make due allowance in Fabre's writings for certain preconceptions, which, strangely enough, seem actually to heighten the merit and beauty of his work. He was trained as a physicist, chemist and mathematician and when he came to study insects he carried with him the point of view of the student of the inorganic sciences and was therefore interested in establishing clean-cut laws. Owing to this tendency and a belief in the scholastic conception of instinct he naturally stressed and schematized the normal course of behavior in the insects. Although he noted many variations in their activity, these evidently appeared to him as so many perturbations or accidents which were interesting only in so far as they helped to define his essentially static interpretation. They were, in other words, merely the exceptions that prove the rule. Hence his descriptions and discussions leave an impression of elegance and finality like a demonstration in mathematics or physics and therefore appeal more strongly to philosophers like Bergson than to the modern biologist who has been so often deceived by clean-cut theories concerning living organisms that he has grown timid and suspicious. Then it must be remembered that Fabre was unable to appreciate the variations of behavior because he was too set in his ways of thinking when the "Origin of Species" appeared to acquire any sympathy with evolutionary theories. If these considerations be borne in mind it is not difficult to estimate the value of Fabre's work. He is, indeed, so preeminent in the wealth and precision of his observations, in the ingenuity of his experimentation and in literary expression, that his "Souvenirs" will always endure.

The variations which to Fabre were more or less negligible necessarily at once assumed great importance when biologists became evolutionists. In fact, the variations in behavior, because they were considered to be the essential materials of evolution, became, if anything, even more interesting than the routine, mechanized activities. The first among entomologists to recognize the evolutionary importance of behavioristic variations was Paul Marchal in 1887 in his study of a solitary wasp, *Cerceris ornata,* and since that time all students of insect behavior have focussed their attention on the variations. This is as apparent in the present volume as in the works of Marchal, the Peckhams, Adlerz, Ferton, Iseley and others, and could not well be otherwise, for all biologists are now thoroughgoing evolutionists.

In one other respect, also, the Raus have followed a commendable tradition in the presentation of their observations. Réaumur in his "Memoirs," published in 1734 to 1742, was one of the first entomologists to write on the behavior of insects in such a manner as to attract and instruct the general reader. Fabre adopted a similar method of presentation but greatly excelled his eighteenth century predecessor in literary power. That the American is as appreciative as the European public of this form of writing is shown by the success of the Peckhams' work on the solitary wasps. I feel sure that "Wasp Studies Afield" will meet with a like reception.

W. M. Wheeler.

Harvard University,
June 10, 1918.

# CHAPTER I

## Some Bembicine Wasps

*Bembix nubilipennis* Cress. [S. A. Rohwer].

The *Bembix* population burst upon us with a suddenness which startled us into full attention at once. We had crossed the field day after day, and, on that very day, June 16, 1914, had passed by this certain bald, bare space in the field which the boys of the neighborhood had, for a number of years, kept packed hard for their Sunday baseball game (fig. 2); but all had then, only an hour before, been as quiet and lifeless as the grey earth itself. Now the very air above the surface of the bare ground seemed vibrant with the low-flying wasps, which formed a wavering, yellowish-green haze over the smooth, dusty earth.

Any estimate of their numbers was very difficult to obtain from the swiftly-moving swarm, but we suspect that at least one or two hundred were present. The ground was dotted with newly-opened holes,[1] less than one-fourth inch in diameter, which seemed to go straight down and had no trace of excavated dirt around their mouths; this evidence led us to conclude that these wasps had all simultaneously emerged by these exits from their winter quarters, to mingle in this first social frolic or dance. They remained in their unceasing flight at a uniform and constant height, all keeping, with

[1] We counted forty-four holes in one area three feet square, but we could not be certain if all were holes of the emerging *Bembix*.

Fig. 2. The baseball diamond. This bald spot in a large vacant lot in St. Louis was for four summers the nesting-site of *Bembix nubilipennis,* for three years of *Sphex pictipennis* and *Odynerus dorsalis,* and for one season, of several *O. geminus* and one *Philanthus punctatus.* None of these wasps nested at other parts of the field, but at its extreme upper end *Priononyx atratum* abounded, and likewise its enemy *Stizus unicinctus.*

surprising accuracy, on a level about one and one-half to two inches above the ground. No digging or any other enterprise could be seen; every citizen of the colony was mingling in the graceful sun-dance, doing his part blithely and heartily but not too obtrusively. The whole was not a helter-skelter commotion, but a merry whirl to the music of a faint, eerie hum of many wings, with every few moments a rather musical crescendo, which sounded like "zip!," when a whirling pair would suddenly dash off at triple speed on the wing, in the final fling of joyful abandon, for five or six feet, at a speed the eye could scarcely follow. But only for a part of a second did this shrill note come from the highly-vibrant wings; for then the pair separated and returned to the swarm and were instantly lost among their fellows, weaving their way in and out the maze, hovering back and forth in large circles or, with other partners, whirling once around in tiny circles.

In these wild dashes, in which two wasps invariably participated, they grasped each other as if in a violent embrace for just the instant, but we could not ascertain further details, for their movements at this point were so rapid that the eye could not follow them; in the twinkling of an eye they had returned to the common maze again. While we suspected that these embraces were acts of copulation, we had no actual proof. We at once called the performance a sun-dance, yet it must not be understood that they followed an up-and-down or vertical dancing movement; on the contrary, they flew with a rhythmical, gliding motion, like a skater taking one long, smooth stroke after another with scarcely a pause between them. They glided thus to and fro in the prescribed area singly, but frequently two would playfully or flirtatiously whirl around each other without touching (this movement we called waltzing), after which both would usually drop back into the glide with the others, although sometimes they would conclude with one of the wild dashes and embraces just described.

The liveliest part of the dance, when the participants were most numerous, occurred from 9:30 to 10 a. m. By 10:30 they were fewer in number and droning wearily along, and by 11 o'clock, when we were obliged to leave the field, both the activity and numbers were greatly reduced, although we could not discern whither they were disappearing.

Two days later we returned to the field at 7 a. m., eager to witness the continuance of this performance and learn more of its mysteries. The holes were all open, as before; but some minutes elapsed before the first drowsy *Bembix* appeared and took up the low, gliding flight of the day before. Presently others joined it and by 7:30 five were in the flight, gracefully weaving to and fro and occasionally resting for a moment on the grey earth. We did not detect whence they came. They limited their flight strictly to a bare area, which was perhaps fifteen feet in diameter, and did not venture out above the grass which surrounded it on all sides.

By 8 o'clock and during the hour following, perhaps half as many as on the first day were on the field, pursuing the same characteristic low flight, but to-day there was no perceptible hum of wings, no embracings, no "waltzes" and very few of the wild, flirtatious dashes. Instead, from time to time, many were settling on the earth and beginning to dig vigorously. In this digging, they paid no heed to the old holes from which we supposed they had just emerged; but they began energetically digging new burrows, each with a broader, spreading entrance and going down at an angle of approximately 30° to 45° with the surface. It seems that the old holes were merely direct channels of escape from the place where they had lain buried in the earth through the winter, and they did not turn to them at all as further domiciles any more than a chick returns to its egg-shell.

In the following year we took up a diligent watch early in June for this pretty phenomenon. Our expectations waned with long waiting, until we gave up all hope of seeing the frolic again. But on July 4 we were surprised by the outburst of wasps, as sudden as before. The cool months of May and June had probably retarded their emergence until this late date. Even this hypothesis seems almost incredible when we consider that they came from the eggs laid by many different mothers of the previous year from June to September, and that even their nests, which remain open until the larva is ready to pupate, were closed at widely different periods; yet we can now imagine no explanation for the phenomenon other than that the wasps which had come to their maturity simultaneously, or had been lying dormant ready to emerge at the right conditions, had all responded to the dazzling sunshine and the rising temperature of this bright morning and had all dug their way straight out into the light, to mingle in this first social frolic or dance. None of the characteristic nesting holes of *Bembix* could be seen, but the clear-cut, vertical holes by which they had emerged were even more numerous than in the previous year. It was very noticeable too that the group was limited to precisely the areas where the mothers had nested during the previous few years, and where also the sun-dance of the last year had occurred. Thus, for generation after generation, they live and reproduce in the spot where they are born.

Strange indeed is the constancy of instinct in this dancing performance, which they are never taught and for which they have no further use; nevertheless it occurs year after year with each generation, and is in all details the same. In this the second year we were alert to ferret out the answers to the many mysteries which the first year had left us.

On the first day we arrived at the conclusion that there was a great predominance of males. In all the morning's dance we saw only three mating flights. In one of these cases, the united pair were in flight when they were knocked to the ground by two other males. A struggle ensued in which all the males were trying to gain access to the female. They were so intent upon this affair that we could easily get close enough to see all this. Even as we watched, more and more males left the flight and joined the struggling mass, and strove together on the ground before us for several minutes—or maybe it was seconds. So large an assemblage were they, and so intent upon their business, that we could have scooped up the mass in a handful, and the hand would have been filled to overflowing. Eventually the female and one of the males broke away from the mass and sped off on the wing. The train of admirers which followed them formed one of the prettiest sights we have ever witnessed in the insect world; the wasps extricated themselves, one by one, from the heap and followed the pair in unbroken succession, like the wool spun from the distaff, in a long, smooth line of glinting green and yellow, pursuing them so rapidly that before the fugitive female had gone fifty feet they had overtaken her again and formed the teeming mass around her. This struggle continued again for several seconds until one could not tell what had become of the female; but presently, one by one, they abandoned the conflict and returned to the dance.

As we have described for the previous year, their flight was low, near to the ground. The wasps were in motion for hours at a time, never resting; if one chanced to drop out or fall to the earth for an instant, another, perhaps mistaking it for a female, or for some other unknown reason, would immediately pounce upon it with a heavy thump and thus arouse it to return at once to the dance The other two pairs that succeeded in mating made their speedy escape to avoid rivalry. This accounts for the wild dashes outside the area of the dance which we observed in the first year; the escape from the crowd has become so necessary a part of the act of mating that a dash for safety from the throng has become an integral part of every suggestion of mating or false mating.

In the midst of this pretty play we were driven from the field by the human proprietors of the baseball diamond, and when we saw the clouds of dust rise from the trampling of many spiked shoes, it seemed inevitable that the little *Bembix* would be driven from the homes of their ancestors. In the afternoon we returned, but found another set of ball-players and many spectators doing their best to exterminate our pets. The next day at 8:30, however, true to their fatherland they were there and even more abundant than on the first day, although how they could have escaped extermination during the terrible trampling will always be a marvel. Wasps do not migrate far from the place in which they are born. This in a peaceful locality might show only indifference, but when even a noisy American baseball crowd cannot drive them from their home it proves persistence of a most surprising degree. Where these *Bembix* had spent the night we know not. We certainly do not see how it would have been possible for any of them to locate their former holes from which they had emerged on the trampled and dusty earth, even if they had so desired. They may have slept on the grass and weeds surrounding this area, but in extensive studies of the sleep of insects in this field we have never found a *Bembix* asleep on the vegetation. The bare ground presented no newly-dug holes which they might have made for their sleeping quarters, but there were more of the vertical emergence-holes from which newcomers had probably issued.

It was soon apparent that there were more females present than on the previous morning. There was a noticeable reduction in the rivalry when a mating took place. A dozen or more matings occurred in the low flight near to the ground; since there was less rivalry, there was less need of a quick escape, and mating could go on with impunity. In only two cases was there marked rivalry where the mated pairs were knocked to the ground, but instead of the teeming mass of competitors which we had seen the day before there were only three or four pursuers.

The duration of copulation is brief. The time is hard to estimate, but it usually continues through about fifty feet of flight. The females are polyandrous, and all indications are that the males are polygamous. One certain female, which we could easily follow on account of her exceptional color, mated six times in a brief period. We are sure, from close observation, that all of these were cases of actual matings. In each case also the mating was spontaneous, that is the female was not coerced by the eagerness of the males to mate, nor did the rivalry of the males cause the separation. Each time, after the union had been effected, the pair glided near the ground for the usual distance of about fifty feet and separated; the female returned at once to the dance and whirled in and out until she casually picked up another partner when the performance was repeated exactly. Thus with more females in the field on the second day the rivalry was much reduced, and we saw none of the extreme behavior of the males.

This also points to the habit of priority of emergence of the males, as we know occurs in other insects (*cf.* Saturniids[2]).

[2] Rau, Trans. Acad. Sci. St. Louis **23**: 1-78. 1914.

At 2:30 in the afternoon of the second day all the excitement was gone, and all was quiet excepting a half-dozen or so females which were beginning to dig their nesting-burrows. All of our afternoon observations show that the mating flights occur only during the morning.

Every morning, for ten days, we found *Bembix* in the field in the characteristic flight, but as the days passed, the number of those in the sun-dance became less and less while the number of females busily burrowing increased proportionately, until July 14 when the dancing behavior ceased. During the latter part of this period, only an occasional mating was to be seen. What becomes of the males? Do they fertilize the females once for all and promptly die, or do they hide away among the grass to be at hand when needed? We suspect that the former condition holds, for we have never found *Bembix* males in the grass or anywhere except for this one occasion, and I have never seen these wasps mate while nest-building.

Thus it seems that the one gala day which we so fortunately witnessed was not only the first but also the chief festivity of the *Bembix* year, for, although we saw a certain amount of this behavior on subsequent mornings, we never again saw the whole population give itself up to the dance as on this first occasion. After this had waned, only a few wasps were to be found above ground at a time. We do not know whether the males had migrated or perished, but we have every reason to believe that a large number of females were busy working in their underground nests or foraging for food for their young, so that now only a small proportion of the population at a time was in evidence above ground.

The work of most of our solitary wasps in nest building is characterized by an admirable constancy and zeal, but some labor with calmness and patience, and some even so cunningly that we can seldom spy them at their work. But there is no chance for doubt when *Bembix* is abroad; others may equal her in quiet diligence, but she works with unequalled commotion and bluster. Since these are solitary wasps working in communities and have a habit of robbing each other of prey, as we shall see later, they must work nervously. A wholly solitary wasp, or one which works in cooperation instead of competition with others, can afford to work much more calmly and deliberately. She alights upon a spot on the bare surface of the field—a spot without a trace of anything which we can discern to distinguish it from all the rest of the large, bald area several yards in width, yet this particular spot seems to be her choice, and there is something about it whereby she can remember it and distinguish it from all the remainder of the large area in returning to it again and again. Here she at once begins her digging. In this task she always works with an intensity which makes her appear to be driven by some fury. She cannot wait to calmly carry out load after load of dirt, as her sister species do, but, after having torn the earth loose with her mandibles, she scratches or kicks it back with her forelegs straight between her hind legs and far out behind her, in a spurting stream or jet. Much of the time, when she is working on or near the surface of the ground, she throws an almost unbroken stream of dirt out behind her as she digs, often hurling it as far as ten inches back of her. The front legs are provided with bristles which serve as brushes or rakes, with which she sweeps back the dirt. To do this, she is compelled to stoop forward; this gives her a comical appearance of "sweeping with her elbows," as the Peckhams suggest for another species of *Bembix*.

Often she seems dissatisfied with her location and makes several beginnings in as many different places, although we have never been able to see the slightest reason why the old place should have been abandoned, or that the new was in any way its superior. We watched one wasp begin one hole after another. Frequently others would fly down and alight with a thump beside her and violently bump her (but without actually seizing her). Thus disturbed, each time she arose on the wing at once and went off a short distance—a few inches or a few feet—and began a new hole. After eight such interrupted attempts, she seemed to learn not to mind the intruders further, and continued to work on this hole while twenty-four others, one by one, flew down and butted her in this fashion, but finally she gave up this one also after it was well begun. After this we lost sight of her.

This case which we have followed in detail was no exception, but only a sample of the conduct of many of the swarm; some continued work upon their first or second hole, but all who attempted to dig were annoyed thus by the intrusion of others. The significance of this strange form of attention we have never been able to determine with certainty; but we have come to suspect that the intruders, seeing the owner of the burrow digging, suspected that she was entering her nest with a fly and pounced upon her to rob her of it. The Peckhams find the same habit in *B. spinolae.*

On two different occasions, when some of the *B. nubilipennis* were in a bumping mood, one swooped down upon a *Sphex pictipennis* that was carrying her caterpillar. A short struggle ensued, but both times when *B. nubilipennis* flew away, *S. pictipennis* resumed her walk. On one occasion a *B. nubilipennis* dropped a fly which she was carrying to her burrow, and, almost before it struck the ground, a sister wasp swooped down upon it and carried it away.

We do not know how long a time is required in which to dig the burrow, but we have one record of a nest that was begun on July 14, 1915. When we excavated it on July 26, twelve days later, it contained a larva three or four days old, together with four flies. Since the cell at the bottom must have been completed before the egg was deposited, this leaves eight or nine days for the construction of the nest and the incubation of the egg. This seems indeed a long time for so rapid a worker as *B. nubilipennis.* We have occasionally found her resting or loitering in her incomplete or newly-finished burrow, and we know that she does not work on cloudy or rainy days; so when we have made ample allowance of time for these indulgences, this may after all be a fair estimate of the normal time devoted to the making of a nest.

The normal burrow, three-eighths inch in diameter at the top, pierces the ground obliquely and continues downward, at an angle of about 30° to 45° with the surface, for five or six inches to its horizontal oval terminal pocket, which is one inch long by one-half inch in diameter. This cell is hollowed out more from the roof than from the bottom of the burrow. The tunnels are usually approximately straight, and only occasionally swerve to the right or the left; the slope of the tunnel rarely varies.

Most of the nests are normal, as the first two illustrations in fig. 3, but there are occasional exceptions. One nest went down at an angle of 60°; the tunnel was about twelve inches long, with the usual pocket one inch by one-half inch; another nest had a normal gallery, but a cell an inch and a quarter long and one inch wide. Another was normal at the entrance, but soon curved straight downward and then back under itself (lower illustration in fig. 3). But the most novel form of nest which we have yet discovered was one which started down and eastward, at an angle of 30°, for two inches; then turned sharply to the south and downward, at an angle of 45°, for four inches; then con-

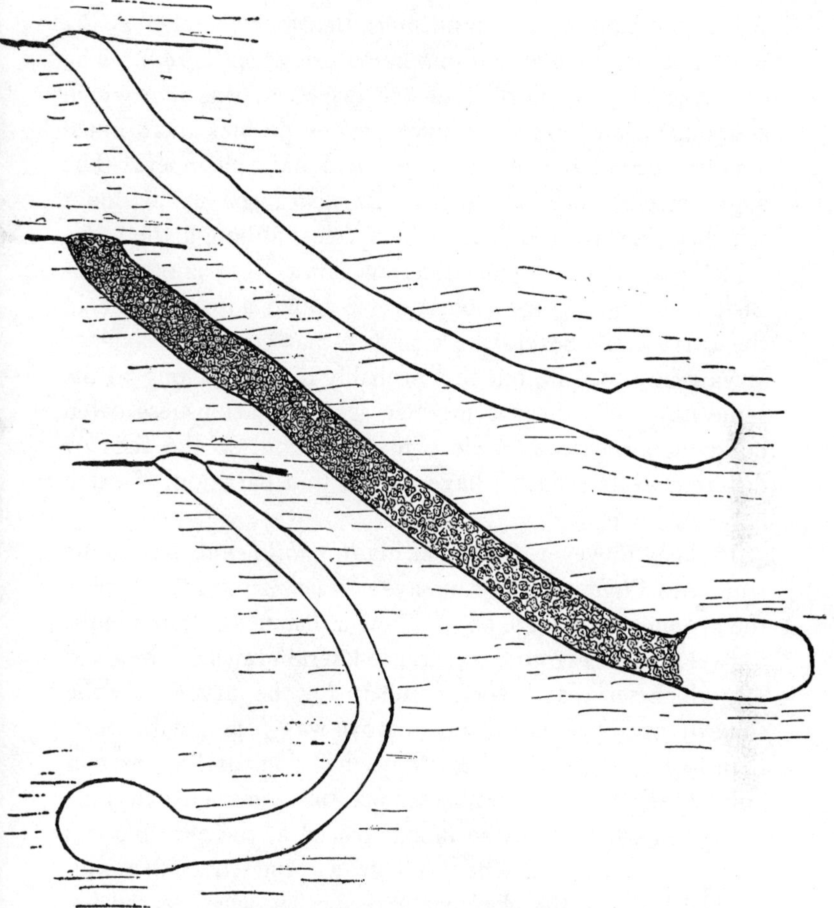

FIG. 3. The burrows of *Bembix nubilipennis.* Two-thirds natural size.

tinued south, at an angle of 30°, for two inches to the unfinished pocket where the owner was at work. It is strange that she should still be extending it after she had worked on it for several days and it was already beyond normal depth.

While we have opened many nests during the two years and found them in various conditions and of slightly varied forms, we have never found more than one chamber at the bottom of the tunnel and one immature wasp therein. The only nest having more than one organism was one which contained a medium-sized larva feeding on flies and a much smaller second one in the same and only chamber. The slight resemblance of the two larvae caused us to doubt whether they were of the same species, although the additional one was a Hymenopterous larva. On another occasion, in digging up a burrow we found a second one in the earth close beside the chamber that contained a large larva ready to spin, but this probably did not belong to the same nest. The wasps in their semi-gregariousness often build their burrows in close juxtaposition, so the cells of different nests seem to have only a thin partition of earth between them.

Parker,[3] however, finds that his *B. nubilipennis* has habits similar to *Philanthus,* for he says: "The burrows * * * enter the ground at an angle of 45°. At a distance of from eight to twelve inches from the entrance lateral branches are given off, which serve as brood chambers for the larvae. At the time of my observation no burrow was found with more than five of these chambers; most had four and a few had only three. In the chambers more than one larva may be reared, in which case the first is placed at the extreme end of the chamber and when full grown and encased a wall is placed across the chamber and another larva reared between this and the main part of the burrow. * * * These observations were made on August 18 and 19, and although many burrows were opened only larvae were found. Many

[3] Ohio Nat. **10**: 163-165. Despite the fact that Cresson described the species in 1872, this is the only paper that we can find which has biological data on this species, excepting Robertson, Trans. Acad. Sci. St. Louis **6**: 458, 1894, who found the adults feeding on the flowers of four species of plants.

of these had completed their growth and were encased in cells * * * but in every instance an immature larva in some stage of development was also found in the burrow. In no case, however, was more than one developing larva found in any burrow. In one burrow with four branches three contained matured and encased larvae and the fourth, just newly constructed, contained two recently killed house-flies, on one of which was found an unhatched egg. From the data given above it would appear that the wasp rears only one larva at a time."

This interesting note recorded from Wilson, Kansas, which differs so widely from our observations on the number of chambers to each burrow, shows that the wasps of Dr. Parker's little colony of *nubilipennis* have acquired the economical adaptation of using their burrows for more than one chamber. It has been a matter of doubt whether *Bembix* makes one burrow and carries that larva through its infancy before beginning the next, or whether she keeps up more than one domicile at a time. The Peckhams think, from some experiments, that *B. spinolae* takes care of only one nest at a time, and from our observations on the permanent closing of the nest early in the season with only a single young one within, we think it probable that, in our colony, the second burrow is constructed only after the first has been completed. When we consider (as will appear later) how poor the dissemination is in this species, we can easily see how a digression of making three to five chambers to a tunnel may easily become a habit and finally a family characteristic and may become constant in the colony. Dr. Parker states that these wasps had nested in this spot annually for a number of years.

Hence the establishment of a very pretty and economical habit. At the same time one must recognize a new habit, correlative of the multiplicity of cells, having arisen here, which, like the new habit just described, would go entirely outside the genus *Bembix*. We know that the digger wasps, *Bembix, Ammophila, Priononyx,* are essentially diggers, but Dr. Parker finds the *Bembix* in his colony taking up mason work also, building partitions to form new cells. "A wall is placed across the chamber and another larva reared between this and the main part of the burrow." It seems incredible that *nubilipennis* could build the wall of dry sand or dust, unless she too has acquired the water-carrying habits of certain *Odynerus*. The fillings of loose, dusty earth, such as she scoops into her holes here, could never be made to serve as a wall across the bulging middle of the chamber. It would be well worth while to make an effort to see how general this new habit has become.

We have so many times found the mother *Bembix* in her burrow when we opened it at any time near or after sunset that we have arrived at the conclusion that she sleeps in her nest, when she has one. We have also found her here safely hidden away on dark or rainy days, for *Bembix* loves only warmth and sunlight. The tunnel is always temporarily closed under these conditions. This is accomplished by the *Bembix* going down into the hole and pushing up loose dirt from below until the mouth of the burrow is completely closed. One morning we found that the dashing rain during the night had packed the soil hard and washed down the loose earth, leaving the hole open. We arrived just in time to see the mother *Bembix* cutting a small area about the opening and kicking the dirt thus loosened into her burrow until the aperture was closed. It seemed that this mother had remained in her burrow all night, with only the usual temporary covering over it, and that the rain had washed down this dust covering and she, unwilling to have herself and her nest exposed thus to danger, was hastening to cover her burrow again, even though she had to dig up the hard-packed earth with her jaws to obtain the necessary filling.

The same morning another *Bembix* alighted upon a particular spot which to us was absolutely indistinguishable from all the rest of the smooth-washed "diamond." She fell industriously to digging, and in a moment opened her tunnel and entered. She had evidently been away from home during the storm and found shelter elsewhere. Even this new condition of the soil about the nest did not confuse her. Some minutes later, upon returning, we were surprised to see the hole again covered, and the topography smooth, but about six inches from the hole (the place was marked or it would have been quite indistinguishable) was much loose dirt which had been swept well away from her door. On one occasion of exceptionally heavy rains the earth from the upper side of the area washed down and deeply covered every trace of their nests; but before evening about a dozen had worked their way out of their holes, none the worse for wet weather.

It was on July 2 of the first year of our observations, or just two weeks after the first emergence and dance of *Bembix,* that we dug out the first nest that was completed and occupied. The waspling was only a tiny larva one-fourth inch long, and was feeding upon its first fly, a delicate little yellow-winged Dipteron. On many occasions thereafter, when we found a very tiny larva feeding, the prey invariably was a very soft, delicate little yellow- or green-winged fly—not the coarse, heavy kind such as house-flies, stable-flies or horse-flies, which the mothers bring in when the larva is stronger. Can human intelligence do better in delicate, maternal care? It was startling at first to see a tiny larva and fly fairly "rattling around" in so large a cavity; but it only proves again the maternal solicitude of Mother *Bembix* who, it seems, knows how to estimate the future needs of space for her growing infant, its food and the usual residue.

We have already stated that this wasp stays with her nest and daily brings in enough fresh flies to meet the needs of the young one until it reaches maturity and pupates. Just how many flies are brought in each day we have never ascertained with accuracy, but we suspect that the food supply varies with the needs of the infant. Also, as we shall see later, this instinct of the mother for providing the daily food for her young is sometimes defective and leads the mother to do various unprofitable things. However, what she does is so wonderful that we shall not presume to criticise her for occasional failures or erratic behavior.

When foraging and bringing in flies, they come and go with surprising rapidity, often making three or four trips in twenty minutes. They alight upon the nest with the fly so well concealed under their bodies, clasped between the middle legs, that we can hardly see it. They never waste a second's time in searching to and fro for their nests, but drop down from flight directly upon them every time. This homing instinct is truly marvellous when we consider that the bare area occupied by their colony is devoid of any apparent landmarks by which they could locate their holes amid the numerous holes of other insects. They work fast and furiously from the instant they arrive, probably to evade parasites, which soon shadow them if they are more than a moment in their work, or to escape attack from their sisters which are hot after them. In a fraction of a minute they dig through the temporary closure of the burrow and scramble in with the fly; in a few seconds they emerge head first, turn around at the brink of the hole, and re-enter at once. For an instant this performance seems strange, but only for an instant; they enter just far enough to go past the loose dirt which has rolled down the sloping channel from the temporary closing, and pause to kick this dirt up in a heap (from within) which almost or entirely closes the hole just beneath the level of the ground. They gauge the strength of the kick with such remarkable accuracy as to throw the dirt to exactly the right point near the top of the burrow, but never out on top of the ground. They usually leave a tiny crevice at the upper side of the hole. This done, they later come squeezing and scrambling out through the loose dirt. Even as they draw their bodies out of the soft earth, they scratch the dirt back to close the hole completely but loosely. They do not leave it open an instant, or in any way give the parasites the least chance of slipping by them. This loose mound is so near to the top of the hole that a few more strokes usually suffice to finish filling it. We have seen the opening smoothly covered with only five strokes. In making these temporary closures, they give little or no attention to packing or smoothing the surface of the ground over the closed nest. Sometimes a wasp will pause a moment to sweep back the surplus loose dirt from around the top of the burrow to a distance of six inches or more before flying away.

The Peckhams, who quote Bates on *Bembix ciliata,* say that this wasp sometimes leaves her door open when off on a fly hunt; she probably does this to save time. *B. nubilipennis* invariably closes her hole on leaving, but we fear she does not burden her soul with anxiety for the value of time, for we have often seen her scrape and scratch at the hard-baked soil about her nest until we thought she would wear her finger-nails off, working for more than an hour to raise a little dust from the hard-packed earth to fill in her burrow.

Thus the temporary closures of the burrows are made when the wasps are coming and going each day, bringing food for their young. In contrast to this we see the final or permanent closure which is made only at the end of the larva's feeding period. The contrast in the methods of effecting the two closings will be at once apparent.

When the wasp has finished feeding the larva, she emerges from the open hole but does not turn around and go right back in, head first, as previously. Instead of going in and kicking the dirt up from the lower part of the channel, she begins scratching and kicking the loose dirt from the surface into the hole behind her, moving forward as she does

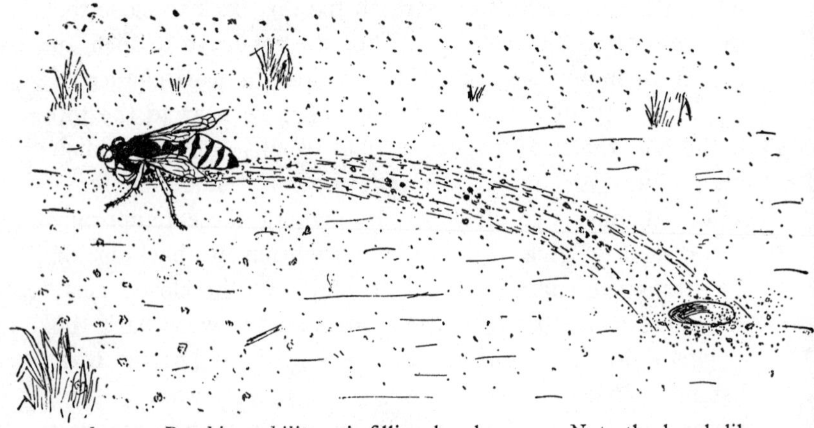

FIG. 4. *Bembix nubilipennis* filling her burrow. Note the brush-like forelegs sweeping the soil under the body, and the accuracy of her aim. Natural size.

so until she is two or three inches away from it. Then she runs to the hole, peeps in, turns around and backs in, kicking, scratching, clawing and crowding the dirt deeper down into the hole and out of sight. Then she comes out and exactly repeats the whole performance several times, each time beginning at the margin of the burrow to scratch the soil back in, and working gradually outward with her face away from the opening. (Fig. 4.) Thus she continues until the hole is filled so near the top that she cannot back down into it any more; then she assumes the same position backwards on the hole and crams and packs the dirt down with her hind pairs of legs and pounds, rubs and punches it down with her abdomen; then brushes more dirt back upon the depression and repeats the packing process two or three times, until the fill is brought up exactly level with the surface of the ground. Having finished tamping the earth she begins sweeping all around, as usual, to remove all traces of her nest from the surface of the ground. Her conduct at this point varies with the conditions; if there is a surplus of loose dirt near the site of the hole, she sweeps it well away and scatters it evenly over a considerable area; if it is bald so that traces of the filled hole may be seen, she sweeps other dust back over it from a distance until no trace of a scar may be seen. When sweeping away from the hole she begins at the outer edge of the patch of dirt, faces the hole and kicks the dust back of her as she moves from side to side and gradually nears the opening, all the time with a stream of dirt spurting out behind her; then she backs off to the periphery of the dusty space again before beginning anew, scattering it further and further from the nest. If, however, she is sweeping dirt toward the hole, she displays far greater skill in estimating the distance and the force necessary to throw the dirt in precisely the right spot. She always works with the hole squarely behind her, so she can throw the dirt back of her. She works fast and furiously in the hot sun, brushing lightly when near the hole and increasing the strength of her throw as she moves further away from it, and, with wonderful judgment of direction and distance of throw, hitting the region of the burrow with astonishing accuracy, from various distances. (See fig. 4.) She moves from side to side as she works, so that her path practically describes arcs of ever-widening circles the center of which is the burrow. When she has reached the limit of her distance from the hole, she does not wander aimlessly over the area, but always returns to the hole to begin a new series of arcs. This marvellous system of covering the ground is more easily made clear by the accompanying diagram (fig. 5). It is interesting to note that the wasp usually confines its sweeping to the area in front and at the sides of the hole, but is rarely seen working behind the hole. Of course this may be due largely to the fact that the loose dirt all lies in front of the burrow where it has been thrown during the digging.

Thus she sweeps, spreads and redistributes the loose surface dust for a foot or more, until, if we have not the exact location of the nest marked, we can seldom find it, so well is it concealed. Then she circles to and fro on the wing an inch or so above the area, surveying it carefully for several seconds, and goes whirling off flirtatiously with the other wasps, which, from time to time, have been dabbing down beside her and bumping her. One *B. nubilipennis* accomplished the permanent closing of her nest in twenty minutes, but they usually require a longer time to finish this critical piece of work.

When we see such highly developed instinct for the care and safeguarding of the young, we are surprised to find that these mothers are often guilty of committing gross errors in the most fundamental points. We watched one wasp working with great care and precision in closing her nest. After the last superficial trace of the hole had been carefully obliterated and the surrounding ground swept clean and she had departed, we opened the burrow in the full expectation of obtaining a mature larva, but we were shocked to find that the larva had pupated long ago and had been dead and rotten for some days at least. No fresh or uneaten flies were in the chamber; only the old débris. What she could have been doing there, or why she was so

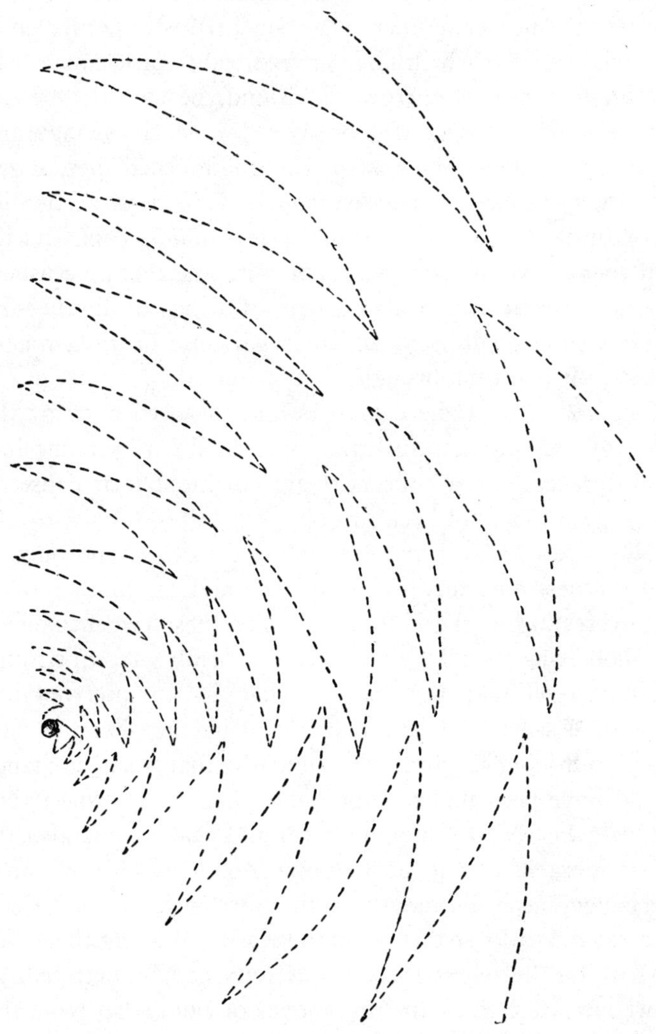

FIG. 5. Diagram showing the systematic method of *Bembix nubilipennis* in sweeping the dust back into her burrow for the permanent closure.

particular in sealing up that dead larva will always be a mystery. Another mother spent equal pains in permanently closing a burrow which later proved to be stark empty. In yet another sealed burrow we found, besides the newly-pupated larva, a spoonful or more of débris—wings and legs—and besides this sixteen whole untouched flies, showing how her solicitude had oversupplied the larva. The flies were all dead; never in dealing with *B. nubilipennis* did we find them alive or paralyzed, nor with the thorax crushed. In this nest we found also a pair of wings of the bee-fly, *Spogostylum anale* Say, which is parasitic on mud-wasps, but here it had been brought in for food.

The contents of the chambers and the occupancy of the holes by the diggers are little understood;[4] as yet, the line of difference between the normal and the abnormal use of the burrows has not been drawn.

Not a few holes have been followed to their end only to find the nest all ready for occupancy and the mother wasp calmly resting at the bottom. Under these circumstances, the hole was usually closed, fairly firmly, from within. Of course, it may be that we chanced to interrupt her at a time when she had just completed her burrow, but this condition occurred so frequently that such a chance would have been highly improbable; hence we suspect that she uses her burrow not only for nidification but also, to a considerable extent, as her own domicile. To be sure, the gallery near the mouth of the burrow is always closed by a mound of loose dirt when the wasp is digging the lower part of the hole, but then the activity can be detected, at short intervals, when the dirt moves or humps up from the

[4] On account of the frequent use of the field by the ball-players, it was impossible to keep in connection with one mother or her one nest long enough to get a connected story. Every effort was made to revisit marked nests, but in every case the boys with the spiked shoes obliterated them.

pressure of the wasp pushing up from beneath, or occasionally the wasp itself will come pushing its way out backwards through the loose soil, emerging not a little dishevelled, and shake itself vigorously to free it from the clinging dirt, precisely as a dog shakes himself upon coming out of his bath. She then proceeds to dig out and sweep back the dirt she has brought to the top of the hole. But at these resting-periods mentioned above, no such movements are seen for days at a time, so we suspect that she is merely resting and enjoying the security of her home. But is she only gratifying a whim, or may she be waiting for the maturation of her ova or some other physiological phenomenon? The population diminishes at the end of the season; perhaps the old adults simply go off and die after they have completed their season of nidification.

On this occasion we might mention one other form of mortality which is yet unexplained. Early each year, when digging out the burrows of various species, we come upon a few subterranean chambers, which have never been opened, containing a dead *Bembix*. Whether these are young wasps which have safely arrived at maturity but have died before emerging, as often happens in other species, or whether they are parent wasps which have died while in the burrows, we had no way of ascertaining.

The contents of a few nests have puzzled us utterly. One hole[5] had long roused our curiosity as we watched and waited for its permanent sealing. Finally, one evening at twilight, we broke open its temporary closure and found therein six *B. nubilipennis* ready to spend the night. Two of these were captured and proved to be females. Since we now know of the male priority of emergence and disappearance, we feel fairly safe in assuming that all of these were

[5] The Sleep of Insects. *Ann. Ent. Soc. Amer.* 9: 240. 1916.

females. On one occasion we saw a *Bembix* having much difficulty in keeping out a sister wasp, whose home it seems had been destroyed and who did not seem to care that it was not her own hole which she was entering. This gives us a possible clue to an explanation of the presence of six wasps in one burrow; perhaps they had returned to the field at twilight, found themselves homeless after the ball-game, and had found it convenient to crowd into the same opening for a night's shelter.

The *Bembix* do not seem to be so discriminating in regard to the choice of their prey as are some other wasps. So long as they can pick up flies, they do not seem to be particular about the variety. We have found in their burrows: *Lucilia caesar* Linn. [F. Knab], *Spogostylum anale* Say [F. Knab], *Sarcophaga sp.* [F. Knab], *Sparnopolius brevirostris* Macq. [F. Knab] house flies, stable flies and many more species which could not conveniently be identified.

The amount of food consumed by one of these youthful gourmands is quite astonishing. One which we brought up from infancy by hand consumed seventy-nine house-flies before it spun its cocoon. Another consumed the forty-nine house-flies and one large stable fly which had been given it, and then attempted to spin its cocoon. In the smooth tin box it made only a silky carpet (fig. 6 *a*). After that, thirty-six more house-flies were introduced, and it devoured twenty-six of them in spite of the fact that it had already begun to spin. How many flies the mother provides for a single larva has never been ascertained; but after its pupation there is usually from a teaspoonful to a tablespoonful of legs and wings remaining. Occasionally we find that a mother has devotedly brought in more flies than the larva has been able to consume; but some of our work leads us to suspect that these gluttonous young are more often willing and capable of consuming even a larger amount of food than the mother provides.

The larvae kept in tin boxes or in vials were unable to spin the usual cocoon, owing to the fact that there was no dirt to blend with the silk. The pupal cases spun in the natural habitat are hard, tightly woven cocoons made of silk blended with earth. (See fig. 6 *b, c, d.*)

In keeping *Bembix* pupal cases at home we often found

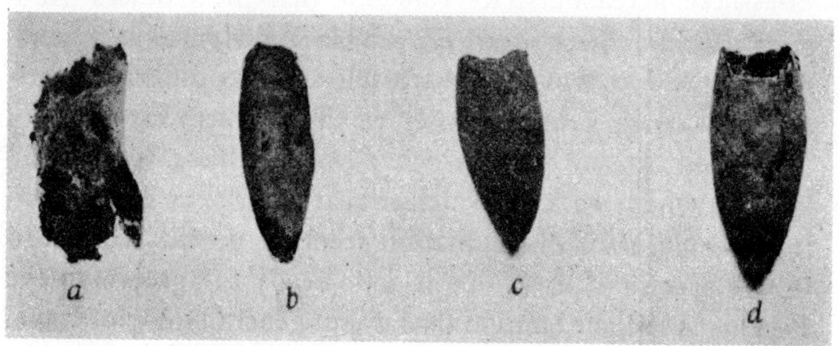


FIG. 6. The cocoons of *Bembix nubilipennis.* Exact size. *a,* abnormal cocoon; *b,* normal one; *c* and *d,* empty cocoons showing apertures made by emerging wasps.

the organism within infested by the tiny Hymenopterous parasite *Melittobia sp.* These no doubt had escaped from some *Pelopoeus* nests in the same room, and very probably, under natural conditions, *B. nubilipennis* is not pestered by them. One *Bembix* burrow was observed which was normally filled in, but many ants were coming and going through the small passageway which they had made through the loose dirt. When this nest was opened it became apparent that they were after the débris of dead flies—wings, heads, legs, etc. The wasp larva had pupated, unharmed, but the musty débris was alive with two species of mites. Dipterous parasites shadow *Bembix,* and a small female Mutillid abounds in this area, but neither of these has been seen to actually enter their holes.

Our present evidence indicates that there is only one generation per year of *B. nubilipennis*. From the time of emergence, in June or early July, the females go on with nidification until the middle of September. We do not know how many nests each constructs during this season, but they ought to make several in order to offset the high mortality and keep up so large a population. The numbers gradually diminish as autumn approaches; since we never see them elsewhere hereabouts, we conclude that the mothers gradually die off. They spend the winter in the pupal stage and, despite the fact that they reach this stage at different dates, they all emerge simultaneously when the warm rays call.

The persistence with which *Bembix* adhere to the one location which we have watched year after year is astonishing. Truly, their dissemination seems to be *nil*. In regard to this species at least, one is soon ready to agree with the Peckhams in their opinion that wasps generally do not travel far from the place of their birth. Here the wasps of our particular colony have had at their disposal a pasture equal in size to six city blocks in which to choose their nesting-site, yet year after year they limit themselves strictly to two distinct corners of a base-ball diamond, in the middle of this field. Here they suffer weekly, and sometimes daily, persecutions under the spiked shoes of the boys; they are routed from their work in the middle of the day and their nests are obliterated in the powdered earth, and not a few must suffer death in the mêlée; yet not even this pressure causes them to move twenty-five feet to one side, where they might enjoy peace and prosperity. The fact that each successive generation should show the same choice and the same persistence is all the more astonishing. In another vacant lot a mile away was another colony which, to our knowledge, persisted in like manner on a small area for three years. Finally a building was erected on the site and the *Bembix* population must have been exterminated, for afterward the country roundabout was scoured in search of them, but no trace of their having settled elsewhere was ever found, although just across the road from the lot was a large tract of vacant land thoroughly suitable to their needs. In the two colonies in corners of the baseball diamond the numbers are becoming fewer and fewer, so if they do not migrate they will probably soon meet with extermination.

*Bembix spinolae* Lep. [S. A. Rohwer].

Other observers, notably the Peckhams[6] and Parker,[7] have already written upon the life of this species, so we offer no new data excepting a contribution of one or two eccentric circumstances.

One burrow which we discovered on Howard's Hill on September 25, 1916, seemed externally a typical *Bembix* hole. It pierced the earth diagonally, and much loose sand was strewn about the mouth of the burrow. It went down thus for an inch and a half, then turned abruptly at right angles, and from there it continued downward in a spiral, so that the pocket was directly beneath the entrance. The total length of this spiral burrow was six inches, and the terminus was three inches below the surface. We saw no obstructions in the soil which would necessitate such contortions in the channel. In the normal nest (according to Peckhams) the tunnel goes down obliquely to a point from three to five inches below the surface of the ground.

At the bottom of the hole we found the mother *Bembix* together with a medium-sized, healthy larva, thirty large

[6] Bull. Wisc. Geol. & Nat. Hist. Surv. **2**: 58-72. 1898.

[7] Proc. U. S. Nat. Mus. **52**: 127-131. 1917.

living Diptera larvae, four adult bee-flies, *Sparnopolis brevirostris* Macq. [F. Knab], the remains of eighty-five more of the same, and the remains of one *Lucilia caesar* L. [F. Knab]. Judging from the enormous amount of food remains when the feeding stage of the larva was as yet far from completed, and the presence of a healthy medium-sized *Bembix,* we can only conclude that the Diptera were not true parasites, since they had not attacked the larva of the *Bembix,* but merely inquilines or impostors who depend upon the mother *Bembix* to work extraordinarily hard to keep them, as well as her own young, supplied with meat. What a terrible toll, that she must provide constantly for thirty others in order that her own may live!

One wonders why the Dipterous larvae, so many in number, spared the *Bembix* larva, for it certainly would have made a fine meal. We do not wish to speculate excessively, yet it is probably only fair to breathe our suspicions on the subject. If they should devour the *Bembix* larva, it would satisfy them for only a short time, but with the demise of the mother's child their further supply of food would be cut off, since probably the rightful infant in the cell is the stimulus for the mother to continue replenishing the food supply for all of them as fast as it is exhausted. With these thirty-one mouths to feed daily, it is little wonder that the mother had to sacrifice all of her leisure that might have been applied to improved methods of domestic economy.

We do not pretend to say that the fly larvae knew the result of this action and behaved accordingly, and numerous other instances of the same kind would be required even to prove that this is a case of habit or blind instinct; yet if it were proved to be such, it would be no more wonderful than many of the delicate adaptations already known to exist in the insect world.

*Microbembix monodonta* Say [S. A. Rohwer].

We saw this little banded *Microbembix* open her hole and enter, and close her nest preparatory to leaving, whereupon we captured her. The hole went down diagonally for seven inches, then turned at right angles and continued its downward course for six inches more, where it terminated without either pocket or prey. The end was six and one-half inches below the surface of the earth.

A second one was seen to leave her hole, after carefully covering it up. The illustration (fig. 7) tells better than words the nature of the burrow. The nesting-site was the semi-barren, sandy area (fig. 8) along the river at Lake View, Kansas. The total length of the hole was fourteen inches. The pocket was hollowed out from the ceiling of the burrow. Great was our surprise upon finding in here two beetles, *Neoharmonia velutina* [H. S. Barber] and *Hippodamia 13 punctata* [H. S. Barber], two tree-hoppers, *Draeculacephala mollipes* Say [E. H. Gibson] and *Phlepsius irroratus* Say [E. H. Gibson], one spider, a *Xysticus nervosus* Banks [C. L. Shoemaker], and one ant, *Pheidole vinelandica* Forel [W. M. Wheeler]. All six items of prey were dead, dried and hard. No egg was found with the food. We can hardly, indeed, call this collection by the term prey, because it was only a collection of dead carcasses which the wasp had garnered. Hartman too finds that *M. monodonta* takes home insects that are already dead. His list includes: slender red caterpillars, the leg of a grasshopper, small queen ants, large red ant, flies of various kinds, bugs belonging to five different genera, tree-hoppers, polistes wasp, freshly-killed grasshopper, a dry Mutillid and old Orthopterous pupal cases with dry, dead pupae inside. A lengthy and very interesting account of the mating behavior, the nesting-habits, food habits, etc., of this species is included

FIG. 7. The burrow of *Microbembix monodonta*

in the paper by Parker.[8] His records of nest provisioning, based on several observations, differ from ours above. He

[8] Proc. U. S. Nat. Mus. **52**: 134-140. 1917.

says that when the burrow is completed, a single egg is placed in the brood chamber, at the extreme end. This is firmly fastened in an upright position in the sand of the floor. No food is placed in the burrow until after the egg has hatched in the course of two or three days. Our single wasp had already provisioned the nest with six dead insects and had left the nest presumably for more, but a very careful search revealed no egg nor larva. Whether the Ohio wasps differ in their ways of housekeeping from the Kansas wasps, or whether ours was only an eccentric individual we do not know. The crooked nesting burrow described above seems also to be only an eccentricity. These points only show that wasps as well as other beings may express, consciously or unconsciously, their individuality.

Barth,[9] in speaking of this genus and also of *Bembix*, says the "Larvae are fed from day to day, nests remaining open during excursions." This sweeping statement cannot apply to *Microbembix monodonta*.

*Bicyrtes quadrifasciata* Say [S. A. Rohwer].

In a semi-barren, sandy area (fig. 8) beside the Kaw River at Lake View, Kansas, we found our only specimens of *B. quadrifasciata*. Parker[10] has described very well her manner of approaching her nest as she returns to it. She returns on the wing, flying high in the air, and poises in mid-air ten or twelve feet above the hole, then drops straight down, as if with a parachute, digs a moment at her very feet where she alights, and lo! her burrow opens. Truly, the students of animal psychology who are trying to solve the homing of insects have here an interesting problem.

[9] Bull. Wisc. Nat. Hist. Soc. **8**: 118. 1910.
[10] Loc. cit. p. 134.

She follows the same method in departing from the nest or in starting homeward from the field when foraging. She rises straight up in the air, so high that it is difficult to follow her with the eye in the dazzling sunlight, then darts away horizontally above the heads of most living things.

We once watched one climbing in and out among the branches of a cocklebur plant, carrying her little bug snugly beneath her, resting once or twice on a leaf. All at once, without provocation, she leaped up into the air and flew straight upward, higher, higher, until we lost her in the dazzling sunlight, but in a few seconds she came down from her highway in the skies, straight down to a spot only ten feet distant from where she had started. Here she scratched on the ground at her feet, opened her hole and went in without letting go her prey. She remained within for about fifteen minutes, and closed the hole lightly behind her with loose sand when she came out before departing upward.

The prey which she brought into the nest was, in all cases observed, a small bug. She clasped it beneath her abdomen, and in the one or two cases which we have been able to observe minutely, carried it with the bug's ventral side toward her own. The four bugs found in one nest were all somewhat similar but of different species, all nymphs of Pentatomidae [E. H. Gibson].

The two holes which we dug out were unlike. They resembled a *Bembix nubilipennis* hole in general appearance, penetrating the ground at an angle of thirty to forty degrees with the surface. One was twelve inches long, and straight; the other was seventeen inches in total length, and the large, terminal pocket was nine and a half inches below the surface of the ground. The burrow curved irregularly, forming half a spiral.

FIG. 8. A sandy area on the Kaw River where *Microbembex monodonta* and *Bicyrtes quadrifasciata* abound.

*Sphecius speciosus*[11] Drury [S. A. Rohwer].

Three individuals of this species, in company with Diptera and a *Papilio* butterfly, were busily feeding upon a mass of foamy sap that exuded from a wound near the base of a huge sun-flower stalk. They were determined to get the sap, and when we attempted to take them they expressed their indignation at being disturbed by the loudest noise that we have ever heard a wasp make. They buzzed and flew about, and always made attempts to return to their bacchanal. The sap seemed to have fermented in the summer heat, so perhaps like ensilage it was particularly exciting to animal appetites.

The next day we again found these *S. speciosus* attracted to the sap, greedily drinking their fill, and boisterously buzzing, bumping and whirling around at intervals. Now they had for their companions several horse-flies, *Tabanus exul* O. S. [F. Knab], many smaller Diptera, one click-beetle, *Ludius attenuatus* [J. A. Hyslop], a half-dozen *Polistes annularis,* one spotted cucumber beetle and one blue *Papilio.* Hence it seems that their pulque was popular in insect society.

Hungerford and Williams[12] found that this wasp quarreled with *Chlorion caeruleum* for the sap oozing from the willows. Riley[13] has worked up a beautiful account of the behavior of this species, a popular version of which may be found in Howard's Insect Book, pp. 22-25, or Weed's Life Histories of American Insects, pp. 157-160.

[11] Of the sub-family Stizinae.

[12] Ent. News **23**: 246. 1912.

[13] Insect Life **4**: 248-252. 1892.

# CHAPTER II

## Behavior of Wasps Belonging to the Family Pompilidae

*Pompiloides tropicus* Linn. [S. A. Rohwer].

One mild, sunny September morning we were walking across the field when we were startled to espy a telltale hole in the path. It was only the beginning of a burrow, but in a most hazardous situation, right in the beaten path over which hundreds of workmen passed daily, and also at its intersection with the wagon-road; yet, because the spot was void of vegetation and sunny, the wasp had proceeded to make her nest there, as if unaware of any danger. The ground was dry and hard enough almost to break a pocket-knife to dig in it, while the surface had been ground by the tread of many feet into deep, fine dust. The hole was perhaps one-half inch deep; the spider, occasionally twitching, lay only an inch away. From this it is at once apparent that this wasp does not dig the hole first and then fetch her prey, for this hole was only begun, and the spider, an immature male *Lycosa frondicola* Em. [N. Banks], lay in front of it.

The black Pompilid, conspicuous against the grey dust, with its broad orange band on the abdomen, was seen hunting diligently all about the vicinity, eight or ten feet away. She returned to the hole once, but we had tampered with it, knocking in a lot of loose dust in trying to break through the hard crust of earth for her, so she left it at once and continued her search six feet to the west. She eventually came back and tried to dig in three or four places near her original location, but the loose surface dirt always rolled in upon her. She left again and wandered on foot down the road; finally after ten minutes she returned on the wing, found the spot without difficulty and again dug in a hole which promised to be successful. A caterpillar hurried by very near to her and seemed to make her uneasy, so she drew her spider back three or four inches. Again she departed for a while on an unexplained jaunt. Meanwhile we brushed the loose surface dust aside to give her access to the soil which was firm enough for her to dig in, and, with a knife, began a new hole. Her spider still lay near by. A parasitic bee-fly, which had been hovering about inquisitively from time to time, hovered over our hole the same as over hers. The wasp came back thrice but did not seem to recognize the area.

Round and round the dusty margin the wasp searched anxiously, and finally ventured to cross the area (six inches in diameter) from which the dust had been removed, peeped once into the hole which had formerly been hers, and scuttled away—frantic. During her absence we replaced some dust around the hole; still she did not recognize it nor her spider, one inch distant. She came within a few inches of it on several occasions, but always searched over the dusty periphery and avoided the open area with the artificial hole exactly where her own had been. We finally placed the spider on the dust in the region where she searched most. She returned to the familiar spot where she found it, looked at it for a moment but showed no particular agitation, dropped her excited manner, walked straight to the hole and began digging inside it without a moment's delay, and as calmly and business-like as if nothing had gone wrong! After digging out a neat little pile of dirt she came and examined her spider once more, pulled and turned it around, legs up, and went back to her digging. Presently she returned again to the spider and proceeded to bite it on the ventral side of the body between the second and third pair of legs; we could distinctly see her palpi move and we suspected that she was sucking the juices. When she withdrew after about a minute she stood "licking her chops," repeated the performance and then left promptly with such a strange flight of abandonment that we doubted if she would ever return. We inspected the spider and, sure enough, the body wall was broken at the point mentioned and a large drop of clear juice had exuded.

The morning passed and we saw no more of her. Whether she became disgusted with the hard soil or offended at the disturbance we know not. But it was interesting to see how she was determined to get some good out of her spider by at least having a meal before abandoning it.[1]

The tiny parasitic fly had been hovering over the hole—not over the spider—during this entire performance, and was still poised in the air over the burrow when we left the scene, long after the wasp had given up the enterprise.

The spider was taken home. At 10 o'clock that evening it responded slightly to stimulus, but by the next morning it was dead.

On another morning, as we were walking across the field past a spot from which all the grass had been trodden, we suddenly scared up from the edge of the grass a *P. tropicus*. She had been engaged in carrying a spider, *Lycosa frondicola* Em. female [N. Banks], not quite mature, but larger than herself. After a quarter of an hour she appeared

[1] It is a question whether *Pompiloides tropicus* does not live entirely on animal juices, for while Robertson found many species of Pompilidae feeding upon the nectar of various flowers, he has not one record as far as we know of *P. tropicus* coming to the flowers.

searching vaguely in the general region, but most of the time six to twelve feet distant from her spider. She searched by walking a few inches, then hopping and flying a foot or two, occasionally taking a circle on the wing just above the grass-tops. She seemed to gain no headway in her search, so presently she went over to a small patch of cockleburs, which was six feet from the spider, and hopped and circled over the plants with an air of getting her bearings. Her behavior made us wonder if she had originally found the spider near these plants and had gone back to retrace her steps. Then she started out in the direction of the grass-plot, but missed her prey, so she went back to the cockleburs again, repeated the performance, and this time went almost directly to her spider. She pounced upon it viciously, as if she thought it necessary that it be attacked vigorously, and got a good grip, grasping it by its ventral side back of the third pair of legs.

She dragged it thus a foot or so, walking backward and pulling like a dray-horse; then poised it in some grasses and went back to hunt a place for a hole. She found a depression in the earth, a place where we had dug with a trowel the day before. The ground was dry and hard, with much dust on top. She tried spots here and there in the side-walls of this hole, scratching and biting furiously in eight different places, but she found the ground too hard and the surface dust fell in on her. After trying thus a long while, she went straight back to her spider two feet away and brought it nearer, then returned to dig, as if satisfied that this place was as good as she could expect to find. Then she seemed suddenly to decide upon her spot, and, after just a few strokes of digging, for the first time she swept the dirt back from the space immediately in front of the hole. It was hard digging, so while she was gone to visit her spider again we pierced the firm surface crust

FIG. 9. *Pompiloides tropicus* transporting her prey, *Lycosa frondicola*. × 2.

to help start her nest. After this she dug rapidly, coming out and visiting her spider six times while it lay in this position. We do not know if she examined the spider frequently in order to see if it was behaving properly, or to gain an accurate idea of the required size of her hole. Next she lugged it one foot nearer to the opening, dug out more earth and again moved the spider nearer, to a spot only nine inches from the hole. She always grasped the spider by the middle of its ventral surface and carried it vertically, the spider's hind legs dragging behind while the front ones hung limp (fig. 9); she did not at any time drag it sidewise by the legs as other Pompilids do. Furthermore, she always walked backward when she had the burden and could not see her way very well, so she constantly struggled over obstacles that she might as easily have avoided if she could have seen where she was going.[2] At one time in moving her spider she struggled through grass and over a tangle of weeds for fifteen inches, when a perfectly smooth clear path lay beside her, all the way, less than two inches from her at all points.

She seemed now to feel the enthusiasm of seeing her work nearing completion, and dug furiously for a few minutes more; then she brought the spider very near and hung it carefully on the tiny weed nearest to the hole, only four inches distant, removed a few more mouthfuls and kicked back the dirt, then dragged the arachnid to the mouth of the burrow and attempted to take it in; but it was too large, so she left it at the opening of the burrow and proceeded to deepen the hole, vigorously kicking the dirt out all over the spider. She dug on and on in this way for an

[2] Another *P. tropicus,* in a different locality and year, moved her spider in precisely the same manner, holding it vertically by the middle of its ventral surface. She always walked backwards, galloping lightly up absolutely perpendicular places, and even backing up overhanging spots without evident difficulty.

hour, only occasionally kicking or sweeping a little dirt off the spider. We suspected that she did this, not for the sake of keeping her spider cleared, but merely to follow her habit of occasionally clearing away the débris around her doorway. Some tiny ants hung around a bit inquisitively; the wasp came out of the hole and bit at them, kicked at them and curled up her sting at them menacingly until they withdrew.

Once when the wasp had swept the dirt off the spider it stirred, scrambled to its feet and walked away three inches, whereupon she promptly pounced upon it and the pair rolled over in a tumble—she probably stung it—then as it lay quiet she calmly mounted its back and precisely curled her abdomen around its body and planted a deliberate sting in the ventral part of the thorax, just in front of the last pair of legs; then she took it back and laid it up-side-down with care, at the mouth of the hole and resumed her digging and kicking dust all over it. So, to try her, when she was deep in the hole we drew the spider back two inches and turned it right-side-up. When the wasp emerged she saw it but paid no attention to the fact that its position had been altered. On her second appearance it began to wiggle its legs; she pounced upon it ferociously and tumbled over, probably stinging it, as the spider did not resist further; then she casually stung it again, as if for good measure, between the third and fourth pairs of legs; then as it lay on its back she most deliberately placed her sting between the second and third right legs, near the center of the body, and left it there for several seconds, while the spider convulsively drew up its quivering legs and stirred no more. Tiny drops of juice oozed out of the wounds; she paused and seemed to drink this. Then she marched away with a most triumphant and self-satisfied air.

By this time she had apparently learned that she could

not profit by keeping her prey lying at the mouth of the hole, so she carried it to a spot five inches away and proceeded with her digging, visiting it often, as if to see that it was behaving properly. She worked by digging up the loose dirt in the hole and then backing out, pushing it up in a mound behind her. But, we asked ourselves, why did she dig so deep and not make the hole wide enough to admit the spider?

Time dragged by—perhaps she spent another hour in enlarging the hole. At last! for the first time she came pushing her way, head first, up through her mound of loose dirt. Once more she visited the spider and shook it enquiringly by the left leg, went in and pushed out the last bit of loose dirt, emerged head first again, grasped the spider by the left coxa and, with much labor, dragged and tugged it in. Thus we see that she made her exit head first only when the nest was ready to receive the provisions. The spider fitted in the hole so tightly that its legs were all doubled straight back. At the last her economy was better than we had judged, for the hole was wide enough after all, with no wasted space, and the spider fitted in the hole so snugly that it could not possibly use its legs to kick or work itself free. After the prey was in the hole she continued pushing up loose, fresh dirt, evidently clearing the way as she moved it back in the gallery. The passage must have been of greater diameter below the surface, however, in order to allow both her and the dirt to pass beside the spider. After ten minutes she had thrown up enough fresh dirt to completely close the mouth of the burrow, so we could see no more of her doings. She did not come out on the surface any more, since her property was no longer outside.

The quarter-hours passed, yet she did not reappear. Thrilling indeed! Two rational human beings squatting in the burning sun, watching a motionless spot of earth!—But how consoling that the poet who best knew patience has said:

"He also serves who only stands and waits."

At length we were preparing to dig her up, when suddenly a speck of the loose dirt in the middle of her mound quivered and a tiny hole appeared; she was hollowing it out from underneath and slowly packing it firmly back into the channel as she came up, until now the door was falling in. She emerged gradually, slowly, packing the loose dirt back into the hole with all her legs and punching it down with the tip of her ventrally curved abdomen. She filled it in tight to the top, swept the dust back over it loosely and departed so promptly that we had trouble in intercepting her.

When we dug out the burrow the spider kicked so vigorously that it seemed it would dislodge the egg. The long,

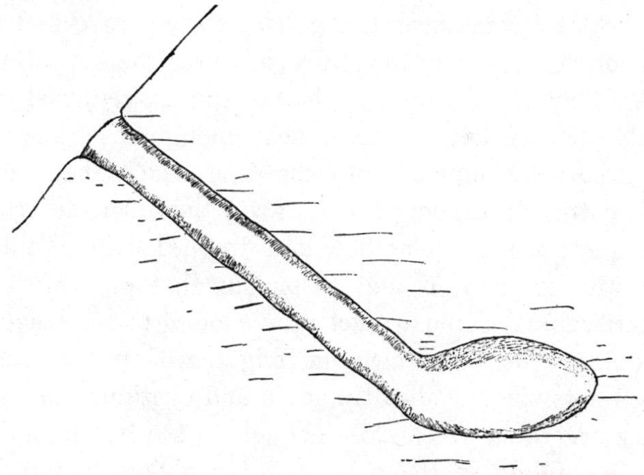

FIG. 10. The burrow of *Pompiloides tropicus*. Natural size.

white egg was slightly curved and fitted nicely to the side of the abdomen where the larva would be in position for the juicy, tender part of its food first.

The hole (see fig. 10, exact size), one-fourth inch in diameter, went downward at an angle of 40 degrees with the surface level, for about two inches, and terminated in an oval, horizontal chamber an inch long and a half-inch wide.

From these observations we may be sure that the egg was deposited and the spider entombed at about 11:45 a. m. At 10 o'clock that evening the spider was active and would make the characteristic threatening spring back when touched. The legs could move actively but not coordinately, and were unfit for progression; the mandibles attempted to close, but could do no more than quiver, when tickled with a straw. After this activity we were surprised the next morning to find it dead. By the following day we were quite certain that the egg too was dead.

One mid-September morning we saw a lot of dirt thrown out of a hole in the side of a depression made by a horse's hoof. As we came nearer, a *P. tropicus* emerged and flew away in alarm, but slowly returned, found the spot and entered. Thus she fled in affright and timidly returned three times, when we tried to come near enough to observe her activities. She jumped into the hole which then lacked only a half-inch of being full, bit away the soil from around the edge of the irregular hole and dropped it in. Still the wasp was so nervous and suspicious that only with the greatest caution could we get near enough to see what she was doing. She often flew out, frightened, then nervously flapped her wings, walked in again and continued her task. At last we could creep close enough to see her smoothing down the filling in the hole with her abdomen, but in a strange way quite new to us. The abdomen was curled under the body, making the dorsal surface of the tip appear ventral; this convex portion, pressed against the ground, proved a very efficient sad-iron, smoothing and at the same time compressing the loose soil.

When the filling was packed into the hole up to within one-eighth inch of the surface level, she kicked in some dust from the tiny embankment overhanging the nest—not the yellow dust that had originally come out of the hole. (The surface earth here was grey and the subsoil yellow.) She then kicked all of the little clods of grey earth in a heap on top, went a few inches away and made another neat pile of exactly the same kind, then kicked more loose dust over the hole, completely covering it, and also flung in any stray lumps, large or small, that lay near. When they were too large, she carried them in her jaws and loosely dropped them on the site of the nest. At no stage did she attempt to compress the mass on top with her abdomen; it seems that this treatment is reserved for interior work. Just when we were happy to think that the two piles of grey clods were placed there to deceive any enemy that might come near, *P. tropicus,* as if forgetting herself, kicked half of the second pile over the hole, so all notions of actual rational deception being practised by this Pompilid were shattered.

When she considered her work finished, she flew to a spot fifteen feet distant. There she deliberately and restfully made her toilet for five minutes, then flew high in the air and away.

We opened the burrow and found it as illustrated (see fig. 11), with the bottom of the chamber three inches below the surface of the ground. The maximum diameter of the chamber was one inch. The spider therein was very active, moving the legs and mandibles violently and giving good promise of recovering from its abusive treatment. The white egg adhered to the dorso-lateral surface near the basal part; it never hatched. Eleven days later the spider, *Lycosa carolinensis* Walck. [C. R. Shoemaker], was dead.

During the same week two *P. tropicus,* in company with

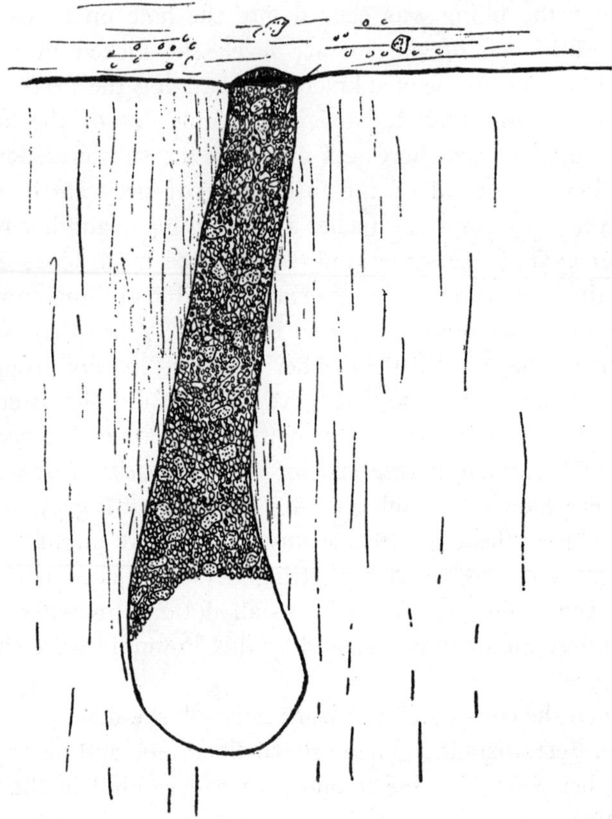

FIG. 11. Another form of burrow made by *Pompiloides tropicus.* Natural size.

two individuals of a much smaller species of *Pompiloides,* were discovered out foraging. We watched them for an hour or more as they walked along on the ground somewhat nervously, examining with particular care the base of all clumps of short grass.

A month later we chanced to see a *P. tropicus* foraging more actively. She alighted boldly upon a large spider-web in the grass (one of the spreading kind with a den or lair in one corner) walked over it with wonderful lightness and rapidity and entered the lair. She came out at once without the spider, however, walked without the slightest entanglement to the edge of the web and flew off. Perhaps the spider spied her and escaped, but it was surprising that the *Pompiloides* was not ensnared in the web, as so many of the larger insects are, especially since this is the whole purpose for which the web is constructed. We have elsewhere remarked that dead *Chalybion caeruleum* and Eumenids are often found in spiders' webs.

Others were seen in other regions and at other times, apparently foraging. Some were out in the grassy fields, and others in barren, clay-covered areas. They seem to be generally distributed, whereas *Bembix nubilipennis* and other wasps are found only in specific places.

It seems, from what we have noted, that the primary sting is insufficient to paralyze the spider and that whenever *P. tropicus* is aware of any activity on the part of her prey, she re-stings it.

One record shows that a spider may recover from the sting. A small female *P. tropicus* in alarm left her spider, a medium-sized specimen of *Pellenes coecatus* Htz. [N. Banks] at our feet on June 12, 1916. This tribute was cherished, even though it appeared to be dead. It was daily stimulated, but it was not until four days later that the stimulation brought forth the slightest movement of the legs. Every day the spider was mildly stimulated with the same sort of response, but it was not until the fifteenth day that the spider showed tendencies to revive. On that day, June 27, it moved the legs more actively and jumped slightly. On July 4 it was so lively that, when the box was opened, it jumped out. It had also just spun a web in the box. The next examination, July 10, found it very active, as did also the inspection on July 20, so it was released in the garden, apparently fully revived and capable of carrying on all the duties of spiderdom. Of course we must not forget that the spider revived only after fifteen days, and had he remained buried with the wasp's egg upon him, he would have been devoured long before the days of his resuscitation.

The fluid of the sting must have had some preserving influence, because without being stung, it is doubtful if the spider would have lived five weeks without food, under like conditions.

*Pompiloides marginatus* Say [S. A. Rohwer].

We followed this little black and orange-spotted Pompilid on the ground for a half-hour; she appeared to be foraging. She kept close to the ground amid the sparsely growing grass and only once or twice climbed the grassblades for a few inches. The twitching wings showed that she might easily be aroused to anger, although the head was kept close to the ground, in a very intent manner, often moving from side to side as if in search of something. At one time in particular, it seemed certain that she could not be bent upon any other mission than the quest of prey, for when she came to the small turret of a young spider she became very much agitated and lingered about the place for some time, possibly waiting for the spider to come out, and several times violently rammed her head against the turret. Finally, seeing the fruitlessness of her wait here, she continued her wanderings. Hancock[3] records finding *P. marginatus* in the tube of the castle-building spider, *Lycosa domifex*.

An hour later we watched another of the same species going through exactly similar foraging behavior.

We found one on the sunny afternoon of August 31,

[3] Ent. News **10**: 29. 1899.

digging in an old hole of some larger insect (wasp, spider or beetle), which had been closed by a recent rain, but not tightly packed, so there was still a marked depression on the surface of the ground. She stood head downward, worked the dirt loose and burrowed down through it, and only carried out a chunk occasionally, when it crowded her too much. She was rather clumsy or indifferent about clearing away the débris, and did not dig as neatly and scientifically as most wasps do; the dirt was constantly falling back upon her as she worked, and, even when she carried out a clod at a time, she usually laid it down on the sloping earth at the side of the hole so it promptly rolled in upon her again. We watched her carry out one lump five times, and each time she laid it in the same place on the side of the funnel-shaped depression so it rolled down and bumped her again. She did not work systematically at all, but scratched first on one side of the hole, then on the other, and occasionally paused to clean herself for a while. Finally, after ten or fifteen minutes of this, she left the place indifferently and performed similarly, but for a shorter time, at another old hole near by, but soon abandoned that likewise.

We dug up these holes but found nothing in them. Was she seeking for prey in them, or was she prospecting for an easy place to dig her own burrow? We could find no spider near. Others of this genus use spiders which they catch before they dig their burrows. She remained in this immediate vicinity, and later commenced to dig, for only a moment, in two other old covered holes. She moved and worked very indifferently, almost stupidly.

It may be possible that this one was merely looking for a spider for her own food. One which we saw in the grass a little later in the afternoon was chewing at a small spider, the remains of which were identified as a young specimen of *Phidippus sp.* [N. Banks]. She munched and sucked at it as if heartily enjoying her meal.

Hartman[4] describes the nest-building of *P. marginatus* in this way. She had chosen for the home of her offspring the middle of a much-used path through the sandy woods. "Here she began to dig with vim and in a few moments had dug a hole an inch or more in depth and was bringing out sand at regular intervals, which increased in length with the increase in depth of the nest. The sand was pushed up in loads with the hind legs and the end of the abdomen. The wasp did not appear with a load each time, but often five or six loads would be allowed to accumulate at the entrance when the whole pile would be pushed out and scattered away from the entrance more or less carefully."

We discovered another one October 10, just in time to witness it doing a marvellous feat of strength. She was walking backward dragging a spider, a *Trochosa avara* Keys [N. Banks], much larger than herself. She was holding the spider in a vertical position, grasping it by having her mandibles inserted in the ventral surface of the spider between its legs. It was remarkable that the little wasp could move such a huge victim at all; but when she proceeded to drag it up a bank eight feet high, part of which was actually vertical and a small portion slightly overhanging, we could hardly believe our eyes, and cannot yet understand how it was possible (see fig. 12); yet the little wasp seemed not at all disconcerted about it.

This method of transportation of prey, as illustrated, does not seem constant. While Hartman says the wasp grasped the spider by one of the coxae, which would probably make the carrying position very near to that illustrated, the Peckhams describe one as "going backward carrying a medium-sized spider," and another "dragging a small

[4] Bull. Univ. Tex. **65**: 52-54. 1905.

FIG. 12. A marvellous feat of strength: *Pompiloides marginatus* dragging her prey up-hill. Two times natural size.

Thomisid * * *, the spider was so small that she held it in her mandibles well above the ground, and we speak of her as dragging it only because she walked backward and acted as though she were obliged to exert herself. Quite often the spiders taken by this species are too large to be carried and then it is necessary to drag them; this habit is so ingrained that when it would be much more convenient to go straight ahead, they stick to the ancient custom, and seem unable to move in any other way." On another occasion they found that she seized the spider by one leg and dragged it off, and again: "We have twice seen a *marginatus* pick up her spider and fly with it backward for a long distance, as much as four or five feet."

When we see the constancy of some wasps in the way of carrying their prey, such as *Priononyx atratum, P. thomae, Bembix nubilipennis, Ammophila pictipennis, Odyneris dorsale* and others, each of which species transports its prey unvaryingly according to the fixed ways of the species, and then we see the variety of methods of *P. marginatus,* one can only wonder if natural selection will some day eliminate the less favorable methods.

The spider figuring in the above incident was taken home. When examined the next day it appeared entirely unaffected by the sting, but jumped up and walked away. Its abdomen had been bitten into and the juices removed, so it was not at all surprising when, on the third day, the spider was dead. Thus it would appear that *marginatus* sometimes indulges in animal food, although Robertson finds that it frequents the flowers of *Solidago nemoralis.* We have often noted that the prey of the Pompiloides exhibit a good deal of energy and activity, after they recover from the first shock of the sting, and soon afterwards succumb suddenly. Hartman finds that the spider is stung to death, while the Peckhams record that the spider of this wasp, which they dug up after two days, was alive, as was shown by the quivering of the legs; four days later this quivering was scarcely perceptible, and it died two days after. They also mention one instance where the spider was stung to death.

The one characteristic that is constant for both Hartman's and Peckhams' wasps is their method of concealment of their prey in among the blossoms, under a lump of earth, or on a leaf high above the earth, while the nest is being dug, and the habit of visiting it at short intervals while the work is in progress.

One interesting record of the Peckhams[5] we beg leave to quote, since it seems as though practical judgment or some other intellectual faculty must have been involved.

The spider was hidden, and then began the usual hunting performance, which soon resulted in the discovery of a cavity which had a very small opening. The wasp crept in, remained a minute and then came out and brought this spider to its new hiding-place. The head went in easily, but it took a great deal of tugging to get the rest to follow. At last both spider and wasp were out of sight, and everything remained quiet for a long time. When the wasp came creeping out, she went on an extended tour. She doubtless selected another halting-place, for when she returned it was to try to get the spider out of the hole by pulling at one of the hind legs. The task, however, was not an easy one; she exerted all her strength so that they expected to see the spider torn to pieces, but still it did not come. At last she seemed to realize that there was more than one way to accomplish her end, and turned her attention to cutting away the earth to make the opening larger. After a few minutes' work she tried again and although the passage was still much too small for convenience the spider was at length dragged forth.

[5] Loc cit. p. 150.

*Psammochares scelestus*[6] Cress. [S. A. Rohwer].

On October 7 this wasp was found carrying an immature spider, a *Dolomedes sp.* [C. R. Shoemaker]. She did not hold it vertically, but drew the spider's middle leg conveniently under her body, grasped its tarsus in her mandibles, and while she walked forward, dragged its body along bumpity-bump over sticks and stones. After travelling this way for a short time, she hid the spider under a clod and flew about over the sandy bank for some little time, where she probably found a suitable spot or hole; then she returned to her spider and again, in the same way, attempted to pull it up hill. This time, however, she failed to get a firm foothold and both rolled down to the ledge below. Here she carried it to a small depression and left it. When she failed to return after an hour, we took the spider, which was then motionless. By the next day it had regained its vigor to such an extent that it could slightly move the body sidewise. Three days after its capture, while it could not move its body, the legs responded to stimulus. The next day it was so active that it could hop for some distance with surprising agility, but on October 13, six days after its capture, it was dead.

One day, in searching for insects, we dug a little cave several inches deep into a bank, near its base. Two days later, October 5, this black wasp was at work digging a hole at the extreme end of this little dugout. The hole must have been deep or large, for already there was a goodly pile of fresh earth thrown out about the orifice. It was rather dark back in this little cave, but with the aid of light reflected upon the wasp from a mirror, we were able to follow its maneuvers. The wasp went into the hole head first, remained inside a good many minutes, and, when

[6] This wasp is the same as *Pompilus scelestus* (*fide* Rohwer).

finally she appeared, she brought with her, under her body, an astonishingly large load of dirt. One could easily spell out her method: during her long stay in the hole she loosened the soil and kicked it under her body, then on coming out of the hole backwards she had only to spread her forelegs in such a way as to make a fence or rake, and by passing out she would automatically drag out the loose soil. When one sees the slope of the burrow in fig. 13, one

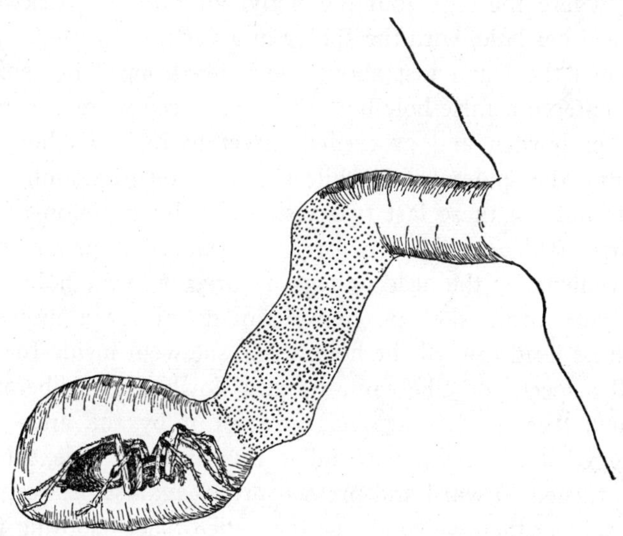

FIG. 13. The burrow and prey of *Psammochares scelestus*. Natural size.

realizes her tremendous task in pushing her load up-hill backwards. Sometimes the load was so large that the wasp had to force her way with much effort out through her doorway. Occasionally the loose earth at the top of the gallery was kicked out, but no attempt was made to clear away the débris from her own door.

We looked for a spider which we suspected she must have near by, but found none. Once when we intruded too close she fled to the top of a bank some fifteen feet away, but soon returned to her hole. After a few minutes more of digging she flew again to the same place on the top of the bank and picked up the prey she had deftly concealed among the vegetation. She at once grabbed it by its ventral center, where the legs join the body, and walked backward toward her hole, with the spider in a vertical position. She reached the ledge just above the hole, dropped her spider and entered a false hole but soon discovered her error, took up her burden and proceeded direct to her own burrow, leaving the spider twice while she went on to examine the nest; but, on these last two visits, she did not stop to get a firm hold upon it as before, but grasped it in any way convenient, by the head or legs, to drag it to the hole. At the very brink she laid her victim down for a moment, with its head toward the hole, while she went inside for the final inspection. She came up and slowly and deliberately turned the spider around, grasped it by the anus and dragged it in. As it was pulled thus into the hole, all the legs turned forward and pressed firmly against the body of the spider; then we could see the logic of her choosing that position. But what impressed us most was the deliberate and careful manner which the wasp displayed in turning the arachnid around, so that the rounded and appendageless part could be grasped. It was no accident, but a deliberate act.

She remained within for one hour. When we opened the nest, we found the spider resting still with its head toward the exit (fig. 13, exact size), and on its right side was the wasp's egg. The wasp's last hour had evidently been spent in closing the hole, from bottom upward, but she had not yet reached the surface. The spider was motionless. The next day it showed faint response to stimulus; then it died. On more than one occasion we have noticed that the prey of this species of *Pompiloides* are so severely stung that only after two or three days do they show the faintest signs of reviving.

The Peckhams in both of their wasp publications have a splendid account of the behavior of this wasp, under the name of *Pompilus scelestus;* in several details our notes substantiate theirs. No other biological notes have been located in the literature, excepting that the insect inhabits mountains at or above an altitude of 5500 feet (*fide* Slosson).

*Pepsis dubitata* Cress. [S. A. Rohwer].

The following paragraphs are merely a description of the efforts and difficulties of a *P. dubitata* on her homeward journey; if the recitation of the trials and struggles seems wearisome to the reader as he sits at ease, let him consider how much more wearisome was the reality for the little *Pepsis* under the midday July sun.

We first discovered her at 1 p. m., July 29, walking nervously about on the ground in irregular circles, as if seeking something lost. Suddenly she dropped into a tunnel in the earth, made by some rodent. We watched at this hole for twenty minutes but she did not reappear; when we gave up the vigil and walked about thirty feet away, we found her where she had emerged from another point in the tunnel. She was intensely at work dragging a spider. These insects are rarely met with, so we turned all attention to following every detail of her behavior.

It was now 1:20 p. m. She had a huge spider by the

head, probably five times as heavy as herself, and was walking backwards, dragging it over sticks and stones, green and dried grass, up logs and down.

After four minutes the wasp stopped dragging the spider, and for five minutes she rested and cleaned her antennae, body and legs. Twice during this interval she left her spider and went under a leaf near by, but each time she returned to keep watch again in front of its prostrate form, while she made her toilet. But we were mistaken in thinking that her burrow was under this leaf; for at 1:29 she grabbed her property and continued her journey, in the same manner as before, for six minutes. Twice she left the spider, walked about in circles with the same nervous, jerky gait, but in a moment she seized it and hurried on again, making good time over a bit of smooth road which chanced to be in her way. She certainly seemed not to trouble herself to find a smooth way. One of the spider's legs was seen to quiver several times.

At 1:35 the wasp enjoyed a perfect rest near her prey, for a half-minute. The spider's second right leg still quivered occasionally; but the wasp was not perturbed by it, but calmly rubbed herself down. She cleaned her abdomen with her hind legs and her antennae and head with the forelegs. For nine minutes she loitered about, making her toilet most of the time, and occasionally moving her position for a few inches, sometimes behind, or to the right or left of her spider, but always near enough to keep a watchful eye upon it.

The spider's right leg gave a more marked twitch. The wasp darted at once to her position at the right of the spider's head. At 1:44 she left it and went under a dried leaf, as if reconnoitering. After a few seconds she came out and dragged her prey under the leaf with her, the legs of the spider protruding. We followed eagerly but cautiously, thinking that here she would bury it. But no, she could be seen, through a rent in the leaf, quietly at rest before her spider. The wasp occasionally walked about slowly under the leaf; apparently she only wanted a more sheltered spot wherein to rest and loiter. Up to this point she had travelled about sixty feet.

Two o'clock came and there was no change; the sun beat down hotly and our patience was strained. With the forceps we gently pulled the spider out by its leg for a half-inch. This instantly aroused the wasp to action; she snatched the spider by its head and dragged it under the leaf clear to the extreme opposite margin, paused a moment, as if undecided, and then impetuously seized her prey and resumed her journey in earnest. There was much difficulty in following her, owing to obstructions, vegetation and poison ivy. She showed by her actions that she now felt anxious and skeptical in our presence; from 2:06 to 2:12 she remained at rest, but this time holding the spider in her jaws all the time. Finally she regained enough confidence to lay it down while she made her toilet for three minutes. We should be glad to know if she purposely laid down her prey so often in order to clean herself, or if she only rubbed herself for a pastime when she paused to rest. We have also wondered if all this was for the purpose of personal daintiness, or if a part of this practice served as a massage or an athletic rub-down of the tired muscles after the strain of labor.

At 2:15 the wasp made a very graceful attempt to climb a log which lay over her path. How the insect became aware of its presence without facing it to see it, or bumping into it we cannot imagine, but she seemed somehow to sense the location precisely. She backed up near to it, dragging her spider until she came within reach of the log, when she lifted her hind pair of legs high up in the air until they came in contact with the rough bark; then she continued backing up until soon she had all six of her legs in action. Just as she reached the top with her heavy burden, however, she grasped a fallen leaf which lay loosely upon the log, and leaf, wasp and spider rolled to the ground. Finding her lost prey after a few seconds' search, the wasp resumed her travels in another direction, this time up a steep hill-side. She resorted to no diagonal inclines, but pluckily struggled straight up the steep slope, pausing only once, for a few minutes' rest, when half-way up the hill. Presently she slipped and fell and rolled part way down the hill. This seemed to discourage her a little, and she left her prey and strolled a dozen inches away, then back to it thoughtfully, and settled down to spend the next ten minutes in resting, toilet-making and short, jerky walks.

At last she resumed her wanderings, carrying the spider still further up the hill, and reached an area blackened by a recent fire, where there was no green vegetation and the ground was literally full of the holes and tunnels of rodents. But nothing here seemed to appeal to her, and again she took up her burden and went down the hill beyond, for ten feet, and then up the next hillock, always walking backwards and holding the spider by its head. About this time she dropped her spider two or three times and made short side-trips, looking over the vicinity, returning to it as though to continue the trip. Suddenly and without warning she disappeared with her prey into a rodent hole. We watched and waited long, and wasted much effort in digging up the tunnels and a considerable portion of the surrounding country, but could discover her no more.

Over the very roughest country this wasp had dragged her burden for a hundred yards. Since she seemed to have an especial liking for rodent holes, one wonders why she did not use for her nesting-place the first tunnel wherein she found the spider, and thus save herself the labor of dragging such a load for three hundred feet over rough roads, or at least choose one of the many which she passed by in the burnt area.

After following this wasp mother through the details of her prolonged trials and difficulties, we respect her for her faithfulness and pluck in continuing her heavy task to the end. And yet we have a lurking feeling (which we regret to express) that this type of faithfulness may have been an exhibit more of brawn than of brain. However, we must not judge the species by this one female which may have been very individualistic in her behavior; perhaps her sisters would have shown as fine instinct and economy as is found in any of the other species.

*Priocnemis pompilus*[7] Cress. [S. A. Rohwer].

Verily, if boils were sent to try the patience of Job, then *Priocnemis pompilus* must have been created to try the patience of naturalists. One sees an animated little black wasp darting nervously here and there in a hot, sandy field, and one follows eagerly, confident that some interesting activity will ensue at any moment. She runs in this direction and that, absolutely without any system or general direction, peeping into every crevice or behind every obstacle, often hopping and twitching the wings nervously. Thus she lures us on and on almost interminably, until our eyes feel strained with watching her in the glaring sun. Sometimes she plunges into a crevice or a mole's tunnel, and we wait until she comes out empty-handed, or she may walk about the tunnel and emerge far beyond, and leave us watching for ever so long at the place where she entered,

[7] This species is listed in Dalla Torre's Catalogue as *Salius pompilus* (*fide* Rohwer).

before we discover that we have been deceived, scramble to our feet and go scurrying after her again. Or perhaps she darts under a grass-blade and there she sits, and sits, and sits, occasionally scratching a bit at the ground or peeping out as if to make sure that her secrets were not being spied upon, and eventually darts out without doing a thing and resumes her crazy journey. Probably these are foraging trips, but in the summer months we have never seen their activity lead to anything more than this vain search. It may be because of the scarcity of spiders of adequate size at that time of year, or due to the sexual immaturity of the wasps. Later in the season, September and October, their work seems to be more purposeful and their efforts lead eventually to some results.

On the afternoon of October 3, 1916, we met with one such instance. A *Priocnemis pompilus* was rushing hither and thither over a small area of broken ground. We had so often seen this species wandering about on the bare ground inspecting crevices, and had been so constantly disappointed in seeing them do nothing that we paid no attention to this one. Upon returning an hour later, however, and finding apparently the same wasp running about in the same small area, we suspected that there must be spiders in the many depressions in the earth, so we sat down and waited.

The retina of one's mind, as well as the retina of the eye, grows dull when weary of gazing at one thing, so our thoughts were far away when, perhaps a half-hour later, suddenly there was a great commotion—hurry-tumble-topsy-turvy! The wasp had her spider and was stinging it. The shock was so great, and the work was done so quickly, that we could not see just how it was done. The wasp left her victim, ran around like wildfire for several seconds, returned, stung it again and dragged it some distance away, left it and, in the same wild manner, looked for crevices, went from one to another and eventually carried the spider to a shallow one. Not satisfied with this the wasp dragged her burden further and, in an uncertain way, wandered about with it. Presently she lost her prey, but continued roaming about, possibly looking for it.

Being unable to wait longer, we took the wasp to make sure of the species. While the story here is incomplete, these observations show that these wasps are persistent in remaining in a spot, when they are suspicious that their prey lies hidden thereabouts, and that they get their prey first and then hunt for a suitable crevice wherein to deposit it.

Even later in the season than this, October 26, the active *P. pompilus* were more abundant than at an earlier date. While these wasps had frequently been seen before in search of game, on this day four were discovered with spiders, on a clay bank. One in particular was followed and watched. She had a medium-sized spider in her mouth and was nervously and quickly moving with it. We say moving because her gait has no name; she was walking and flying without lifting her legs from the ground and doing both equally well, either pushing her burden forward or going backward and dragging it with her. She would often leave her prey to explore the region for suitable holes. At last one was found on a perpendicular bank, eighteen inches from where the spider lay. This bank was almost straight up and down, and we wondered how it would be possible for the wasp to carry the prey up to the hole. It seemed for a time as if it were not possible, for in the twenty or more attempts that she made walking backward and climbing up the bank, invariably both fell down; either she tumbled down holding to her prey or she dropped it and flew down after it. She made a few examinations of other nearby holes, as if considering the advisability of a change of plans, but for some reason she always returned to the one of her first choice.

Eventually she mastered the art needed and her perseverence was rewarded with success; at last she got the spider up to the hole. However, the ledge in front of the hole was so narrow that it would tumble off just as fast as she got it there. It seemed that she had an aversion to dragging the spider into the hole without first going in herself, and this seemed impossible. She later learned to place—or better to say succeeded in placing—the spider just over the mouth of the burrow, and there it hung while she very dextrously wedged her way into the hole, to see if all was right, before entering with the prey. But here new disaster came; she could let the spider lie on the outside over the hole while she squeezed herself in, but when she came out her head butted against the spider and down it went again into the valley below. Her patience and strength seemed inexhaustible; we had long ere this lost all estimate of the number of times she had skilfully carried her spider up this precipitous bank. Three times in succession this last mishap occurred, when finally (and this may have been accidental, but we shall always hold it as a case of profiting by experience), she took up her spider, carried it some distance to a point where the bank sloped gradually, and climbed up, walking backward and pulling the spider with her; then she dragged it back horizontally and let it rest on a ledge three inches directly above the hole. Next she went into the nest, examined it once more, and came out and got her booty. Here we thought the insect showed wonderful intelligence; it would be easier to carry her spider down three inches to the hole than up eighteen inches and still it would be within easy view while she went for her final inspection of the hole, which she deemed so necessary. This arrangement, we thought, would obviate that examination and the subsequent sliding down of the spider into the chasm below.

She emerged from her burrow and walked directly up to where the spider lay and dragged it down to the hole very easily. She did not immediately take it in, as we had expected, but squeezed in alongside it exactly as before for that supremely important final examination. Then, alas, she came out and as usual bumped against the spider so hard that it plunged down the eighteen inches, and she went tumbling after. The instinct of unnumbered generations of always examining the depths of the nest while the prey is at the door was not to be undone, even if she must go only three inches from the hole since the last scrutiny.

Her next scheme was to drag the spider up the steep declivity under the hole, then a little to one side and let it rest in the crotch of a protruding root while she again entered the hole.—Now there is really and truly a limit to the patience of a naturalist, so we helped her, and glad she seemed to receive the aid. When she stepped aside again to get the spider, we pressed a notebook against the bank to form a shelf just beneath the hole. When the little wasp came with her ponderous prize she found that it would rest securely and exactly flush with the hole. She went in, as always, to examine the bottom of the burrow, came up and protruded only her head, grasped the spider and attempted to bring it in. Alas! the hole was not large enough to admit it! Is it not remarkable that, through all her dogged determination to examine the hole immediately before taking her prey in, it had evidently never occurred to her that the hole was far too small to admit the spider at all? This is very different from the accurate methods of many other species discussed in these pages. She did not seem at all disconcerted, but shoved out her spider, removed several mouthfuls of dirt at the opening and then had no trouble in getting it in.

Both disappeared in the depths. After more than an

hour's weary waiting for the wasp to emerge, we stirred her out with a probe and dug away the earth to explore the nest. It went in horizontally about six inches (it had probably been a beetle's hole); then the channel or crevice was lost. The prey was not found. Probably her last hour was spent in filling and packing the hole within up to this point, much after the manner of other Pompilids mentioned.

This species of wasp uses a variety of spiders. We have at various times and places found it carrying off the following species: *Pardosa minima* Keys [N. Banks], sp. of Lycosidae, immature [N. Banks], *Lycosa helluo* Walck (young) [N. Banks], *Pardosa nigripalpis* Em. = *P. cana-*

FIG. 14. *Priocnemis pompilus* travelling backwards and dragging her prey. Twice natural size.

*densis* Blk. [N. Banks], and *Clubiona abbotti* Koch [N. Banks].

It soon becomes apparent that in many of the affairs of wasp life, *P. pompilus* is not such a stickler for conventionality as are many of her sister species. She takes such prey as she can get, and does not reject good spiders because they are not of the species which Habit specifies as proper for her; she uses such holes as she can find in the moment of need and modifies them to suit her needs; if she cannot ascend a precipitous slope directly, she will in time contrive some indirect way to scale it. In fact, like most individuals who go outside the pale of convention, while she may at times seem bizarre, yet her action contains an increased portion of refreshing multiformity and resourcefulness. And so also in her way of carrying her prey, she has not one fixed way, but a variety of ways. She seems, in fact, to be entirely without any fixed habit in this point, excepting that she grasps it in her jaws. This is really the only way possible for her, since she is so small that she could not possibly straddle spiders of the size she catches. Her most common mode of locomotion is to walk backward, pulling her prey (fig. 14), but she also sometimes walks sidewise, dragging her burden at right angles to her own body. Her method of half-running and half-flying with the feet on the ground, while she either pushes or pulls her spider, has already been described. In making ready to drag her prey, she seizes it by any of its members that may offer themselves as a convenient handle at the moment. Each place of insertion of her jaws in the spider's anatomy gives it a different aspect. For instance, when she grasps the spider by the base of one middle leg, this stands the body on its side; when she grasps it by the middle of the ventral side of the thorax, the ponderous abdomen bobs up and down as it passes over the rough ground in a way that must be annoying to the little worker. Another of her favorite methods is to seize it by the palpi. The loose sand often gives way under her feet, and both captor and prey roll headlong.

Another species of *Priocnemis* (*P. flavicornis*) according to Needham and Loyd[8] transport their prey by flying above the surface of the water and towing the load too heavy to be carried. Out onto the surface of the water the wasp drags the huge limp spider, "and, mounting into the air with her engines going and her wings steadily buzzing, she sails across the water, trailing the spider and leaving a wake

[8] Life of Inland Waters, p. 330. 1916.

that is a miniature of that of a passing steamer. She sails a direct and unerring course to the vicinity of her burrow in the bank, and brings her cargo ashore at some nearby landing."

*Arachnophoctonus*[9] *ferrugineus* Say [S. A. Rohwer].

This large red wasp[10] was observed on July 7, 1908, walking up the perpendicular stone wall of the abandoned ice-house at Meramec Highlands, near St. Louis. She was walking backwards, dragging a very large *Lycosa* spider, much heavier than herself, straight up the wall. She held the spider's head between her mandibles, and was making very rapid progress. Thinking that she was climbing to some height in order to fly down to her nest (in this conjecture we were probably mistaken), we captured her and her prey before she should get beyond reach. The spider had a long gash surrounded by a large swelling on the dorsal side of its abdomen, but we had no way of knowing whether this was a wound inflicted by the wasp's sting or a cut from her mandibles, or only a laceration from the stones over which it had been forcibly dragged.

While looking for mud-daubers' nests about the stone foundation of another abandoned building in this vicinity, we frightened another specimen of this formidable-looking species out of a crevice. The cracks between the limestones of the foundation were filled with well-weathered mortar. She flew to the ground near by and crouched low under some grass; when we attempted to examine her, she

[9] Mr. Rohwer writes that this generic name is one of Ashmead's divisions of the old genus *Pompilus*.

[10] This wasp is comparatively rare in this region; besides the few mentioned here we have seen only five, four females and one male, in five years.

flew further, but she was recognized immediately by the bright red of her abdomen and, in the bright sunlight, her bluish-tinted wings. Her brilliant coloration and her nervous, defiant manner certainly render her a formidable looking creature (fig. 15). In cabinet specimens of this species, the red of their bodies looks far more dull, and the wings,

FIG. 15. The Pompilid wasp, *Arachnophoctonus ferrugineus* Say. Exact size.

which are a conspicuous royal blue when vibrating in the sunshine, are but a smoky color with a slight blackish-blue tinge at the base.

After having frightened her away, we proceeded to examine the loose mortar for her nest or prey. We were attracted to a pile of loose, dry plaster-dust on the damp earth; this pointed up to the third tier of rock, probably eighteen inches from the ground, where a large *Lycosa* spider lay in the crevice, about an inch from the opening. It was removed and found to be fresh, limp and motionless; it was probably dead, so we replaced it and waited. After fifteen minutes the wasp flew into the vicinity again, but became shy upon seeing us there. After another ten minutes she ventured near again and alighted on the stone wall at a height of six feet, and east of the nest; then walked down and westward, entering and examining several holes and remaining in some of them for a few seconds. She eventually found the crevice containing the spider, entered and examined it so intently that we wondered if she recognized that it had been tampered with. Then she turned her abdomen toward the spider and held it thus, hugging it closely for some seconds; we suspected that the wasp was stinging it again, but she was so deep in the crevice that we could not see distinctly. She then went deeper into the cavity between the stones and flung out another half-dozen kicks of dust. Unfortunately, at this point she spied us lying flat on the ground to scrutinize her, so she darted away to another part of the wall and entered another niche, and remained there so long that we thought she would carry her spider there. She suddenly emerged from this retreat and escaped. We waited an hour for her return, but she seemed shy, so we wandered away, returning every three or six minutes to look for her.

While thus loitering about waiting we took a trowel and, at a point in the wall about thirty feet away, idly removed from the foundation the hard, black cement which covered the soft mortar beneath, thinking thereby to make an attractive spot for other wasps. After a time, we lost patience, however, and decided to work elsewhere. We knew the species of the wasp, the place where her spider lay was marked, and we knew where she had dug her cavity in the mortar, so it was decided to leave her in peace and return later to get the spider with the egg on it.

Upon returning in a half-hour, imagine our surprise upon finding the spider gone. It seemed scarcely probable that another had come along and purloined it, because, from her previous actions, it appeared that she was going to change her nesting-place. Now it was a task to find the spider, and for another half-hour we dug into the mortar in various suspicious-looking places in search of it. Suddenly a passing gleam of color caught our eye; the wasp flew past, ignoring her old location and alighting on the wall thirty feet beyond. We watched her carefully as she tried to find her new apartment. She accomplished this with difficulty; twice she had to fly away and return on the wing to the same spot to get her bearings. Eventually she located her hole and entered—the very one we had, only a short time before, begun in order to attract some wasp! We were almost too astonished to believe the story ourselves, and yet the evidence seems sufficient to warrant the surmise that it was the same wasp. We knew that she had become dissatisfied with the place that harbored intruders, and that no others of this species were seen all that day. Her actions indicated that she was looking for a new abode, and we are sure that this second hole could not have been there for more than a half-hour—the exact time since the first nest had been deserted—because it had been accessible only since we pulled away the hard outer cement.

She went in and remained about fifteen minutes, when she was captured in a vial placed over her hole. We worked for a long time trying to dig out her spider and egg; but the probe showed that the crevice between the rocks was eight inches deep, so we were obliged to give up the quest without getting her prey or learning anything more about her nest or egg.

This also solves the problem of seven years previously, when an *A. ferrugineus* ascended the old stone wall of the ice-house, walking backward and dragging her *Lycosa.* No doubt that wasp also was directing her course to a chosen crevice in the old stone wall.

In other species of Pompilids, as previously noted, when the wasp is digging her burrow, she often leaves her work to examine her prey and frequently moves it closer to the hole. The notes that follow will show that *A. ferrugineus* does not drag her prey along until she comes to a suitable spot, but in transporting her prey she has a very definite notion of where she is going.

On August 19, at 4:30 p. m., one was discovered dragging a large Lycosid spider by one mandible, walking backwards with a jerky motion, travelling without much difficulty over the long, fallen blue-grass in the front yard. She carried the spider right-side-up and brought it about fifty feet after being discovered. Twice in that time she left it and took a quick, circling flight, as if exploring, over to the old log smoke-house with plaster-chinked crevices; then she returned, without difficulty, to her spider and continued her course very directly, as if she knew precisely what she was about. When finally she got it to the bald area a few feet in front of the smoke-house she paused, left it again and flew to the wall, alighted on it and took a quick, surveying gallop over the two lower logs and their interstices; then went right back and got the spider, took it hastily over to the wall and hid it deep in a crevice in the foundation. She then took on a very nervous attitude, running and flying all over the two walls, examining nooks and crannies everywhere, with wings and antennae nervously vibrating; finally she sat down for five minutes' rest and "meditation," then resumed the chase and search. We cannot believe that the wasp travelled from the spider to the smoke-house so often to see if the smoke-house was still extant, but we think perhaps that was her way of ascertaining whether she was travelling in the right direction; she knew where she wanted to go, and retraced her steps often to see that she was going there.

Presently the wasp disappeared in one of the crannies. Meanwhile the spider was examined. It was limp, but responded to stimulation by slight movements of the legs, although it was so completely paralyzed as to be almost dead.

After a half-hour in hiding, the wasp again apppeared and made her way to the spider and rested in the crevice beside it. When we intruded too near, she flew to the log above, rested, made her toilet and visited the spider for a few seconds. Then she went forth on another tour of inspection of the log walls clear to the very top and down again, by a circuitous route, examining every crevice on the way. Once more she rested a while and made her toilet, then went to the original crevice and carried her booty into a nearby cranny, which she had just passed with casual notice, and dragged it far in out of sight and beyond our reach.

This wasp, then, seems to have a propensity for building nests in the crevices of stone walls, and the propensity probably had its origin in the days when the loose stones of bluffs or hillsides was the only place for the species' abode.

*Pseudagenia (Agenia) architecta* Say [S. A. Rohwer].

Under the loose bark on a log, tangled in a mass of spider-web, was a pretty little two-celled nest of mud. It was treasured until *P. architecta* emerged from it, revealing its authorship.

Later in the season several similar cells were found at Cliff Cave, near St. Louis, Missouri. They were always in pairs (see fig. 16), neat, thin little cells joined end to end like sausages.

The Peckhams[11] found a similar dainty mud nest hidden away in the folds of a flag when they unfurled it on July 4. Each cell contained a dead spider and a wasp larva. They spun their cocoons on the 7th, 8th and 9th of July, and on July 29 a male emerged and on August 2 two female adults appeared.

Wickham[12] found one in Iowa dragging off a spider, a

[11] Bull. Wisc. Geol. & Nat. Hist. Surv. Ser. I. **2**: 165-166. 1898.

[12] Ent. News **9**: 47. 1898.

*Trachelas tranquilla* Hentz, which was much heavier than herself. The spider's legs had been bitten off at the junction of the coxae and trochanters. She dragged it with its

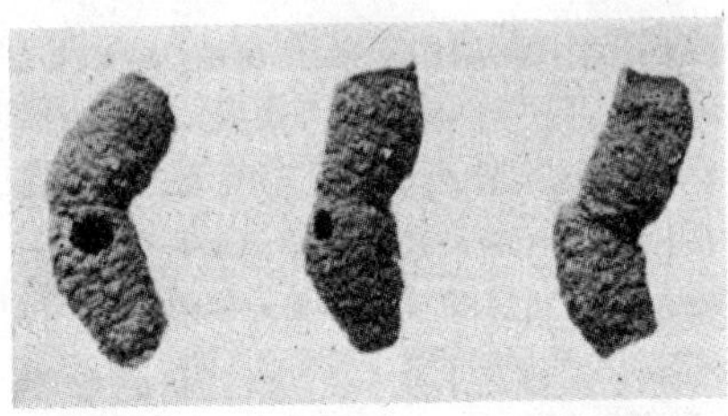

Fig. 16. The twin-celled nests of *Pseudagenia architecta*, showing the holes made by the emerging wasp. Exact size.

smooth, rounded back downward, to prevent friction, and grasped it with jaws near the tip of the ventral surface of the abdomen.

Ashmead,[13] in citing Walsh and Riley, says that the thimble-shaped cells occur under bark, logs or rocks, and are parasitized by *Pteromalus sp.* and *Osprynochotus junceus* Cr.

*Pseudagenia pulchripennis* Cress. [S. A. Rohwer].

This medium-sized black wasp was found walking along a path at Creve Coeur Lake on October 7, carrying a spider, *Phidippus andax* Hentz [C. R. Shoemaker]. The wasp was holding the spider by one of its chelicerae and walking sidewise, the combination of spider and wasp forming a right angle (see fig. 17). It moved in a very strange manner, walking sidewise. This was the first wasp we had ever seen travelling thus. Night was approaching and train-time was drawing near, so we were obliged to abandon

[13] Psyche 7: 66. 1896.

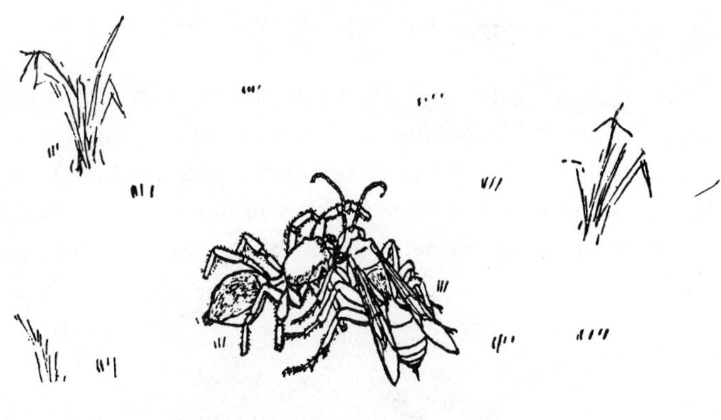

FIG. 17. *Pseudagenia pulchripennis* escorting *Philippus andax* to her burrow. Two times natural size.

further observations on their free behavior and take both. The spider showed signs of life for three days.

Long afterward, another wasp was found actively engaged in running about on a fallen log. Suddenly it leaped to the ground and chased a medium-sized spider. The arachnid made one leap and escaped. The wasp became frantic; the sight of the spider and the fact that she had been fooled so excited her that she acted as though mad, walking, flying, running about the ground in indescribable directions until she tumbled headlong into a mole's hole. After a few moments she emerged from the burrow carrying a spider by its anus. She walked forwards, backwards or sidewise over the ground or low vegetation, in a manner indicating intense excitement, and eluded us many times before we finally captured her. All this occurred, not in the hot sunshine where most Pompilids choose to work, but on a path in the cool, shady forest.

*Pseudagenia mellipes* Say. [S. A. Rohwer].

We have recorded and illustrated the fact that *P. mellipes* emerges from cells made in the walls of the mud nest of *Sceliphron.*[14] The figure here reproduced (fig. 18) shows the nest of the mud-dauber with two hilly protrusions which were cut down to show the cells that contained the pupal

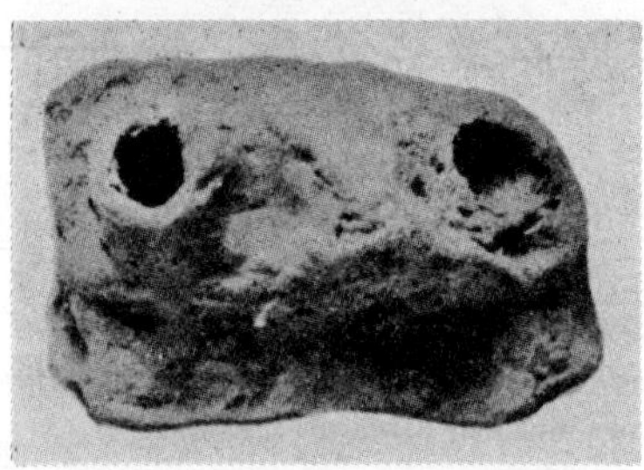

FIG. 18. Two protuberances on the nest of *Sceliphron* which gave forth adults of *Pseudagenia mellipes.* Natural size.

cases of *P. mellipes.* Elsewhere on the nest, mandible marks were in evidence, so we suspect that *mellipes* dug out a small cavity and then carried mud bitten from other parts of the nest and built up and around it until the cell was completely enclosed and hidden from view.

This, we find, is not the only method of nidification of this species. At Moselle, Missouri, on June 30, 1916, while breaking away some loose bark from a fallen tree, we found a little three-celled nest, very beautifully constructed, which we carefully guarded since we expected some species of *Agenia* to emerge therefrom. We were surprised when on July 8 and 11 two adults of *P. mellipes* emerged. The nest did not adhere to the wood, but lay loosely under the bark. The accompanying figure (fig. 19) shows this nest and also the builder (exact size).

[14] Journ. Animal Behavior **6**: 27-63. 1916.

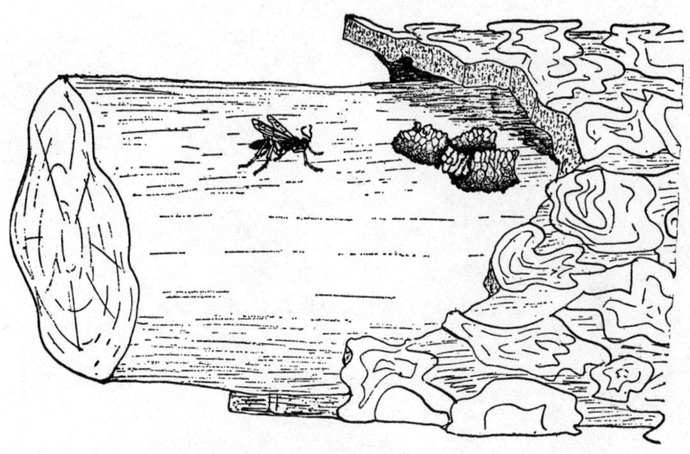

FIG. 19. The three-celled nest of *Pseudagenia mellipes* under loose bark, and its author nearby. Both natural size.

An old oak-apple taken from the tree on June 20, 1917, had the four-celled nest within it. (See fig. 20B). Two cells were sealed and two unsealed. The unsealed cells were perfect; this goes to show that this wasp does not fill each cell as it is finished, but makes several before hunting for prey. The apple was perforated by a small, round hole, one-fourth inch in diameter, through which the wasp had entered and departed. The big, brown oak-apple had made a most comfortable home. On July 10, one male *P. mellipes* emerged.

How many other places of nidification *mellipes* has remains to be discovered. Ashmead, citing Walsh and Riley,[15]

FIG. 20 A. The mud cells of *Pseudagenia sp.* from which adults of the Mutillid wasp *Sphaerophthalma scaeva* emerged. Natural size.

says that *Agenia mellipes* makes thimble-shaped cells under bark, logs and stones, and that they are parasitized by *Pteromalus sp.* and *Osprynochotus junceus* Cr. The cells here illustrated can hardly be called thimble-shaped.

A collection of *Pseudagenia sp.* mud cells was found under the loose bark of a tree (fig. 20A), and another

[15] Loc cit. p. 66.

group of identical cells was found under a plank which covered a depression in the ground. Both lots, however,

FIG. 20 B. A mud nest of *Pseudagenia mellipes* within an oak-apple. Slightly enlarged.

gave us not *Pseudagenia* wasps, but both sexes of the parasitic cow-killer, *Sphaerophthalma scaeva* Blake [S. A. Rohwer].

## CHAPTER III

### Some Fly-catching Wasps

*Hypocrabro stirpicolus* Pack. [S. A. Rohwer].

An old railroad tie lay half buried in a heap of dirt. Under the protruding rotten end was a miniature hill of sawdust, or rather particles of wood bitten out, and above this a clean-cut hole pierced the log. We found after we began digging into it that only a small portion of this was rotten, and under the surface the wood was very hard. The long tunnels leading in from the surface aperture were made in the softer, decayed part of the wood. This tunnel led to a series of three cells which were five mm. in diameter and were partitioned to make neat cells fifteen to eighteen mm. long. Another tunnel branched off from the main channel, and, going into a lower stratum of wood, there branched into four similar cells as shown in fig. 21 (slightly enlarged), each containing a definite successive stage in the development of the young. The material used for partitions was the sawdust tightly packed to a thickness of ten mm., so it made a remarkably strong wall.

The prey in these cells was two-winged flies of several species. Two cells that were filled and had very small larvae had four flies each, and another had four flies plus one head. In some cells were many heads, wings and thoraces of flies. One cocoon was of a dark brown color, and all the débris in the cell had been shoved to one end before spinning (fig. 22). Two adults emerged on July 1 and 3.

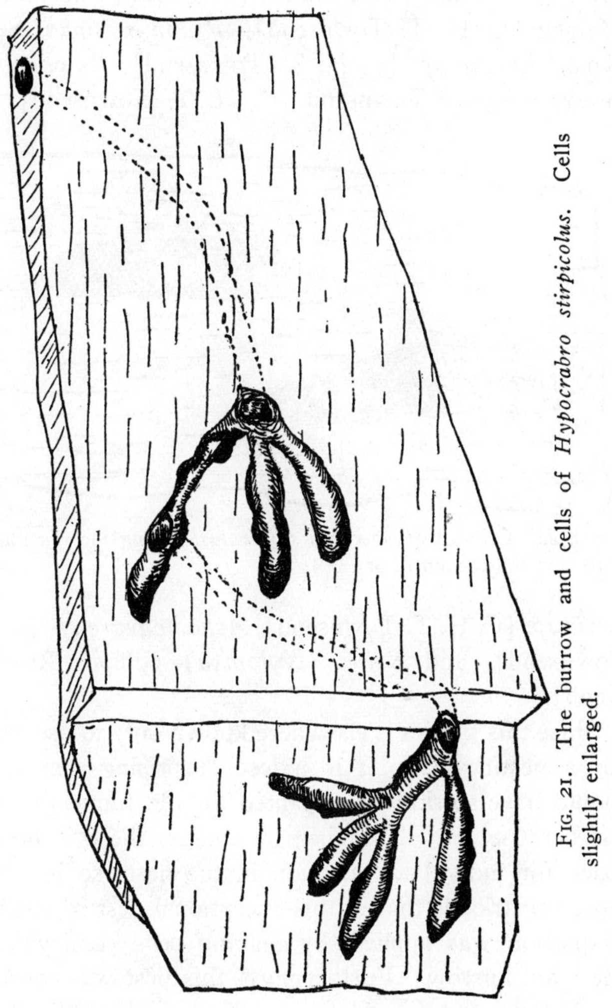

Fig. 21. The burrow and cells of *Hypocrabro stirpicolus.* Cells slightly enlarged.

A variety of flies are used by this wasp. Those found in these and other cells are: *Atrophopoda singularis* Townsend [C. H. T. Townsend], *Ravinia quadrisetosa* Coq. [C.

H. T. Townsend], *Phorbia sp.* [F. Knab], *Phormia regina* Meigen [C. H. T. Townsend], *Psilopus sipho* Say [F. Knab], *Lucilia sp.* [C. H. T. Townsend], *Emphanopteryx eumyothyroides* Townsend [C. H. T. Townsend], *Sarco-*

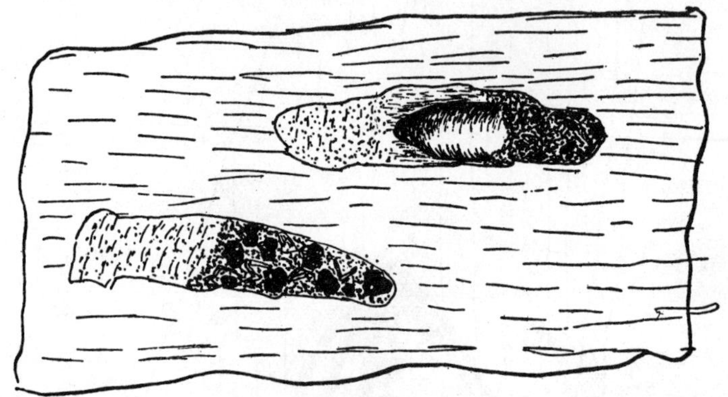

FIG. 22. Cells of *Hypocrabro stirpicolus,* having the remains of the feast and the cocoon in one cell.

*dexia sp.* [C. H. T. Townsend], *Achaetoneura sp.* [C. H. T. Townsend], and *Solva* (*Xylomya*) *pallipes* Loew, [F. Knab].

Since this species is elsewhere known only to use brambles for a nesting-place, it is indeed surprising that this one should have so skillfully adapted the old tunnels in the log for her use. In the stalks, of course, there is no lateral space for individual variation in the nest; so it is all the more remarkable that in this exceptional nest so much good adaptation was applied, by making cells ramifying from one main burrow. Furthermore, this nest was constructed horizontally, while all other nests recorded have been in upright stalks.

On one occasion an elder twig was broken off and examined for twig-dwelling insects, but it was unoccupied. In less than five minutes we passed by this spot again and found a *H. stirpicolus* boring into the soft pith. It had in this brief time made a hole one-sixth inch deep. Another was found still at work burrowing in the pith at so late a date as October 25.

One fine nest in an elderberry twig was found in November. The burrow in the pith chamber was thirteen inches long and one-fourth inch in diameter. The gallery was not at all points in the center of the stalk, but oscillated from side to side. Perhaps the wasp in digging it out had merely followed the line of least resistance and had chosen the softest spots. The partitions were made of the soft pith firmly packed together. The thickness of the partitions and the length of the cells were variable, as the following table shows:

| Partition. | Cell. | Partition. | Cell. |
|---|---|---|---|
| 1⅜ inches | ⅜ inch | ⅜ inch | ½ inch |
| 1 inch | ½ inch | ¼ inch | ⅜ inch |
| ½ inch | ¾ inch | ½ inch | |
| ¼ inch | ⅝ inch | | |

The upper five inches of the tunnel was open and unused. All the six cocoons in the cells rested with the heavy end toward the bottom, leaving the thin, easily opened covering on the top. We do not know, however, whether these wasps habitually emerge by boring through the side of the twig, or by struggling through the pith to gain the top exit. In another series of cells in a twig eight inches long, the partitions in the upper half were broken and crumbled, as if the occupants of the nest might have escaped by that way. Of course, if they emerge by the open, upper end of the stalk, the priority of the lower inmates offers difficulties. These nine adults emerged during our absence, from April 12 to 28. Another neat nest very similar to this is illustrated, exact size, in fig. 23. This had fourteen cells and eleven cocoons. The cells varied in size from 2 to 6 mm., and the cocoons fitted nicely into them. There was no fly débris remaining; every evidence of the feeding proclivities of the tenants was gone.

Packard[1] says that they avail themselves of plants whose stem has a pith which they can readily excavate, and Cresson[2] found their nests in blackberry stems. The Peckhams found that this wasp uses the stems of plants; in fact, this is the famous insect that worked for forty-two consecutive hours with only a ten-minute intermission. They found all tunnels of this species to be from thirty to forty centimeters in length, and the completed cells contained flies of four different species, all dead. Our notes show that the species uses various species of flies. Perhaps Packard was mistaken in stating that the females of *stirpicolus* provision their nests with caterpillars, aphids, spiders and other insects.

Cresson[2] says that the Hymenopteron *Diomorus* hatched from the nest of *H. stirpicolus.*

*Hypocrabro chrysarginus* Lep. [S. A. Rohwer].

A log of wood was lying on the ground, and just beneath it a heap of fine sawdust. This cone-shaped mound pointed to a hole in the log directly above. Presently a black-and-yellow *H. chrysarginus* flew into this hole and remained therein until we lost patience. Among the sawdust on the ground were four flies, apparently dead but quite fresh, *Sarcodexia sp.* ♀, *Sarcodexia sternodontis* Towns. [C. H. T. Townsend] and *Anthrax lateralis* Say. [F. Knab]. There was no way of determining whether the wasp had dropped them as she entered the nest and had abandoned

[1] Guide to the Study of Insects, p. 158. 1889.

[2] Psyche 2: 189. 1878.

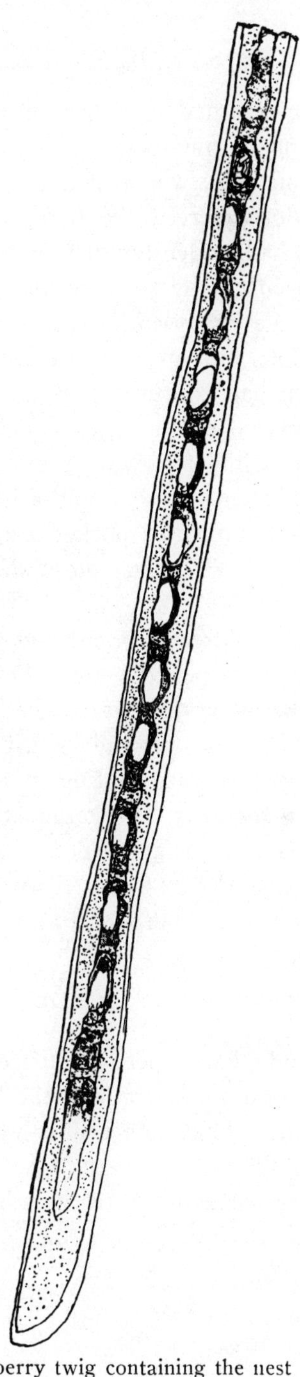

FIG. 23. An elderberry twig containing the nest of *Hypocrabro stirpicolus.* Natural size.

them, or whether she had left them here only as a relay station in bringing in the food. Since the wasp gave no promise of coming out, we opened the log and got her. The entrance-gallery pierced the hard wood for one and a half inches. It had evidently not been made by this wasp, but must have been cut by some beetle during the life of the tree, because the wounded surface was all healed over. Where this previous burrow had reached the rotten wood beneath, the wasp had continued the gallery. The length of this tunnel was seven inches, not exactly straight but oscillating a little, while following the same general direction. The tunnel came to an end and a little to one side of the terminus was a completed pocket containing four flies, 3 ♀'s and 1 ♂, of *Promusca domestica* L. [C. H. T. Townsend].

Neither egg nor larva was found and we could not tell, upon rudely chopping open the log, whether this cell was connected with the gallery, or even whether it was sealed. We suspect that the wasp was only storing this cell.

Barth has found this wasp nesting in an old log in company with *Crabro obscurus, C. montanus* and *C. sexmaculatus.* The adults are nectar feeders, as recorded in the papers of Banks and Robertson. All of these records appear under the generic name *Crabro.*

*Paranothyreus*[3] *cingulatis* Pack. [S. A. Rohwer].

In a steep, sandy bank, perhaps fifteen feet wide and twelve feet high, near the margin of the lake, was a fairly large colony of these black-and-yellow wasps. There was no vegetation on this sandy area (fig. 24), but at some recent time a large pile of straw had been dumped and

[3] The generic names of this species were formerly *Crabro* and *Thyreopus, fide* Rohwer.

FIG. 24. The bare portion of the sand bank was inhabited by *Paranothyreus cingulatis.*

burned there. This is mentioned merely to show that the smoke and flames had been unable to put the insects to rout. A survey of a large part of the shore revealed no other colonies of these wasps. While the community was large, nothing in the way of communal life could be discovered. Each wasp conducted its own home independently.

The open holes were conspicuous because of their form. While the burrows themselves were round, the entrance was shaped like an arched doorway with a flat bottom, and was one-eighth inch larger than the inner hole. The wasps were coming and going, each bringing a Dipterous morsel under her abdomen, darting into the hole with it, without stopping at the entrance or leaving it at the doorway until an examination of the interior could be made.

Several of the wasps were enlarging their nests. The method was to bite out and loosen the sand, and rapidly kick it out under the body, through the doorway, where it rolled down the slope below. When biting out the earth from the sides or ceiling of the nest, they turned around, sometimes quite upside down, and the abdomen squirmed as they forcibly attacked each bite. In many cases the nests were under, and sometimes concealed by, a little natural hood or projection of the earth (fig. 25, burrow in the upper left-hand corner).

The nests were found, when excavated, to be of various shapes. The accompanying illustration will give an idea of the diversity of form and their general nature (fig. 25, one-fourth natural size).

We have never seen lateral cells directly connected with these channels, but have often found from two to eight isolated cells near by. Perhaps they had been made as branches, but when the short, lateral galleries leading to them were closed, the connection could not be distinguished in the sand. Whether or not this wasp digs a long burrow and makes several cells from the main gallery, we cannot say with certainty. In nests excavated later the cells were sometimes found to be so numerous that we could only suspect that other wasps were responsible for them. The burrow in all the nests was about one-eighth inch in diameter, and the entrance one-quarter inch wide. When the mother was found within, with some flies at the bottom (showing that the nest was being provisioned), it was seen that no perceptible chamber or cell had been excavated, but the completely filled and closed cells which we came upon in the sand were of very pretty oval form, one-fourth by one-half inch. In one such case we found fourteen flies forming a pretty heap, all piled up like cord-wood, one atop the other, all with the head laid in the same direction. In two other cells close together, twenty flies each were taken. Others contained from eleven to twenty flies. All of the flies used by these wasps were *Paralimna appendiculata*

Loew. [F. Knab]. All which we took from the nests or from the wasps in transit were dead.

The following week we again visited Creve Coeur Lake and further studied the contour and contents of the burrows. It was strange that, in one mass of homogeneous material like a sand-bank, with no roots, stones or other

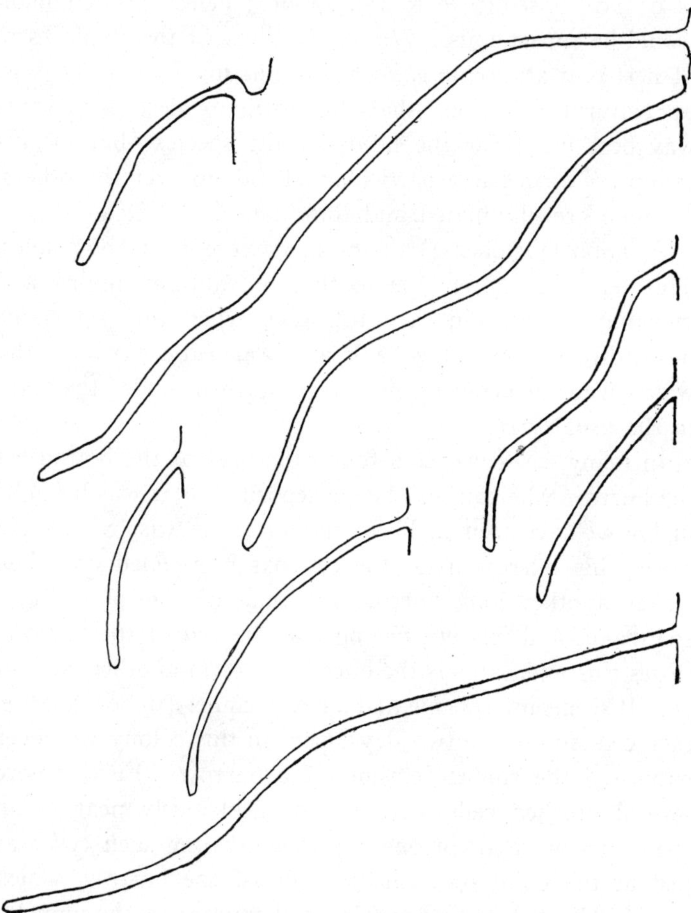

FIG. 25. The burrows of *Paranothyreus cingulatis.* One-fourth natural size.

obstructions, no two burrows were alike. Of course there is some reason for *Philanthus* and *Xylocelia metathoracicus* making a tortuous gallery in a clay bank which is full of rocks, roots and rubbish; but here this extreme variety in habit makes one think that either there is instability of the species, or that so far as natural selection goes this point is of no consequence to the species; hence a fixed habit would be superfluous. We like to think of the staple form of nest that all *Ammophila pictipennis* make as being fixed by Natural Selection—that this form of nest is in some way best fitted for the needs of the species—but in this group no form has a particular advantage over the others, so none are eliminated and thus none is selected.

At noon (October 2) the mothers were all in their holes. This may have been due to the cold autumn nights and mornings. Later in the afternoon, when the sun shone more directly upon the bank and warmed it, two of the wasps were carrying in flies, hugging them under the body in the usual way.

In many cases we have found the prey at the bottom of the burrow where it was being deposited as it was brought in, but we have been unable to find out if the wasp completely closes this burrow after the cell has been filled and then makes another long burrow for the same purpose, or if she makes and fills one chamber at the end of the burrow, closes this and extends the burrow to form another, and so on. It seems improbable that a new channel can be made for each cell, for in the two days spent in this colony we never witnessed the surface closing of a burrow. Furthermore several finished cells were found suspiciously near to an open burrow, and, in one nest opened, one such cell was just at the point of a sharp angle of the burrow, which would indicate that they are dropped down from the tunnel.

One interesting item about this species is the tenacity

with which they cling to the fly. We have caught them in a test-tube, and only with the hardest shaking could they be induced to relinquish their hold. At the time when we were afield we never thought of the probability of their holding the fly by the aid of their sting. The figure (26), drawn from a pinned specimen which was placed in the cyanide jar with the prey and later shaken loose, shows clearly the position of the abdomen and sting, and reveals how it is possible for the fly to be carried on the under side of the body, with the curved abdomen and sting holding

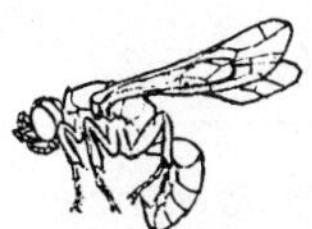

FIG. 26. *Paranothyreus cingulatis.* ♀. Twice natural size.

the prey like a hook. This detail, however, needs further clarification. Parker finds that a near relative, *Oxybelus quadrinotatus,* enters the nest with the fly firmly impaled upon her sting.

The only biological note on this species is recorded from Washington State by Kincaid,[4] who saw it flying about clumps of *Lysichiton kamtschatinse.*

[4] Ent. News 11: 358.

# CHAPTER IV

## The Enemies of the Plant-lice

*Xylocelia metathoracicus*[1] Mickel. [S. A. Rohwer].

The picture herewith (fig. 27) will give the reader an idea of the physical features of the site of the only colony of *Xylocelia metathoracicus* which we have observed. This perpendicular bank, six feet high, was the side of a gully which had been washed through a vacant lot by many rains. The wall at this point faced directly southward, where the sun beat down with burning glare, and not a breath of breeze could enter the hole walled in by dirt and tall vegetation.

On September 3 we came here in quest of large game, but found instead a swarm of these tiny black wasps dancing in the sun on the face of the bluff. We were startled to find them here in so great numbers, for none had been in evidence when we had visited the place only the week before. At that earlier date, however, in digging out a *Philanthus* burrow in this same bank, we had exhumed a tiny cocoon from which emerged one of the *X. metathoracicus*, the first we had ever seen. This one incident leads us to think that the normal time of emergence of these wasps was September 1, and that the entire population had come forth at this

[1] This wasp has been only recently described by Mickel, *Ann. Ent. Soc. Amer.* **9**: 349. 1916. Mr. Rohwer writes that *Xylocelia* is the correct name for *Diodontus* in the Pemphredonini as treated by Fox.

FIG. 27. The clay bank where *Xylocelia metathoracicus* build their burrows.

time, in the same manner as *Bembix* and other wasps, to participate in a sun-dance at the opening of their season of activity.

They did not wander far from the general region; neither did they keep in a strictly defined swarm as some insects do, but wavered lightly and leisurely to and fro in front of the face of the bank. As they hovered and flew they always kept their heads toward the wall. Occasionally they sat down at the foot of the bank to rest and rub their abdomens. Frequently, while one was resting thus, another dashed down and bumped against it, or pounced upon it and stirred it into flight again. Only twice on these occasions did we see real matings accomplished. One mated pair on the wing was soon lost to view; the other remained in copulo, the male surmounting the female, for five minutes before we lost sight of them. The pairs seemed to be equally at ease walking, resting or flying. While at rest, however, they were disturbed frequently (eight times in one brief resting-period), by other males eager to mate.

Presently we realized that the size of the swarm (or rather colony, for it was not unified enough to be called a swarm) was gradually diminishing; occasionally one wasp would alight on the bank and slip quietly into a tiny hole, so small as to be almost imperceptible. The holes must have been of their own making, for they were so neat a fit for the insects and of a very uniform size. We dug out some of them to a depth of two or three inches, but at this early date found no nest. They usually slipped into their holes without any confusion, alighting on the very spot where the opening was. Sometimes they almost flew into the burrow.

Their flight was a lazy, droning flight, poising and wavering to and fro in the air more than dancing. It all seemed the more wonderful because the wasps, burrows and all were so tiny; the adult wasps were only a little larger than gnats.

The foregoing observations were made between 11 and 12 o'clock; it was 3 p. m. when we returned to the place the next day. By that time the wasps were behaving not at all as they did on the first day, but this difference may have been due to either the hour or the day. Other wasps which indulge in these sun-dances in the morning of their lives usually dance only in the morning of the day, and then turn their attention to more serious occupations after the second or third day and in the afternoons. (See account of *Bembix nubilipennis*). It may well be that these wasps were already in the second or third day of their existence when we found them.

On this day most of them, when they approached the bank, would fly into these burrows. The apertures were temporarily closed from within, and the wasps spent only a few secouds there, when they would come out and fly away.

The holes were quite inconspicuous, and they were perceived only when the wasps entered them. If the openings were as inconspicuous to their enemies as they were to us, there was little need for their closing them.

None of these wasps seemed to be making burrows. It is possible that these were the holes from which they had originally emerged. We see no reason why they should not serve perfectly well as places of nidification as well. To be sure, the wasps may have dug them before they were discovered, but we saw none of them digging at this time.

On the second day, instead of dancing or digging, all were busy carrying in prey which consisted of aphids, *Aphis setariae* Thos. [J. J. Davis]. These they carried in their jaws. The wasps clung tightly to their booty, and even when taken in a test-tube and violently shaken they would not release their hold.

The bank was of "made" or "filled in" ground, with pieces of glass, crockery, cinders, etc., strewn thickly through it, so it was impossible, at this stage, to trace out the delicate burrows to the end; but some that we followed for a distance showed that they were usually very crooked and gradually wandered downward in their course.

From time to time, until the end of September, we visited these tiny black wasps in the dirt bank. While they continued plentiful, they were by no means so abundant as they were on the first day, when they performed the sun-dance. This might have been due to the elimination of the males. The specimens present later and those entering the holes were all the larger ones, probably females, and at no time did we again find the mating behavior; hence we suspect that *X. metathoracicus* mates once for all time.

Approaching autumn did not seem to cause their industry to wane. On October 6 many of them were out. They were all females, coming and going busily at their nests, carrying aphids as usual. No males were present, and the sun-dance seemed quite forgotten. The dance is no doubt a sign of their having just emerged, so probably the date we have recorded for that event might be accepted as approximately the date of the first appearance of this species.

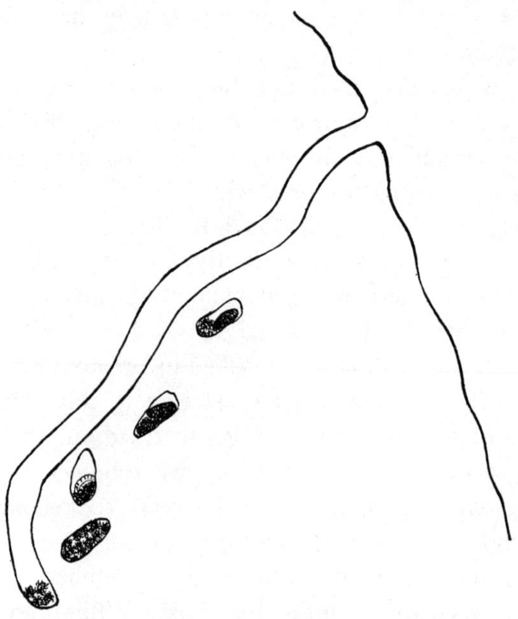

FIG. 28. The burrow and cells of *Xylocelia metathoracicus.* Enlarged.

We succeeded at last in tracing one hole to its terminus. The opening and gallery were about three mm. in diameter. The channel was tortuous, owing partly to the rocky condition of the soil, and its total length was less than four inches. At the bottom of the gallery (fig. 28) were four aphids. Doubtless the mother was carrying in prey when we intruded. A short distance to one side in the earth was a little cell, sealed off; this was completely packed with forty-eight aphids, all of the one species, *Aphis setariae.* They were all dead. It was with difficulty that these delicate organisms could be removed, and if the minute wasp-egg was among them we failed to notice it. Just above this was another cell, also disconnected, containing a full-grown larva, but the food-supply had been exhausted. Still further up, in line with the gallery and nearer to the opening, were two cells, evidently older, since in them the pupal cases were already spun.

Hence we see here that the wasp probably uses one tunnel throughout its life, and that it digs a little channel turning sharply downward at the end, fills the end of it with prey and an egg, seals it up, thus forming a cell, and continues the burrow further into the earth in such a way that the little cells are always dropped beneath the gallery. Thus, as we progress inward, we find the young in earlier and earlier stages of development. As the season advanced these galleries and the row of subjoined cells became more nearly complete, while the mother continued, at least in several marked holes, to work in the same nest week after week.

Until the middle of October they were industriously at work on every day that was warm enough for them to venture out, and even on November 3 several dared to come forth as if attempting to continue this work.

No notes on the behavior of this species have been published. A moment's comparison with the ways of allied species may give the reader a more comprehensive idea of the ways of this group.

Westwood[2] says that *Diodontus gracilis* and *D. corniger* provide aphids for food for their progeny, carrying them in the mouth to their cells in the holes in posts. Morley[3] finds *D. tristis* V. der Lind. flying to nests in sand banks.

[2] Introduction to Modern Classification of Insects **2**: 195. 1840.
[3] Entom. **31**: 14. 1898.

Ashmead[4] says *D. tristis* Dahlb. and *D. minutus* Fab. burrow in sand, while *D. americanus* Pack. burrows in hard clay and makes burrows of "considerable depth." On *D. americanus,* one of the "tiniest of all the wasps," the Peckhams[5] have given us a very interesting account, and the only record extant heretofore of an American species of *Diodontus.* They find for this species that in most cases the aphids are killed by squeezing the neck repeatedly between the mandibles; in other cases the disturbance to the prey is so slight that they are able to walk about as soon as released. The wasp never uses the sting. The nests are in the ground, with some grains of dirt irregularly heaped around the edges. It takes the wasp about an hour to dig the nest; she carries the earth out in her mandibles and front legs, backing from the hole. The nest is not closed until the provisioning is completed. The number of aphids in each of six nests varied from five to forty, and sometimes the aphis served as food for the mother also.

*Ceratophorus*[6] *tenax* Fox [S. A. Rohwer].

At Valley Park, Missouri, on June 26, we broke off an elder stem and found this wasp in the hollow within. The lower portion was crammed with twenty-five aphids, *Macrosiphum rudbeckiae* Fitch [J. J. Davis]. The partitions were of the pulverized stem. It was 4 a. m., when dawn was just breaking, and we suspect this mother had spent the night asleep in her nest. Another elder stem taken near by had a few loose aphids of the same species in the top cells and two pupal cases beneath. On July 20, two adult *C. tenax* emerged from these.

[4] Psyche 7: 46. 1896.

[5] Bull. Wisc. Geol. & Nat. Hist. Surv. 2: 99-106.

[6] Commonly known as *Pemphredon.*

# CHAPTER V

## The Bee-killing Wasps

*Philanthus punctatus* Say. [S. A. Rohwer].

The *Philanthus punctatus* is a faithful little creature, but her task of nesting is so prolonged that we have never been able to watch the entire process in a single case. By putting together the parts of the story as we have gathered them, we may be able to get some idea of this shy wasp's way of living.

We discovered one burrow, already begun, August 1, at 8 o'clock. A lot of loose dirt was rolling down a tiny embankment by the roadside; the dirt was freshly kicked or pushed out, and we ascertained with a probe that the burrow underneath it went into the bank horizontally for about one inch. We could not remain with the wasp then, but the next morning we were pleased to find that she was still at work. A good deal more dirt had been pushed out. We knew that this must have been done very recently, because heavy rains during the night had tamped down the previous lot. That evening, too, when we passed by, we were certain that she was still at work.

Knowing that it would be impossible to watch her further, and desiring to know whether she spent the nights in her burrow, we dug her up. The hole went horizontally into the embankment, an inch below the surface level of the ground above, and toward the south for two inches; then it turned at right angles and went westward and downward at an angle of forty-five degrees, for ten inches, the course of the channel being broken at one point by a rather sharp kink, without any obstruction or cause that we could see. It then turned at right angles again and went directly down into the earth for two inches. Here, at the end of the tunnel, was the female *P. punctatus,* probably ready to spend the night. The monotonous details of the channel are mentioned here because it certainly was the crookedest one we ever saw in the work of wasps. No larva nor provisions were present—there did not even seem to be a terminal chamber—so we suspect that the burrow was still in course of construction. If this is only a part of her work, what must be the extent of her finished project! The entire length of the burrow was about fourteen inches, and after its many convolutions it terminated about eleven inches below the surface of the ground.

The burrow was already begun when we found it, and it seemed still to be incomplete; nevertheless, we know that the insect was at work digging for two whole days. The wasp is comparatively small, and when we think of the small burrows of some of her larger cousins, we marvel at the amount of work that she does. It is truly wonderful that this little creature should delve so deep into the earth to find safety for her offspring, which doubtless she will never see. Since the top of the hole is always covered with the loose dirt, and since she is never seen out-of-doors, we suspect that she keeps pushing the dirt upwards with her head and cut at the orifice, thereby keeping her house constantly closed to intruders.

Later in the summer, September 19, we found one insect hovering over her nest, which was temporarily closed. She seemed to be performing her flight of orientation, calmly poising in the air and deliberately swinging, pendulum-like, to and fro, in semicircles, with her head always toward the hole. The arcs or semicircles of her flight gradually grew wider, and suddenly, with a dash, she flew off across the field.

On the same day we found, on the firm, bald margin of the boys' baseball diamond (fig. 2), a little mound of very fine dirt, almost indistinguishable from a small ant's hill. It was neither of pellets nor of dust, but of dirt which was granular like corn-meal. A tunnel five inches long led down under this at a slope of forty-five degrees. The hole was not under the center of this mound, but under one edge; the dirt had been thrown out in a neat pile in front of the bore—not thrown about indiscriminately like the *Bembix* pile, nor carried to a distance like that of *Ammophila*.

We dug it out. The larva had just pupated, but was injured with the trowel when it was unearthed suddenly. The length of the burrow was about twelve inches.

In the same location, another *P. punctatus* flew about and settled upon a characteristic hill of loose soil. The wasp kicked the dirt from the opening, entered and closed the hole by casting up the loose dirt in the tunnel. She stayed in about ten minutes, came out head first by working her way through the loose soil, which fell in and closed behind her, covering the hole. She flew over the nest for a few seconds with a jerky motion (probably the flight of orientation) and then flew away. After some minutes she returned with a bee; this she concealed so well that we could not see it until we got down on all fours to watch her as she opened the nest. She kicked the loose soil away as she did before, and by close scrutiny one could see that she held the bee tightly to the ventral side of her body with the middle pair of legs, while with the first pair she dug out the dirt, and with the hind pair kicked it back. She remained within for about five minutes and left, after closing the hole behind her. But at this interesting climax the boys came romping across the diamond ready for their game, so we were obliged to relinquish the field to them.

For about seven days we had kept our eyes on another burrow and had known that activities were going on inside it, and a few times we had caught sight of the female or had seen some fresh earth thrown out. On September 24 we opened the hole and found its entire length to be about twelve inches. It followed a somewhat irregular slope of approximately thirty degrees, so the end was five inches beneath the surface of the ground. The mother was in the burrow. Near the terminus was a short branch gallery or neck, leading off at a right angle from the main channel; this led to a chamber which was oval and a trifle more than a half-inch long. This neck was snugly filled with soil, and the chamber contained a white pupal case and some heads and wings of bees. Another burrow of an identical general plan, although with the main channel a little more crooked (fig. 29), leads us to think that the mother *Philanthus* digs a long main burrow, then makes, near the end of this, a branch with a pocket which she provisions and seals, and that she then proceeds to extend the main burrow further, with a view to making more cells on the sides. If this species uses one burrow for several young, she is more economical than *Bembix*, which probably digs a new burrow for each larva.

Another of these nests was discovered on July 23. It pierced the side wall of a little depression, and a large quantity of loose earth lay scattered beneath it. One of us chanced to be near when the *Philanthus* came to her hole at 8:30 a. m., brushed out the loose dirt with her forelegs, kicking it backwards under her body in a way very similar to *Bembix,* and darted into the hole. Once inside, she

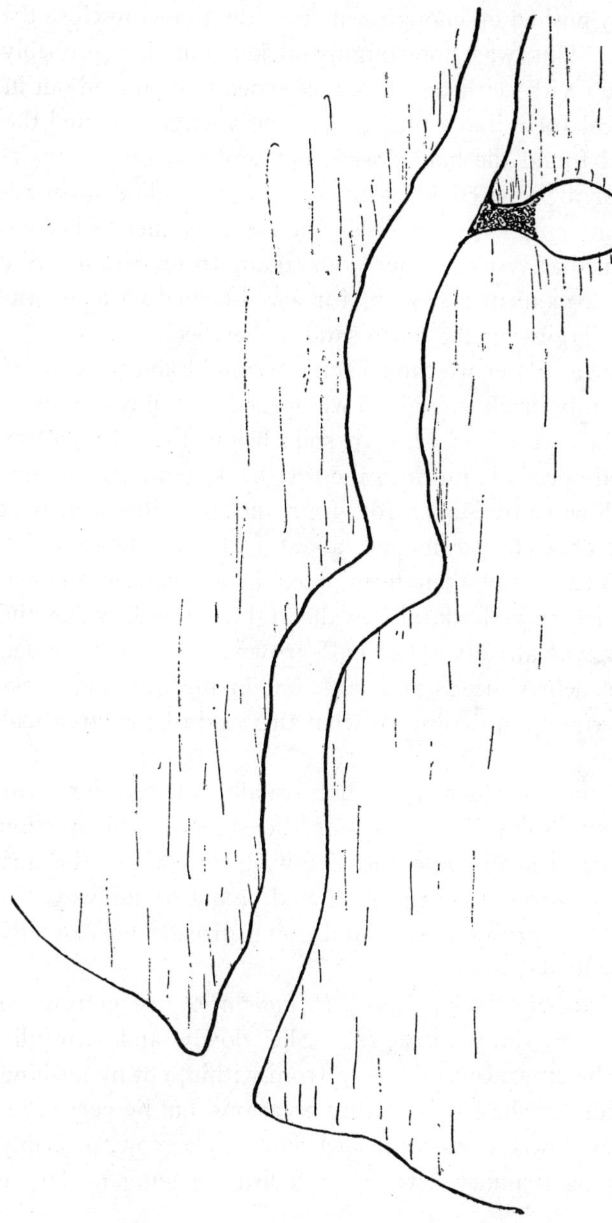

Fig. 29. The burrow and pocket of *Philanthus punctatus*. Pocket exact size, burrow enlarged.

promptly pushed up enough soil from the tunnel to close the burrow. This was not roughly kicked out, but probably pushed up with her head, since it seeemed to be forced out in cylindrical form like a plug. At 2:30 we again visited the spot and found the hole closed; but probably only temporarily, for a probe could easily be inserted. The wasp returned and entered, in precisely the same manner as before, and immediately closed her door again from within. She was not a moment too soon, for a red-bellied parasite was already digging in the loose sand at her heels.

Three days later we came back at twilight and then found it apparently firmly closed, so we opened it. Only the upper few inches were packed with soil; below this, the gallery remained open. It ran into the tiny bank, with only a very slight downward slope, for four inches, after which it dropped at a steeper incline, about forty-five degrees, for eleven inches, and then terminated in a chamber an inch long which turned sharply to the right. The larva in the chamber was already about half-grown; it was surrounded by some débris, heads and legs, but in the growing darkness we could not determine what the food of the larva had been.

Thus they frequently, if not usually, choose for their nesting-site some little slope or the side of a depression where they can dig into the side-wall, and where the dirt cast out can roll down the slope and be out of the way. A number of burrows were found going directly horizontally into clay banks.

We chanced to see a sleepy *P. punctatus* just getting up one June morning at 7:20. She slowly and carefully opened the entrance to the hole from within, not by pushing the dirt out as she does on other occasions, but by very carefully and slowly working it back into the burrow, probably by scraping it under her. First a little opening no larger than a pinhead appeared, then this grew, as if by magic, until the round face of the *Philanthus* was quietly and intently gazing at us. Presently she slipped out through the opening; the loose earth lightly closed behind her and she flew away on the morning air.

*P. punctatus* seems to experience as little difficulty as *Bembix* in finding her nest upon returning to it. She alights from flight upon the very spot where her hole is concealed under a little mound of loose dirt. Only once we saw one in error; she entered a hole in the bank and came scuttling out, then tried once more and emerged again. Then she began digging at a spot right beside this hole and uncovered her own nest only one-quarter inch away from the other hole, the domicile of some other insect, which she had entered by mistake. It is little wonder, however, that she committed the error, when her neighbor's door stood invitingly open only one-fourth inch from where her own lay covered. Repeated observations have taught us to expect to find the mistress within the burrow if the door stands open, but if during the day it is closed, she is probably away from home. Since she makes chambers from time to time alongside her tunnel, she probably alternates the work of excavating and hunting.

The bees, *Halictus sparsus* Robt. ♀ [J. C. Crawford], *H. versatus* Robt. ♀ [J. C. Crawford], *H. pruinosus* Robt., and various other species of *Halictus,* which we found in the wasps' possession, in the burrows, or in the cells were always dead. We saw no marks of violence on them to tell us the manner of their death. Ashmead finds that these wasps prey upon *Halictus disparalis* Cr.

On one occasion we tried to offer a bee with the thorax crushed to a *Philanthus* which was finishing her burrow. Repeatedly we laid it at the mouth of the burrow, but just as often she carried it back and discarded it. A second *Philan-*

*thus* did exactly the same, but when finally she returned to her hole with a bee of her own she seemed to become confused at the sight of ours lying there, hesitated and dropped her own and flew away.

The Peckhams have some very interesting notes on the stinging habits and general behavior of this wasp. They also illustrate a nest which, in shape, is unlike anything we describe here. They find that the males of this species construct lodgings in the sand, and return to them night after night to sleep.

*Pseudanthophilus vertilabris*[1] Fab. [S. A. Rohwer].

On the afternoon of September 16 a little pile of dirt, about two inches in diameter, appeared to have been newly excavated and lay covering the mouth of a hole. A *P. vertilabris* alighted on the pile, carrying an insect snug beneath her body, and walked about as if seeking a place to enter. She dropped her prey for a few seconds while she explored the mound; this gave us the opportunity to see that it was a little bee all yellow with pollen. She soon picked up her property again and, carrying it between her legs to a precise spot on the opposite side of the pile, began excavating and kicking the dirt up behind her, all the while keeping a firm hold upon her precious bee with her middle legs while the forelegs dug up the soil, and an instant later the hind legs flung it back. Her method of proceeding with her work seemed to be: after she had gone inside the channel, to leave her insect in the part of the gallery already cleared, retreat to the opening and kick out the dirt, go back and excavate some more and move the insect down to the new clear spot.

[1] This wasp is generally known as *Philanthus ventilabris* or *P. vertilabris*.

After a minute or two of this work, she came out and began vigorously kicking in the soil. At this point we had to take her or run the risk of losing her identity. Upon opening the burrow, we found the top two inches filled in loosely and the remainder empty. The hole sloped downward at an angle of forty-five degrees, first toward the southeast for ten inches, then it turned west and then reversed sharply and went directly east. We could not accurately follow the sharp curves of the channel, but at the end were found a pupal case and a larva, both surrounded by bits of black chitin. It was one of the longest wasp tunnels that we have seen. It was little wonder that the abundant soil on the surface made a conspicuous mound. Is it then the custom of these wasps to continue using the same hole for several offspring? It certainly appears so, since this burrow already contained two babes of different ages. We do not know whether the bee which the mother wasp was bringing in was intended for food for the larva already in the nest, or to be a host of another egg.

The Peckhams have a short note on *P. vertilabris,* wherein they tell how she takes bees of several genera and species into a ground nest. She carries her prey with her second pair of legs, and closes the door whenever she leaves the nest.

Robertson finds the adults feeding on the flowers of various species of *Solidago*. Packard figures this species in the American Naturalist, 1 : 77, 1868, and his Guide, p. 158, 1885, where he mentions this as "our most common southward form."

The Peckhams tell us how *P. punctatus* males make holes in the sand wherein to spend the night, and we found a male of this species, *P. vertilabris,* hiding one evening at deep twilight, in the burrow of a cincindela beetle.

# CHAPTER VI

## SOME MUD-DAUBING WASPS THAT HUNT SPIDERS

*Sceliphron* (*Pelopoeus*) *caementarium* Drury.

In a former study[1] of the contents of the nests of this species we included many items on the behavior of this insect. We present here a few notes on the biology of this species, not included in those pages.

We learned in the previous observations that the mother sometimes fails to supply sufficient food for the growth of the young, but we did not inquire whether the larvae could assimilate more than the normal amount of food supplied by the mother. The number of spiders most frequently supplied by her is six or seven. In the one case in which we experimented upon this point, we added three more spiders; these were promptly devoured, so we added one more. By the next evening this too was gone, so we gave the young wasp four more fat ones. Two of these were eaten, and the larva was found dead. Whether its gluttony produced its death we do not know, but in the five days it had eagerly consumed six extra spiders.

During the latter part of June we had the good fortune to discover three *Pelopoeus* larvae in the act of pupating. This enabled us to learn accurately the duration of the pupal period at that time of year. One of them emerged nine-

[1] Journ. Animal Behavior **6**: 27-63. 1916. Also Journ. Animal Behavior **5**: 240-249. 1915.

teen days after pupation, and the others twenty-two days after spinning.

The Peckhams gauge the quality of the sting of wasps by the longevity of the victim, but in our opinion the size, vitality and species of the spider should be taken into account. The *Pelopoeus* or *Chalybion* may give a sting of standard size to all of her prey, regardless of their size. It remains unknown whether the larger spiders live longer than the smaller ones. We found great variation in the longevity of the spiders from one new *Pelopoeus* cell. The wasp's egg was still new and unhatched, so we knew that the spiders had not been entombed more than one day at most. On the day of discovery, August 11, they all moved their legs actively, but their vigor gradually waned; on August 19 the first one died, after having lived 8 days after being stung, and the other seven lived respectively 8, 10, 14, 14, 14, 25 and 32 days.

Our actual observations have confirmed Peckhams' suspicions that the choice, tender abdomens of the spiders are first eaten by the young larva, and later, if there is need for more food, the legs are served for a second course.

A completely melanic specimen of male *Sceliphron caementarium* was seen getting nectar from the flowers of smartweed. When taken up in the hand, it pretended to attempt to sting by curling and passing its abdomen over the finger, much in the manner of a more formidable female.

One July day we were startled to see a *Pelopoeus* leisurely flitting from flower to flower, with the entire abdomen gone, only the basal segment remaining. She seemed lively enough, and just as happy as though she were all there. We took her home. The next day she appeared the same, but we could not see how she could escape misery, so consigned her to the cyanide bottle. Packard[2] records a female *Pelopoeus*

[2] Psyche **2**: 18. 1877.

*coeruleus* that lived more than twelve hours after it was beheaded.

FIG. 30. Nests of *Sceliphron caementarium* or *Chalybion caeruleum.* Interior and exterior views. Two-thirds natural size.

One often pictures the male wasps of this species as lazy, good-for-nothing fellows, while the females are incessantly busy, bringing in mud and spiders and making the nest; but the females too like to loaf sometimes. On September 16, 1914, we observed one mother at work during the afternoon. At 3:15 the cell was completed but unsealed and unfilled, and the wasp was bringing mud to reinforce the nest by spreading it thin all over the outside. Up to 7 o'clock she was still thus occupied without paying any further attention to the unfilled cell. Until noon the next day the wasp was absent, possibly loafing. At 4 o'clock when we returned to the nest we found that the cell had been filled and sealed in the interval, but further work for the day had been discontinued. We watched for her the remainder of that afternoon and all the next day, but there was no return whatsoever to the nest. On the following day also we lay in wait for her, and were about to give her up as dead, lost or stolen, when she returned for an hour at midday and finished another cell, after which she seemed to consider herself deserving of another afternoon off. Unfortunately we could not watch her beyond this time, but we have often wondered if this was an unusually indolent individual, or if such is about the usual rate of progress of the work of these wasps.

The nests of this mud-dauber and those of *Chalybion coeruleum* are identical. Figure 30 illustrates the exterior and interior of their homes. Some nests show nicely the details of architecture (upper figure), while in others these details are obliterated by the decorations of mud pellets (see middle figure).

A six-celled nest of a *P. caementarium* was found hanging firmly to a root only two mm. in diameter which ran along its longitudinal axis. It reminded us of the mode of attachment of the potter wasp's cell to the twigs of plants. This was the root of an overturned tree on the top of a sandbank; the soil was washed away from the roots, and on one of these strands of exposed rootlet this nest was very deftly attached. Since this root was so small, it must have required a great deal of deftness on the part of the mother to attach her first cell to it; of course with this one well anchored for a foundation it was easy to build the others. But if this sort of site was generally used by primitive *caementarium*—and this undoubtedly must have been necessary before people provided them with barns and shed-roofs—then we think, in those days of pioneering, a deal more of ingenuity was necessary than in the life of ease and convenience of today. Campers had built fires in the hole under the roots of the tree, and the smoke had blackened the nest, but this did not affect the contents of the cells.

On another occasion we found a four-celled nest hanging to a thread-like vine which grew into the shed through a crack in the wall. Despite the fact that there was hundreds of feet of board surface upon which this wasp could have built, it chose this frail vine. These facts, together with the fact that these nests have often been found plastered to nails protruding from the walls, on umbrella ribs, corn-husks and other unlikely places, suggest that probably the primitive instinct was to build in such places.

At Lake View, Kansas, a fine, large nest was being built on the outside of a schoolhouse. It was structurally complete but the mother was busy daubing mud all over it to strengthen it. In taking it down it became slightly broken, so we left it. The next day the mother had plastered mud all over the broken parts. Some would say: "A wise mother!"; but in this case there was, we believe, no wisdom or intelligence at all; she was daubing mud all over the nest at the time when the accident happened; hence nothing is more natural than that she should continue to spread mud all over the broken places as well. In our opinion it would have shown real intelligence if she would or could have interrupted her momentum of spreading mud all over the nest and constructively repaired, ring by ring, each injured cell. This she did not do. However, we once saw a case where, when the cell was broken while under construction, the wasp did repair it so. Here too it was probably instinctive work, as she was already occupied with the task of ring-making.

We have every reason to believe that *Pelopoeus* suffers at the hands of many impostors. The appalling toll of parasites has been reported previously. We find also, in the laboratory, that mice carry off mud nests or open them on the spot and eat the contents. One wasp was seen dead in a spider's web, and a second one was actually being devoured by a spider, *Theridium tepidariorum* Koch. [N. Banks]. The Peckhams say that this wasp goes in and out of spiders' webs for prey, and it is surprising that it should get trapped in the game.

*Pelopoeus* is, sometimes at least, a flower feeder. We have seen her eating at the flowers of iron-weed and a pink-flowered wild pea.

These wasps do not congregate at night, but sleep individually on the flowers.[3]

Their cocoons differ from those of their near relative, *Chalybion caeruleum* as illustrated in our previous note.[4] Other life history details are very interestingly told by the Peckhams.[5]

Ashmead[6] writes that this wasp is distributed all over North America. Blackburn and Cameron[7] find that this species, introduced by man's agency to the Hawaiian Islands, is now a common species. Cameron[8] finds, too, that

[3] Rau, Ann. Ent. Soc. Amer. **9**: 227-274. 1917.

[4] Psyche **12**: 62-63. 1915.

[5] Bull. Wisc. Geol. & Nat. Hist. Surv. **2**: 176-199. 1898.

[6] Psyche **7**: 65. 1894.

[7] Mem. Manchester Lit. and Phil. Soc. **10**: 233. 1886.

[8] Proc. & Trans. Nat. Hist. Soc. Glasgow II. **1**: 264. 1885-86.

hopper; we do not know whether she had just caught it or had had it there somewhere all the time during her many attempts at digging in this region; but, from what we saw later, we judge the wasp undoubtedly had the hopper in hiding. She carried it fully three feet beyond her hole and hunted for five minutes before she rediscovered her burrow. She then resumed digging earnestly, going in and out mechanically, like a toy wound up, and coming out two or three times to kick the dirt further back from the mouth of the nest. She worked earnestly, as if the work was now full of meaning to her.

Disturbed by a passing boy, she flew around, came back and examined her prey and returned to more digging, brought the hopper a foot nearer and propped the thing up in a tuft of grass and went back diligently to digging, lugging out in her jaws loads of earth as large as her head. She held the masses of soft dirt up against the mandibles with her front legs as she carried it out backwards, to keep the load from falling to pieces, so it looked as if she were carrying a double armful up to her chin. As the burrow grew deeper she backed away from it further, to perhaps a distance of two inches or more, before dropping her load, and occasionally paused to sweep the whole pile back with her forelegs.

We examined her grasshopper, a *Dissosteira carolina* Linn., and were astonished to find that its hind legs were gone. Evidently they had been carefully bitten off, though probably not by *atratum,* for the cut was smooth, and not lacerated as the wounds would have been if the legs had been torn off.

The same day we found another hopper in the field with the jumping legs neatly cut off. Both of these mutilated hoppers displayed all normal activities except jumping.

After about ten minutes more of digging, this one brought

her prey nearer, to within one foot of the hole. She carried it by straddling it right-side-up, grasping its antennae in her mandibles, clasping her forelegs around its neck, and struggling over the ground with her two hind pairs of legs. The wonderful modification of the legs of this species, as shown in figure 36, shows how capable they are of scraping and carrying the soil, as well as long enough gracefully to straddle and ride home a huge grasshopper. After another brief period of digging, the wasp moved the hopper to the very brink of the hole and swung it around so it was directly facing the sloping burrow, although it had formerly been behind the hole. She went in, turned around and reappeared at once, head up, seized the grasshopper's antennae and dragged it in out of sight. The hole was a close fit for the prey; it was with difficulty that she squeezed it in. For only one brief minute she remained inside the chamber with her booty; then she scrambled out and scooped in a few armfuls of dirt, arranging each load slightly but packing it little. As the channel filled, she tamped the dirt down more. She scooped in each armful of earth with a circular stroke, cutting a crescent-shaped area out of the tiny hill, smoothly and systematically like a workman carefully scooping sand away from one side of a heap (fig. 37). Such precision rather startled us, since we were accustomed to *Bembix'* way of scratching over the whole region.

With her head she packed it constantly tighter as she neared the top. When the depression was nearly full she stopped taking the loose earth, but bit up chunks of firm, fresh dirt which she carried in her mandibles and broke to pieces on the site, just as *Sphex* does with little clods, rubbing and pressing down the soil with them until they were ground pieces and became a part of the firm pack of pulverized earth.

Just as she appeared at the mouth of the hole after having

dragged in her grasshopper, a little parasitic Dipteron arrived and hovered about the place, like an evil spirit. It poised persistently over the hole, and tried to get in whenever the wasp's back was turned. The wasp would occasionally whirl suddenly around, glare and jump at it defiantly and it would dart away, only to return at once as teasingly as ever. Such persistence! Such perfect adaptation! On the spot as sure as fate and as inevitable!

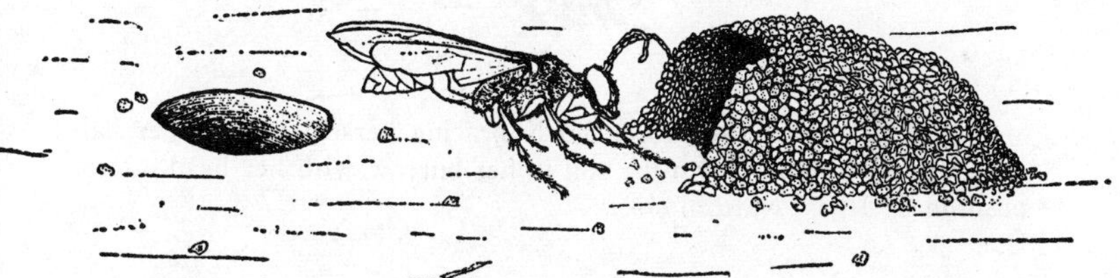

FIG. 37. *Priononyx atratum* filling her burrow. Natural size.

The wasp pounded and buzzed and labored for fourteen minutes, packing dirt in the depression until the ground was so hard and smooth that no trace of a hole remained. She stood squarely on her head, pushing downward so hard that twice she started to turn a somersault and just saved herself with difficulty; after that experience, she ingeniously altered her position for pounding, with her hind legs braced against the dirt and spread to their fullest extent, and one middle leg (the left one) thrown clear over above her head to serve as a prop and keep her from turning a somersault (fig. 38). She showed much mechanical skill in spreading her hind legs and bracing herself by placing one middle leg forward, to hold her balance and yet get more power for her work. When the closing of the hole was completed, she straightened up and took one look at it, then in a flash arose in the air and dashed away across the fields so swiftly the eye could not follow her, and was lost in the distance. Even one unfamiliar with wasps' ways would have said at a glance that her interest in the spot was forever at an end.

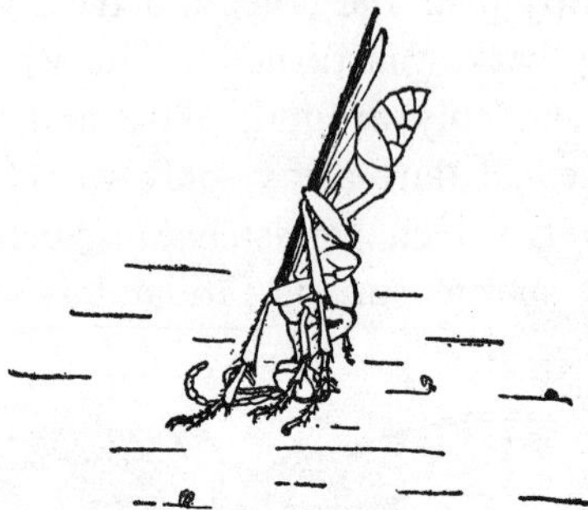

FIG. 38. *Priononyx atratum* deftly bracing herself to hold her balance while pounding down the soil in her burrow with her head. Note position of legs. Natural size.

Then we went back and dug up the first hole for which she had hunted so long and earnestly, expecting to find what she so carefully sealed up in it. It was stark empty! Why had she been so very particular to put the dirt back into all of these empty holes?

Let us add here that this persistent habit of closing up the abandoned holes is not constant. We have one record of an *atratum* which commenced six holes before she was satisfied with a location, but made no attempt to kick back the earth.

The last nest, to which our wasp had given such careful attention, contained the hopper with the wasp's egg cemented, in its usual position, on the hind leg and curved around the side of the body. But the Dipterous parasite mentioned above must have been too quick for the mother wasp after all, for fifteen minutes after the egg was laid, it and the host were already teeming with tiny Dipterous larvae. There is a possibility, of course, that the hopper may have been parasitized as it lay in hiding, but this chance is slight because usually the adult parasites stolidly ignore the prey of wasps while it is left lying idle, but take an interest in it when they see, with surety, that it is going to be buried properly.

The next day at 5:00 p. m., the hopper could still move its mouth-parts and legs, and when stimulated it could flutter its wings. In the interval, the parasites had devoured the egg and were entering and feeding upon the body of the grasshopper at the point of attachment of the wasp's egg, at the base of the left hind leg.

We have never found more than one hopper stored in the burrow of *P. atratum.* Williams[1] found their prey in Kansas to be a mature *Aulocara, Mermiria neomexicana, Melanoplus differentialis* ♀ or *M. lakinus.*

On one occasion we were so fortunate as to catch the *P. atratum* in the act of selecting her nesting-place. On that morning, August 30, at 10 o'clock, we found her searching to and fro in the region of her grasshopper, which lay, already paralyzed, on the grass. We should much like to know whether she had brought it here from some distance or whether she had killed it on this spot. We might add here that the Peckhams are evidently mistaken in surmising that the species first prepares the nest and then catches the wherewithal to fill it. In every case when we saw the wasp at work digging, we found the paralyzed hopper near by. This wasp did not come directly to her prey, nor did she at any time wander further than four feet from it. Judging from her manner of hunting here and there over the region, we thought she was seeking her lost quarry until, after examining one bare spot closely for five minutes, she began to dig. This spot was only about eighteen inches from her hopper, but in selecting the site she did not return directly to her prey at any time.

[1] Kans. Univ. Sci. Bull. **8**: 230. 1913.

The earth was moist and she dug rapidly, carrying out large mouthfuls of dirt as she emerged backwards from the hole, dropping it near the brink and flinging it back under her body and out of the way with her forelegs. When the dirt had accumulated near the hole so as to form a slight obstruction, she would come out and kick the whole pile away to a distance where it would cause no further annoyance. During the next period we timed her; she usually took out five loads of earth a minute, and occasionally six.

After ten minutes of her faithful digging, the hole was deep enough to include her whole body; then her mind turned back to her hopper and she started out in quest of it. Her manner of locating it was interesting to watch; first she walked in the direction of the prey but a little to one side and missed it; when some distance beyond it she turned and came back but passed it again. Then she took a short flight but went too far and landed beyond it again; then another return flight brought her only slightly past it once more, and from there she walked a few steps to it. She mounted it and trundled it half-way to her hole, where she left it on top of a thick clump of grass, and resumed her digging for another quarter of an hour. Once more she moved her hopper nearer to the hole; this time she had no trouble at all in finding it, but walked straight to it. When she brought it near to the hole, we felt sure that she had the burrow almost ready for it, for these wasps have a way of gradually moving their booty nearer and nearer as the work on the burrow progresses, until it arrives at its destination just as the hole is completed. Why do all of the *Priononyx* persist in digging awhile and then bringing their prey closer, several times before its final burial, when they might as well bring it all the way at one trip? Do the wasps grow anxious about the welfare of their prey? Hardly, or they would bring it at one trip clear to their place of work, where they could keep a watchful eye on it. Do they rest themselves by a change of work? Or do they want to compare dimensions and get a more exact estimate of the required size of the burrow in course of construction? Or do they judge in terms of their weariness, *i.e.,* after a long time of digging do their tired muscles (not their "heads") tell them that the hole must be large enough; then when they have tugged at the heavy caterpillar or grasshopper until their backs ache and their legs quiver, do they decide from their muscle-sense (not by their visual estimate) that the varmint must be larger than they had thought and they must dig the hole larger, etc., alternately until they arrive with the prey at the hole?

True to our expectation, this wasp worked at excavating just two minutes longer; then she moved the grasshopper to the very brink of the hole, wheeled it around so it was in position to slide down the sloping entrance head-first, went in to turn around and promptly reached out and dragged it in by the antennae. After only one minute, she reappeared and began at once to fill in the hole by first kicking in a small amount of dirt and then getting into the hole and working this earth down solid with her head, buzzing shrilly as she rammed it down. Sometimes she would break off clods or chunks of earth to fill in; these were not carelessly dropped but crushed to powder and packed tight with the head. She finished her burrow just one hour after she had commenced it.

On another occasion there was a small sandy area on Howard's Hill, where a load of sand had once been dumped and left to disintegrate. Here and there on top were streaks of grayish-white fire-clay and a few cinders, which had been washed over the sand by heavy rains. On one of these clay-colored areas was a very conspicuous spot; a little mound of moist red sand was surmounted by a tiny monument of black cinders thrown out on top of this smooth white surface. It was clearly the work of a *Priononyx,* in all probability *P. atratum,* since the only other member of that genus found here is *P. thomae,* and none of them had yet been seen in this vicinity. The gallery of this burrow was about an inch and a half long. It was tightly packed near the mouth with the material which had been excavated. In form and slope the burrow conformed in every way to the standard specifications of *Priononyx*; hence we may conclude that she finds the same scheme adequate, whether working in sand or firm earth. The adult hopper in the cell, a *Dissosteira carolina,* was active in all its members, kicking vigorously with all of its legs, moving its mouth, antennae and abdomen, and occasionally fluttering its wings. During all of this activity the egg, which was glued at the base of the right hind leg, was not dislodged, although it was badly shaken and occasionally received a full blow from the middle leg. Hence, it was not in the least surprising that the egg never hatched and that three days later it was shrivelled. The hopper was at that time fairly active, moving the hind legs, mouth and antennae; only the first and second pairs of legs seemed helpless.

The site of the nest was particularly conspicuous because of the contrasting colors of the mound and the adjacent soil, while the tiny black cinders laid on top of the gray clay made the contrast only the more striking. In covering and finishing off her burrow in this way, the *Priononyx* had merely followed her usual custom for effecting its concealment, but she had failed ludicrously, by picking up material of sharply contrasting colors. Surely, if this behavior was not blind instinct, at least it was colorblind.

In 1914, while walking along a country road in Kansas one August morning, we noticed a hole in the side of a wagon rut. In a moment the proprietor, a *P. atratum,* returned and claimed it. About twelve inches away and facing the hole was a grasshopper, a *Melanoplus differentialis* Thom. ♀ [A. N. Caudell], lying in the very natural position of one at rest. When it remained there without moving we decided that it, too, was a participant in the drama about to take place.

For fifteen minutes the wasp enlarged the hole, all the time working out the dirt with her mouth and forelegs. The mandibles brought out the big clods, while the legs rapidly worked the dust out behind her. Once she paused to examine the hopper and when she found it resting perfectly quietly except for the pulsating of the abdomen, she at once resumed her work. For eight minutes more she worked at the excavating before she again examined her prey. She had more difficulty in finding it this time, and walked around in an irregular circle twice and a part of a third circuit before she stumbled upon it. She straddled it as it lay, grasped its antennae in her jaws, stretched her legs over the sides of its body, and thus trundled it along (just as in fig. 40). At a point about four inches distant from the nest, she left the grasshopper, went to the mouth of the burrow, poked her head in, turned back and once more scrutinized the prey and immediately took out two loads of dirt, one from each side of the entrance, thereby enlarging the opening. It was difficult for an observer watching this exact work to throw aside the conviction that actual judgment was a guiding factor in such little details of behavior as this. Then she continued deepening the cavity. A buzz, similar to the shrill buzz of a fly ensnared, was occasionally audible; it seemed that each buzz was simultaneous with the energetic pressing of her head as she strove to loosen a pellet of earth. At 9:15 she started for her hopper, mounted and grasped it the same as before, excepting that this time she clasped its thorax with her front legs and struggled forward on her four hind feet. Thus they progressed to the burrow. There she laid it down, with its head at the very brink of the opening; but she left it for only a moment while she stepped inside, turned around and poked her head out just far enough to grasp the hopper by one antenna, and dragged it in. After a brief time, perhaps one-half minute, she came out and immediately commenced to fill the hole, pausing only to chase a Dipterous parasite that hovered about while she was filling it in. How strange it is that only the filling of the tunnel seems to stimulate the fly's desire to enter; she had had abundant opportunity to enter ere this, or even to deposit her eggs on the grasshopper as it lay wholly unprotected, but she seemed to take no interest in the hopper until she was sure the wasp had finished with it.

While filling and packing in the earth, the wasp stood on her head and pressed down the soil, producing with each stroke the shrill buzz. Next she brought large pellets from a distance and dropped them on the depression. Then, in scratching the dirt back, she worked gradually sidewise, with her face away from the hole, so her path formed a perfect arc of a circle the center of which was the nest. Often she would have to go back to the original spot to get her bearings and estimate exactly where to direct her kicks. While thus occupied, without ceremony or warning, she arose and flew away in a straight line. It was then 9:30, or forty-five minutes after the time we discovered her.

We opened the nest. The length of the tunnel down to the grasshopper was five inches. The chamber was no wider than the rest of the burrow and lay horizontally. No earth was in this chamber, and the hopper, with its head to the wall, had ample air space around it. We dug it out and took it home for further observation. It was still alive, but seemed severely stunned, and for the remainder of that day moved its legs and antennae only upon stimulation. By the forenoon of the following day, it had recovered enough vigor to move spontaneously, but the powers lasted for only this one day, when they again waned. During the next two

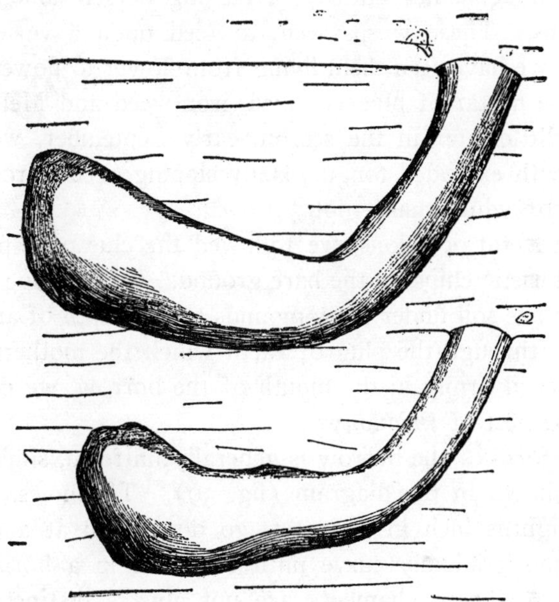

FIG. 39. Two burrows of *Priononyx atratum*. Natural size.

or three days, it moved in response to stimulation and voided excrement, but gradually grew more sluggish until, one week later, it was dead.

In four instances, we found a *P. atratum* nest well covered, and the hopper within being speedily consumed by Dipterous larvae. These parasites destroy the egg as well as the locust, and since they seek to enter the body of the hopper at its softest point, *i.e.,* where the wasp egg or larva is attached, the egg is usually destroyed before it has a chance to hatch.

Adams[2] finds the Tachinid fly *Metopia leucocephala* Rossi hovering over their burrows.

To see a *Priononyx* intent upon the herculean task of making her burrow and burying the grasshopper, one can hardly imagine her blithely refreshing herself among the blossoms. These wasps seem to feed upon a variety of plants; we have seen them flying from flower to flower, sipping the nectar of blue veronica, iron-weed and Melilotus, and a little later in the season, early September, we saw them with extended tongue, lazily sipping nectar from the florets of white snake-root.

On several occasions, we followed the clue of a pile of characteristic chips on the bare ground. By scooping away the surface soil under these mounds to the depth of an inch or two, through the plug of earth which the mother wasp had packed firmly in the mouth of the burrow, we discovered the nest of *Priononyx*.

The form of the burrow is generally uniform, similar to those shown in the diagram (fig. 39). The holes, about three-eighths inch in diameter, go downward at a gentle slope and gradually curve until they end in a horizontal chamber. These chambers are not always distinct; frequently they are little more than a continuation of the gallery. The burrows are three and one-half to four inches in total length, and, at the deepest point, about one and one-half inches below the surface of the ground. We have never chanced to find a *Priononyx* burrow of the form described by Williams,[3] a distinctly L-shaped nest about two inches deep and two and a half inches long. There has been very little variation in the form of the fifteen nests which we have excavated.

The *Priononyx* nests which have come under our observa-

[2] Bull. Ill. St. Lab. Nat. Hist. **11**: 195. 1915.

[3] Kansas Univ. Sci. Bull. **8**: Pl. 33, fig. 2.

tion have always contained one of three species of grasshoppers: *Dissosteira carolina* Linn. nymphs, *Arphia corinata* Scud. ♀ large nymphs, or *Melanoplus femur-rubrum* DeG.[4]

The first named was the most abundant. Riley, Packard and Thomas[5] record them as pursuing and capturing the nymphs of the Rocky Mountain locust, *Coloptenus spretus,* and Adams (*loc. cit.* p. 195) also says they use *Melanoplus femur-rubrum.* The prey was always placed in the oval terminal chamber, with its head toward the wall, away from the exit—a wise precaution which would prevent the hopper's escape in case the stinging should be imperfectly done. The upper portion of the channel was always filled with earth, and near the surface this was packed so firmly as to be indistinguishable from the surrounding soil. The horizontal chamber at the end was not filled with earth, but contained only the grasshopper surrounded by plenty of air space. May it be that this terminal chamber is made in this form so that the dirt will not roll in and pack around the grasshopper?

The faithfulness of these wasps in returning to the unfinished nests is variable. We have described above the case of one wasp which spent a whole hour in diligent search for an unfinished hole, only to fill it up and desert it the moment she found it. On one other occasion, we disturbed a wasp as she was making her nest, and found the next day that she had returned and finished it. In another instance we met exactly the opposite behavior: the wasp with her prey, a large *Dissosteira carolina,* right beside her, was putting the finishing touches to her burrow when our footsteps frightened her away. She returned and found the hole again before we passed on, but when we came back that afternoon

[4] All kindly identified by Mr. A. N. Caudell.
[5] U. S. Ent. Comm. 1877: 318.

to dig up the finished product, we were surprised to find that she had deserted it just as we had left it that morning. The nest remained slightly unfinished, and the hopper nearby was being dismembered by ants.

Two other unfinished and deserted burrows of *Priononyx,* probably *atratum,* were found. One was evidently ready for the closing; even the hopper, a *Melanoplus femur-rubrum,* was in place at the bottom, but the owner was gone, the dirt was dry and the locust was being carried away in bits by ants. The other was almost as far advanced; the prey, an *Arphia corinata* ♀, lay directly in front of the hole and facing it—the last position before the wasp drags it in—but this too was being plundered by ants. There is, of course, a possibility that both of these failures had been caused, not by the faithlessness of the mother wasp, but by some tragedy which had overtaken her. We might add here that the mothers themselves are not exempt from enemies, for Pierce[6] records this species as being stylopized by *Ophthalmochlus duryi,* and in one instance where a male parasite emerged three days after the death of the host.

On one August morning we were interested in watching the courtship of a *P. atratum.* At 8:42 a black female was seen at rest on a small *Melilotus.* After a few seconds a second insect appeared, flew directly to the first, mounted and tried hard to effect a union, and flew off. During the next fifteen minutes this performance was repeated about a dozen times; occasionally the male would fly to a distance of fifteen feet, rest for a second and then return to the female and resume activities, but more often the flights were short. The male would hover to and fro in a space of about three inches in the air in front of the female before mounting; then he would curl his abdomen beneath hers. Mating probably occurred during this coquettish performance, but if so,

[6] Bull. U. S. Nat. Mus. No. 66: 38. 1909.

it must have been instantaneous. Finally the male flew away permanently and the female remained on the same plant, apparently waiting for him to return. Our approach caused her to seek another plant, where she assumed the same position. We watched her for some time, but no suitors appeared.

*Prionony x thomae* Fabr. [S. A. Rohwer].

In a vacant lot adjoining the brick-yard, where the ground was well covered with cinders, we saw this red-bellied *Prionony x* nervously walking about at 4:35 p. m. on July 14. From her manner, we at once suspected that she was looking for a nesting-site. One may imagine the difficulties which confronted a little creature trying to dig her hole in a surface-soil composed largely of cinders; one would hardly think of trying to dig in such material with a pocket-knife.

She already had her grasshopper, a *Dissosteira carolina* Linn., which was in its last nymphal instar. Twice while hunting for a location, she returned to her hopper to see if it was safe. On each visit, she straddled it and carried it a short distance, then wandered away again looking for a site. In two places she seriously attempted to dig, but abandoned the spot on account of the bad cinders. Both of these were at so great a distance from the place where she had left her hopper that we doubted whether, if she remained there, she could ever find and fetch it.

Her third and successful attempt was begun in the rough cinders somewhat nearer to where her hopper lay, but still at a distance of about fifteen feet. The cinders were harsh and heavy, and how she tugged at big lumps in getting them out of the hole! We often thought that if the rough cinders hurt her legs as much as they did our hands and knees as we watched her, she deserved our highest respect for faithfulness to duty.

Her method of digging was similar to that of *P. atratum;* she would plunge into the hole head first, grab a lump of dirt or a cinder, back out and drop her load a few inches away. When the bore was about half completed, she found her hopper with little difficulty, mounted it again, grasped its antennae in her mandibles as usual, and away she went (fig. 40).[7] She did not exactly fly, but she made such rapid speed that she must have aided her progress by beating her wings. She left the locust about twelve inches from the hole until she enlarged it. Then she returned again to her prey, and, despite the fact that she was very near to it, she found it with more difficulty than on the previous occasion. It took her one minute to discover it, and at one time she passed it when only one inch from where it lay. In the usual manner, she mounted it, grasped the hopper's antennae in her mouth, and dragged it to within three inches of the burrow. Here she evidently decided that it was a trifle larger than the hole would yet admit, so she laid it down and removed three more mouthfuls of dirt. She then carried the prey to within one inch, went into the hole once more to make sure that all was ready, came out again and dumped it, head-first, half-way into the opening; then she herself crowded in ahead of it and dragged it in after her. She remained in only one-half minute, came out and began to fill in the dirt. After this, for many minutes she carried large cinders and placed them over the site. The heavy cinders were moved with the mandibles with comparative ease. Sixteen minutes later she stopped piling cinders and for two minutes walked and took short, low flights about the nest, surveying the situation; then she came back to the

[7] Through an error in the figure, the middle leg fails to reach the ground,

very spot and critically added more cinders, took a few more last looks and finally, at 5:29, she flew off and rested on the grass some distance away, as if all her interests were now in the future and the past was a closed book. It had taken

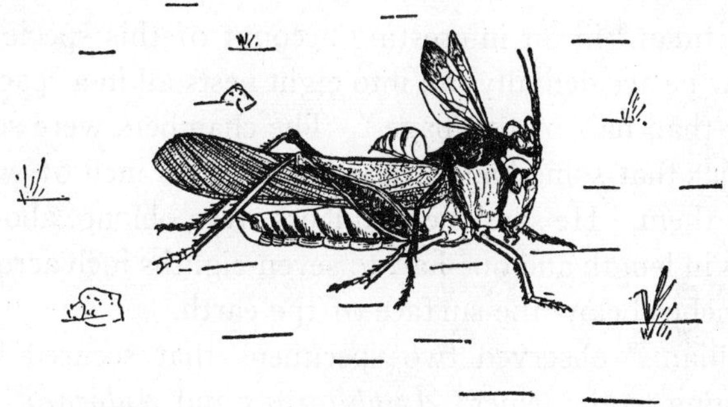

FIG. 40. Homeward bound *Priononyx thomae* transporting her locust to the burrow. Exact size.

her just fifty-four minutes to dig her burrow, bury her prey, lay the egg, and conceal the spot.

After she had gone, we opened the nest and found the hopper with its head to the wall. The chamber was only one inch underground and one inch long, of no definite shape, but it was as well constructed as it could be in such rough material. We found the brown egg on the right femur, near where it joins the thorax. We took the egg and its host home and guarded them carefully. The next morning, July 15, at 7 o'clock, we found the legs, antennae and mouth-parts of the hopper active and excrement had been passed, but the femur upon which the egg rested was immovable. With what delicate accuracy the little mother-wasp had done her work! By the following day the egg was slightly enlarged and had changed from brown to green. The morning of the 17th found a larva, fat and large, still clinging to the femur of the hopper and eating away the thorax near the joint.

July 19 revealed a light-brown cocoon just completed; the hopper had all been eaten. On August 15, scarcely one month later, a perfect adult female emerged. This shows that in this species there is more than one generation each year.

Hartman,[8] in an interesting account of this species, tells of how he accidentally ran into eight nests all in a space "not larger than half of this page." The chambers were so close together that some had but a quarter of an inch of wall between them. He says the chambers were oblong, about two inches in length and one-half to seven-eighths inch across and two inches below the surface of the earth.

Williams[9] observed two specimens that secured locusts belonging to the genera *Amphitornus* and *Aulocara.*

Another chapter in the life of *P. thomae,* the hunting of the provisions, must be taken from another individual.

A terrific commotion in the low grass attracted our attention. An adult grosshopper, *Arphia xanthoptera* Burm. [A. N. Caudell] lay on its back violently flapping its wings against the earth, as if in great distress. A little red lump on the ventral side of the thorax explained the mystery; it was the abdomen of a *P. thomae* with its sting buried deep in the hopper's thorax; the rest of the body of the wasp was curved around the grasshopper's side. The struggle was more violent than that of an insect on its back trying to right itself; besides, a grasshopper seldom has much difficulty in turning over if it happens to become inverted—in fact they are seldom so clumsy as to get into that predicament. The point is, this action was simply an aimless and conclusive muscular contraction, a writhing resulting from the sting of its enemy. A grasshopper is so seldom seen in this position that the wasp must have either attacked it on

[8] Bull. Univ. Tex. No. 65: 64. 1905.

[9] Kans. Univ. Sci. Bull. **8**: 227. 1913.

the wing and made it fall, or attacked it on the ground and caused it to roll over in its agony. We should like to witness the initial attack of the wasp. It is doubtful if the hopper's movements were really an effort to rise or to shake off the enemy. Nevertheless, it is certain that the wasp had much difficulty in clinging to the hopper during this shake-up without removing her sting. The sting was inserted between the head and the thorax, at a point just in front of the fore-legs. She did not make several thrusts as *Ammophila* does, but when we saw them her dagger was already inserted, and there she calmly and firmly held it for over one minute while her victim writhed and fought; how long they had struggled thus before our arrival we do not know.

At the end of the minute the wasp suddenly darted away on the wing to a snakeroot plant ten feet away. Judging from the suddenness of her departure and the absence of any flight of orientation, we suspected that she had fled in alarm and would not return.

We then watched the hopper as it lay on its back violently beating its wings against the earth. Gradually the beating grew weaker, until it was a throb and a quiver; this in turn gradually waned until, at the end of five minutes, the hopper lay motionless on the ground with its wings outstretched. Of course this made us ask at once: "If the wasp returns, how will she right the hopper and close the wings to make its removal easy?" At that moment the wasp appeared on the field, seeking her victim. By a series of walks, jumps, skips and short flights, she attempted to locate it, but she had left it so hastily that she had difficulty in discovering it; although in her fifteen-minute search she came within a few inches of it four times, she could not find it; she evidently knew the general vicinity, but had memorized no familiar landmarks by which to locate it, so presently she flew away permanently.

After waiting in vain for her return, we looked at the hopper again; it had somehow righted itself and sat on the ground with its wings closed. Closer examination showed that it was powerless to use its legs, but it moved its wings in response to stimulation. It tried to walk, but the only result of its efforts was a slight quiver of the left hind leg. We picked it up, a little later, to examine it more closely on the open hand. Imagine our surprise when, with the first puff of wind, it spread its wings and flew a distance of forty feet and was lost in the vegetation. Evidently the legs had been properly paralyzed, but the wing nerves and muscles were unaffected. This condition is usually sufficient by reason of the fact that hoppers cannot normally use their wings for flight without first leaping into the air by means of their jumping legs. As prey they may occasionally escape by some unusual circumstance, as in this case, but such cases are so rare that there is no need of the wasp burdening herself with either the instinct or the task of paralyzing the wings of her prey . As to this hopper it probably lived and grew fat, even if it was unable to use its hind legs, but we should like much to know whether the injured members fell off. We have seen healthy hoppers with the hind legs so neatly trimmed off at the basal joint that we wondered how they came so; may it be that *P. thomae* or *P. atratum* had once had them?

### The Relation of *Stizus unicinctus* Say [S. A. Rohwer] to *Priononyx thomae.* Fabr.

While *Chlorion cyaneum* was working on the cinder-bed, as later described, a *Priononyx thomae* appeared, reconnoitering in the same field. She at once went to work energetically and dug a hole a half-inch deep, then deserted it and attempted another at a spot ten feet distant and abandoned that also; a little later she commenced a third burrow about five feet from the second. This last location seemed to offer more favorable conditions. Here the wasp worked diligently among the cinders, and in ten minutes had dug a hole the length of her body, with an opening one-half inch wide. This was good work, considering the difficulties of digging in packed cinders. It seems that this species has a liking for cinders, for the other that we saw worked in the same material despite the fact that only a small proportion of the available area was covered with it.

The blue wasp, *C. cyaneum,* which was foraging under a brick-pile near by, annoyed her twice by entering her open burrow; but since she entered every hole and crevice in the brick-pile and cinders, this was probably only an accident.

This *P. thomae* followed the same technique in her work as *P. atratum:* she would carry up the soil, cinders, etc., with her mouth, back out with the load and drop it near the orifice without turning around, and run in again, head first, soon to emerge in the same mechanical manner, like a little toy wound up with a spring. When the débris had accumulated so as to be annoying, she paused long enough to rapidly kick and brush it all together, in a neat little heap, some distance away.

After she had dug down about the distance of her own body-length, she turned to a horizontal direction and excavated the chamber. Thus the ceiling of the chamber, when completed, was only about a half-inch beneath the surface of the ground. The opening was large enough to permit us easily to see her moving about inside.

After a half-hour's arduous work, she came out of her burrow and slowly walked about in the immediate vicinity of her nest. We thought she was getting her landmarks preparatory to bringing her booty home. Her slow and deliberate actions indicated this, but presently she changed her mind and again went into the hole to make certain improvements in view of the coming storage, removed a few more mouthfuls of dirt and again strolled slowly about her nest. Then she flew off for her hopper. During this period of her work, we had made a diligent search for her prey, which we were certain she had in hiding somewhere near. But now, without hesitation or uncertainty, she walked directly to a brown brick on the ground at the side of which lay her hopper, almost indistinguishable against its similar-colored background.

Once, while she was at work in the hole, a red-banded *Stizus unicinctus* had poked her head in and walked away without further intrusion; but now, while she was gone, the same meddler returned and wandered about the vicinity, with a "looking for something" manner.

*P. thomae* straddled the hopper, grasped its antennae in her mouth and struggled on her way over the rolling cinders. It was with considerable difficulty that she rode the hopper; besides the grasp on its antennae she gripped the hopper's neck with her forelegs; so she walked with her hind legs, while the middle legs attempted to assist, but, owing to their shortness or the thickness of the burden, they seldom reached the ground. The hopper itself often assisted in their progress in this way: as *thomae* dragged her prey forward, the tarsi of its hind legs would cling to the rough cinders, and, while the heavy body was being pulled forward, the hind legs would thus be stretched out to their fullest extent; of course this process would lift the rear part of the grasshopper and make the body pitch forward. When the legs had reached their full extent, they would snap shut and the process would be repeated, pushing the heavy body slightly forward each time, thus at least avoiding hindrance by friction, if not positively aiding the struggling wasp.

She thus carried the hopper to a tuft of grass about ten feet from her hole and there left it, returned to the burrow and dug for ten minutes more, again went direct to the locust and carried it, in the same fashion, to a spot three feet from her hole and once more resumed the digging. At this point in her work she was again visited by *S. unicinctus,* but this time the bold *Stizus* actually entered the new burrow, where, after a brief tussle, she was chased out by the owner and angrily pursued for a distance of three feet (see fig. 41). *Thomae's* wrath soon cooled and she devoted her-

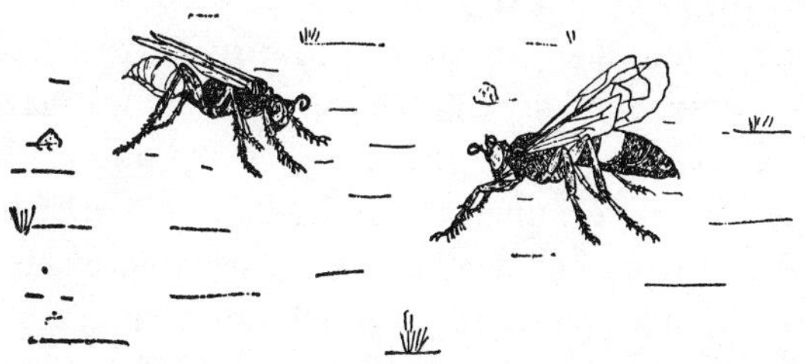

F.G. 41. *Priononyx thomae* and *Stizus unicinctus.* Exact size.

self to digging for about five minutes, and again visited her prey and brought it, in precisely the same manner, to within six inches of her hole, where she left it in a clump of short grass and resumed her task of adding the last critical touches to the future nest of her offspring. During her visits to the hopper, we watched carefully and found that no other stings were given to it, although its hind legs sometimes quivered. She dug for ten minutes more, then got the prey and carried it directly in front of the hole, went in for a moment as usual for one final survey to see if all was in readiness, then reached out and seizing the hopper's antennae, pulled it in. Just a short time previous to this, we had looked into the burrow and had seen a large cinder, which she had failed to remove, projecting into the gallery; this now obstructed the way so she had trouble in getting her property in, but she worked strenuously inside the hole, and, with our assistance on the outside, worked her locust in after five minutes' labor. Again *Stizus* was seen lurking about in the vicinity of the nest.

*P. Thomae* came out and filled her hole carefully, first by carrying in mouthfuls of soil and precisely arranging it on the inside, and then kicking more dirt in and going in after it to pound it down, making a loud hum as she pressed with all her strength against the tightening soil. In getting dirt to fill in, she first took that nearest the hole and when this was gone, instead of taking all of the earth which she had kicked into a hill, she dug at the foot of this tiny hill and hollowed out a semicircular space just as we have seen *P. atratum* do (fig. 37). Of course, as she dug at the foot of the pile, she undermined it and much of the dirt tumbled down and rolled into or near to the cavity where she needed it. When the hole was half covered, she was again visited by *Stizus,* but she at once gave chase and the meddlesome intruder fled. The task of filling and covering was continued, and when this was done, several cinders, large in size but of light weight (see fig. 42, exact size), were brought in the mandibles and placed over the spot. A collection of twelve such cinders was taken from her mouth, with the forceps, as she brought them to the place; this shows how tame she was or how accustomed to our presence she had grown. She surrendered the cinders to us peaceably and without defiance; however, we did not pull them away from her but merely held them firmly with the forceps so she could not move them further. So she gave them up, or she may have merely thought that they were too heavy or too tightly lodged for her to move. After a few more kicks, she abruptly flew away.

FIG. 42. A collection of cinders, exact size, carried in the mandibles of *P. thomae* and deposited on the top of her burrow.

Our flesh and bones were weary of sitting on all fours on the cinders for two hours and it was growing late, but still we were eager to see if *Stizus* would show any further interest in the nest. We waited for five minutes and she did not reappear, so we began to dig up the nest and had removed enough soil to expose one of the hopper's tarsi when behold! *Stizus* appeared upon the scene. We slipped back and she came nearer and nearer to the nest by walking zigzag, following almost arcs of circles around the hole, with her head close to the surface and antennae vibrating, until she came to the nest. She located it apparently with less difficulty than wasps sometimes experience in locating their own nests. She approached in the manner of one familiar with the situation and having business there. She kicked away much of the filling until she had removed the hard plug and arrived at the loose material beneath; then she worked her way into the nest at the right side of the hopper, remained in for about five minutes and emerged at the left side, showing that at least she could turn around inside the chamber. She went in again and this time we removed a little of the soil, yet could not see fully what she was doing; but this much was clear—that she was standing on the hopper with her head near the fore part of the insect, quietly sitting there with the abdomen pulsating for over five minutes. She came out and kicked in all of the loose dirt, then dug up more with her mandibles, kicked it under her body into place, and picked up and placed a few more bits until the hole was once more nicely covered. She then went a few feet away and calmly sat down to rest, when she was taken to secure her identity.

We dug up the nest and found a hole of the type usually made by both *P. atratum* and *thomae,* only the chamber was unusually long in this case. The hopper lay there with its head to the wall. The egg of *thomae* was in its usual position on the right femur, at the base of the abdomen, but lo! it was only an empty sac! Evidently *Stizus* had mutilated the egg by malaxation, or had sucked the contents for food. We found no *Stizus* egg; but it is probable that, in the difficulty of opening the nest in a harsh cinder bed, it was knocked off by crumbling walls. We know that *Stizus* did not deposit an egg during her second stay in the chamber, for we could see her abdomen all the while, but we suspect that she was then mutilating the egg of *thomae,* after probably having laid her own.

We wonder by what sense *Stizus* found the nest. To be sure, she had returned to the spot while *P. thomae* was at work sufficiently often to get the landmarks of the vicinity; but considering the remarkable way in which the nests are covered and concealed we wonder how she could find the exact spot under normal conditions. In this case it may have been easier than usual, since we had already exposed the tarsus of the grasshopper.

After having observed this startling conduct, we were alert for other *Stizus*. On August 31 the morning was bright, dry and sunny on the diamond. When a *S. unicinctus* appeared, foraging after her manner, we followed in eager pursuit. She was flying lightly from place to place, peeping and examining every spot where the bare surface ground (fig. 2) was a little roughened, such as by ant-hills, or little breaks in the bald smooth ground made by hoof or heel. She made no pretense at alighting on smooth or unbroken spots, but flew lightly from one to another. We followed her and watched her for six minutes; in this time, she alighted ninety-one times on the roughened spots and peeped under the clods, but only twice did she alight on the smooth, unbroken earth, although by far the greater portion of the area was smooth. Was she trying to find a *Prionyx* hole by this method? She flew out over the grassy portion of the field bordering the diamond a part of the time; there, in about three minutes, she made twenty stops. When out over the grass she alighted only at long intervals—whenever she came upon a little bald spot among the grass—but here she alighted on every bare spot she found whether smooth or broken. While on the diamond, where all was bare, she paid attention to only the roughened spots. On one occasion, she appeared to be particularly suspicious of a certain hoof-print and examined it all very minutely; she paused and scratched at five different places in the crescent, and once burrowed so deep that her head was out of sight.

An hour later, on the same morning, we followed another *Stizus* for a few minutes, as she flew from place to place over the grassy part of the field, examining bare or roughened spots just like the one described above. She moved calmly and without haste or agitation. After examining about ten spots in a couple of minutes, she arrived at a certain inconspicuous pile of loose earth, in outward appearance very similar to all the others. Instantly her manner changed. She became greatly excited, nervous, quivering with eagerness. She probed here and there in the pile until, in a fraction of a minute, she had located the filled-up hole beneath one side of the pile, and then eagerly began digging. She burrowed steadily and rapidly in the freshly-stirred earth, and pushed and flung the loose dirt out between her legs and under her body. She worked with the furious eagerness of a dog digging out a rabbit; surely, if she could have barked or snorted, she would have done so. In a minute or so she was through the plug of earth and disappeared into the cell. We waited breathlessly, knowing that this was the time when she was probably crushing the *Prionony.x* egg and laying her own—but we nearly fell on our backs when she came out *at once,* washed her face thoroughly, rubbed her legs vigorously and unceremoniously flew away, leaving the hole wide open! There was no indication of her returning or giving any more attention to the place, so we dug it up to see if it really was a *Priononyx* hole, and if she had done anything. The case was quickly explained: the hopper in the *P. atratum* chamber was reeking with parasite larvae, but bore neither *Priononyx* nor *Stizus* egg. Wise *Stizus!* The Diptera larvae had probably devoured the *Priononyx* egg, and the *Stizus* knew at a glance that the same fate would befall her babe if she left it there, so she fled from the place at once. Where will adaptations and interrelations cease!

A few minutes later we noticed several parasitic Diptera

hovering around the wreck of the tunnel, although both hopper and wasp were now gone. How did they know? It did not any longer look in the least like a *P. atratum* hole, all dug up as it was. Did some *Priononyx* odor remain on the dirt which she had handled, by which the parasites, and also *Stizus,* could detect the location?

On one other occasion we opened a carelessly closed, or, as we later concluded, a newly opened burrow which we took to be that of a *P. atratum,* but were surprised to find, beneath the rumpled earth-covering, a freshly-killed hopper and in the chamber with it a live *Stizus.* What business she had there we can only surmise.

To be sure, the above cases give only circumstantial evidence, which is generally not accepted as proof in the courts of law. Yet we think that the evidence here is strong enough to justify our indicting *Stizus* as a cow-bird wasp, and one highly skilled in her profession. In this suspicion we are not alone, for Williams also has suggested:

"While the evidence at hand is incomplete, it seems more than probable that the common red-banded bembecid wasp, *Stizus unicinctus* Say, plays the part of a burglar and uses the locust captured by *Priononyx atrata* as food for her own young. *Unicinctus* is a rather compact insect, somewhat inferior in size to and less powerful than the sphecid. . . . In Stanton county one of these wasps was observed to hover about a freshly-made tunnel, apparently that of a *Priononyx,* which it entered while the sphecid was away. The latter had brought an *Aulocara* near this burrow, which, being occupied by *Stizus,* was finally deserted by the disgusted *Priononyx.*

"In Morton county, July 7, 1911, I came upon a *Stizus unicinctus* engaged in smoothing over a spot with her feet. I unearthed what proved to be a filled-up burrow, which in form and dimensions resembled that of a *Prionony.x*. In the single cell lay a *Melanoplus.* But where the *Prionony.x* egg was to be expected on this egg was only a small bit of soft matter, probably the remnant of a sphecid egg destroyed by the *Stizus,* while cephalad of these remains was a short wasp egg, doubtless that of *Stizus.*

"Certainly the short-legged *Stizus unicinctus* does not appear to be a sufficiently powerful insect to capture and subdue locusts of the size and vigor of those which serve as the prey of *Priononyx.*"

If we consider this idea tenable, it may throw some light upon the circumstances which obtained when once we found, in different places, three open holes, apparently of *P. atratum.* We opened them further; one hopper had been almost all carried away by ants, another was heavily parasitized by Diptera larvae and nearly riddled, and the third had both ants and parasitic larvae. Had *Stizus* opened these and left them open like the one described above? We have at other times also been mystified by open *Priononyx* holes or their grasshoppers ruined by ants. Some such cause must be behind this waste, for it is too frequent to be attributed to mere accident. Furthermore, when *Priononyx* closes her hole, she does it so thoroughly that it takes a sneak-thief to get in.

*Stizus* undoubtedly opens the nests for the purpose of laying her own egg. True, we have not found her egg there, even though the *Priononyx* egg had been destroyed, but this may well have been due to our faulty manipulation in digging. It seems hardly possible that the taste of *Stizus* can be so perverted that she, cannibal-like, goes into the nest only for the purpose of sucking the contents of the egg, for we find she is a nectar-feeeder. We have often seen her feeding upon the flowers of white snakeroot.

From the above observations we see that *Stizus unicinctus* has two ways of locating her host: by inspecting all breaks in the surface of the earth where *Priononyx* nests are likely to occur, in order to locate the nest when closed, and by shadowing the *Priononyx* while she is storing her prey and closing the hole. This evidence shows that Fabre's[10] idea in regard to Ammophila, that the insect is endowed with certain marvellous and mysterious powers, an unknown sense, which draws her to her subterranean prey, cannot apply to *Stizus,* although we are sure that, from a literary standpoint, Fabre's chapter on An Unknown Sense will live. True, her powers are wonderful, but it seems to us after witnessing the above, that she finds her host, not by magic, but by energy and persistence. Here again, "genius is only the capacity for taking infinite pains." We ourselves usually find *Priononyx* holes by examining the piles of dust or earth-clips which look to us suspicious; so does she.

True, she may possess a delicate sense of smell or other faculty, which may help her to detect the presence of the *Priononyx* nest when near it, for she must be highly skilled if she can inspect a mound of dust and determine, in five seconds or less, whether or not a securely-covered *Priononyx* hole lies beneath it. But in the case described above of the *Stizus* opening up the parasitized nest, it seems incredible that the scent alone could have attracted her to open up this spot. It was natural that the Diptera should be attracted to the hole after the earth that had lain next the decaying hopper had been thrown out on top of the ground, all nicely saturated with hopper scent. Since the flies appeared so promptly when the tainted earth was thrown out, it is evident that they must have been plentiful in the field at that

[10] Chapter on An Unknown Sense, in The Hunting Wasps, 371-384. 1915.

time, so why did they not come about before the hole was opened? Probably just because the flies could not scent the hopper through an inch or more of well-packed earth. So if the fly, with its highly specialized olfactory organs, cannot scent the contents of the nest when it is closed with earth, how can we have the audacity to suspect that *unicinctus* finds her way to the burrows by the sense of smell alone? Of course, you may say, it is possible that mother *Priononyx,* when carrying out the earth, leaves her taint upon it. Perhaps so, but even if she does, in this case the condition of the hopper and parasites showed that the nest had been sealed for at least three days, and surely any taint that *Priononyx* could leave at her doorway would, in three days of wind and weather, have been reduced to a minimum. Granting that *Priononyx* does leave an odor, we would again have to prove that *Stizus* has the power to perceive it in so delicate a degree. It is hard to believe that she locates the nest by the grasshopper odor, for the field is at that time of year constantly overrun by hordes of grasshoppers, and certainly she cannot by scent pick out a buried one which is just like all the others except that it is paralyzed.

Thus it seems, from the evidence at hand, that the greater part of the responsibility in discovering the hidden nests falls upon the sense of sight, although it is almost beyond belief that any one sense could be developed to such a degree of sensitiveness.

The highly specialized instinct of *Stizus* to get the hopper only after it is buried is worthy of note. The hopper lies fully exposed for a long period awaiting burial, during which time *Stizus* ignores it, but suspiciously visits and revisits the hole. Would it not have been less complex if her instinct had been so developed as to lead her to seek the hopper as it lay and deposit her egg, and then and there get it out of her system both physiologically and psychologically? But no, the chance of injury to her egg in the transportation of the hopper for burial, and the question of the survival of her young one in a tussle with the infant *Priononyx* proves her way safer after all, and she is right in wanting to see the food safely in place, the *atratum* egg destroyed and the host devoid of parasites before she will take any chances with her own young.

*Chlorion* (*Proterosphex*) *ichneumoneum* L.

While walking over the sparse grass on a clayey plateau, we scared up a large sand wasp, *Chlorion ichneumoneum*. It created a great commotion, buzzing about our heads in threatening manner until we withdrew. It then returned to its burrow, which was near by, and resumed its digging. The hole was already nearing completion; it went straight down into the ground from an opening one-fourth inch in diameter. About four inches distant was a large pile of pellets of earth (fig. 43), which had been taken from the hole.

Presently she stepped aside to get her prey, which she was from time to time bringing nearer to the hole; it was a long-horned green grasshopper. Then, after the usual manner of certain wasps, she laid it down and went inside once more for the final survey of the pocket, came out and brought the hopper to within one-half inch of the opening; she went in head first, turned around and poked her head out just far enough to grasp the hopper's head and then dragged it down out of sight. A minute later she appeared at the surface for just a moment and at once went down and remained inside the burrow for three minutes.

When she emerged again, she flew away directly, leaving the hole wide open. This was at 12:30 p. m. We thought she had gone for another hopper; but when she did not return by 3 o'clock, we opened the nest. The hole went straight down into the hard soil for seven inches, then it turned at a right angle and in the direction just opposite to the pile of pellets, continued for three inches and terminated in an enlargement or pocket (see fig. 43, one-third natural size). (The pocket in this one was somewhat larger than that illustrated by the Peckhams.) In it were four green, long-horned grasshoppers, *Orchelimum vulgare,* one of which bore a young larva which appeared to be a Dipterous parasite. Another female nymph, which was larger (body-length five-eighths inch), bore a yellow, slightly curved egg three-sixteenths inch in length. The other two hoppers were males measuring nearly three-quarters of an inch in length. They were not active, but were still able to move the antennae and mouth-parts when stimulated.

By the evening of July 28, two days later, the wasp larva had grown enormously. It had eaten the contents of three of the green hoppers and was greedily working over the garbage, a few heads and legs, and actually eating the softer parts of the integument, so we gave it the fourth grasshopper. Shortly after this it spun a weak and incomplete cocoon. Two weeks later we found that this had been ravaged by that pestiferous intruder, *Melittobia.*

On the same day and in the same place, a second burrow was discovered near the first. This had the same external appearance, a hole five-eighths inch in diameter running straight downward, and a large, neat pile of loose dirt and small pellets four inches away. The wasp soon returned from her flight of alarm and resumed her digging. She would walk in head first and come out backwards and continue to

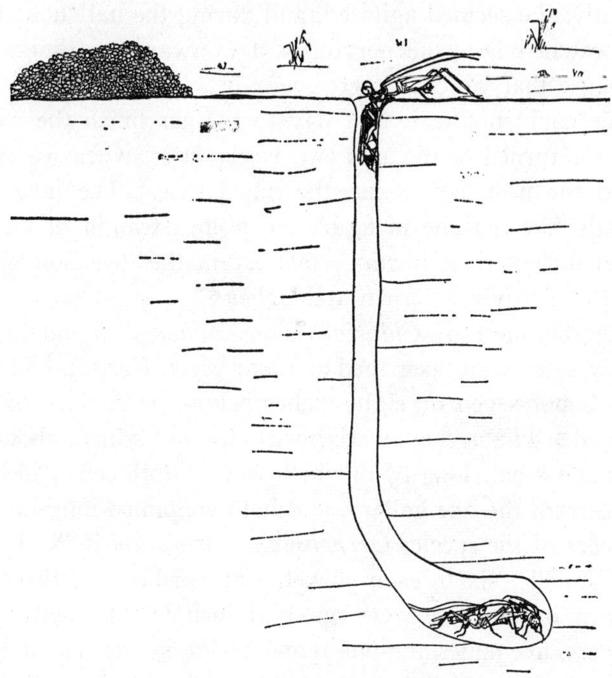

FIG. 43. *Chlorion ichneumoneum,* her burrow and prey. One-third natural size.

walk back until she came to the dumping-place, where she would release her load and go in at once for another, without looking to the right or left. These trips to and fro were repeated with all the mechanical air of clockwork. The load of dirt was carried in the mouth while the front pair of legs helped to hold it in place. She dug out a big mouthful of the loose, crumbling soil for each trip, and would probably have lost much of it on the way if she had not supported it in her jaws with her fore-feet. After carrying out and dropping several loads with mechanical precision, she would pause to clear the path of any débris and to brush up the pile with her legs. Although she worked intently, she seemed agitated, and during the half-hour that we watched her, she nervously flew away five times, for no cause that we could perceive.

We could not wait that day to see her finish the work, so we returned to the spot two weeks later, when we excavated the nest and found the pupal case. The hole was exactly like the one in figure 43, going straight down for seven inches, then turning squarely in the direction opposite the dirt-pile, to form a chamber.

Another nest of *Chlorion ichneumoneum,* found in the sunny side of an open shed at Lake View, Kansas, had two cells about seven or eight inches below the surface of the ground. The pockets were horizontal and sealed, about an inch and a half long by one inch wide. Both cells had been made from the one gallery, and both contained long-horned hoppers of the species *Orchelimum calcaratum* R. & H. [A. N: Caudell], six in each pocket. The orifice and the main burrow of the hole were one-half inch in diameter. The hoppers, five males and one female, were in one cell, and the egg was fastened to one, ventro-laterally, between the first and second legs; in the other cell were three males and three females, and the egg was on the ventral side of one. Barth[11] finds that this wasp has several cells leading off at right angles to the main passage, and that it stores its nest with as many as twelve grasshoppers.

For this species, Hancock's[12] notes substantiate the observations of the Peckhams. In addition, he found the prey to be females of *Orchelimum delicatum* and *O. vulgare* and both sexes of *Conocephalus attenuatus.* He found one wasp to weigh 5 grains and four hoppers weighed 7, 10, 11, and 10 grains. One wasp made two nests in succession close together.

[11] Bull. Wisc. Nat. Hist. Soc. **6**: 134. 1908.

[12] Nature Studies in Temperate America, p. 195-201. 1911.

The prey from our two nests survived their sting and imprisonment equally well. The next day, in one cell, one had rotted, one had died and four responded to stimulation; in the other cell, one had rotted, one responded to stimulation, and four were motionless, but apparently living. Four days later, all were dead.

These *C. ichneumoneum* also are annoyed by various pests. The ever-present *Melittobia* were found in their pupal cases kept at home, although in nature, when the underground nest is closed, it is improbable that they can reach them. A hopper taken from one of their nests had a larva attached to it that was probably a Hymenopterous parasite. Our attempt to bring it to maturity failed.

We have noticed these wasps feeding on flowers, both goldenrod and sweet clover. Robertson records them as feeding upon the flowers of various species of *Solidago,* and Cockerell finds that, in New Mexico, they frequent the flowers of *Cleome serrulata.* Folsom in his Entomology figures an insect of this species with pollenia of milkweed attached to its legs. Fernald[13] finds that they visit the flowers of sumach, clematis, asclepias, mint, etc., and says that the species has probably the widest distribution of any of the Chlorioninae in America. He has seen specimens from various states in the United States, and gives references of their occurrence in Brazil, Guatemala, Nicaragua, Costa Rica, Panama, Guiana, Venezuela, Cuba, Jamaica and Santo Domingo. Howard[14] says that this species is gradually extending its northward range.

Pierce finds this insect to be the host of the twisted-wing parasite, *Strepsiptera.* Adams says that the larva of this species is probably devoured by the parasitic fly, *Metopia.*

[13] Proc. U. S. Nat. Mus. **31**: 402. 1907.

[14] Cir. Bureau Entom. **97**: 2. 1908. Footnote.

Howard gives a good figure of this wasp in The Insect Book, Pl. 5, fig. 18.

Davis[15] found the following prey in the nests which he opened: *Atlanticus dorsalis,* three in each of two nests and five in another, and elsewhere he saw a wasp carrying a *Conocephalus triops.* Packard, in his Guide, says they use *Orchilimum vulgare* or *O. gracile.* Our records mention only *Orchelimum* in their nests. All of these are the long-horned grasshoppers, for which they show a preference.

## A Locust-hunter that Makes Twin Cells.

All summer long we had scoured this bare spot in the field almost daily (fig. 2), yet it was the middle of September before we discovered the first burrows of an unknown wasp. The mouth of the hole, open, is about three-sixteenths inch in diameter, clear-cut, and might easily be mistaken for a beetle's or spider's hole, while the neat little mound of dirt nearby is almost indistinguishable from the dainty little ant-hills which abound in the field. *Sphex pictipennis* carries out and piles up the dirt in the form of little chips; *Priononyx* and *Bembix* kick it out as dust, but this species brings it out and piles it up in granular form, only a trifle coarser than that of the tiny ants. She must understand the art of keeping herself modestly inconspicuous, and must work without all the bombastic commotion in which *Bembix* indulges, for we have never been able to catch her at her work.

One of these piles of granules aroused our curiosity on September 15. We examined all the earth about it carefully, but could detect no trace nor scar on the ground where the soil had been disturbed, so with the trowel we shaved off

[15] Journn. N. Y. Ent. Soc. **19**: 218. 1911.

the surface of the earth for several inches around. This at once revealed a hole, newly refilled, which went down to a depth of less than an inch, when it expanded into a pocket, one inch long and three-eighths inch in diameter, lying almost horizontally. At the far end, this chamber contracted into the channel again with its diameter of three-sixteenths inch and a length of about one-fourth inch; this portion also was filled in with a compact plug of fresh dirt. Beyond this, the hole again expanded, forming another pocket exactly like the first. Each of these cells contained a grasshopper, *Melanoplus femur-rubrum,* neatly tucked in with its head toward the rear wall. Each hopper carried an egg fastened to the femur, near the abdomen, in the precise spot where *Priononyx* attaches her eggs. We took them home but were unable to rear them.

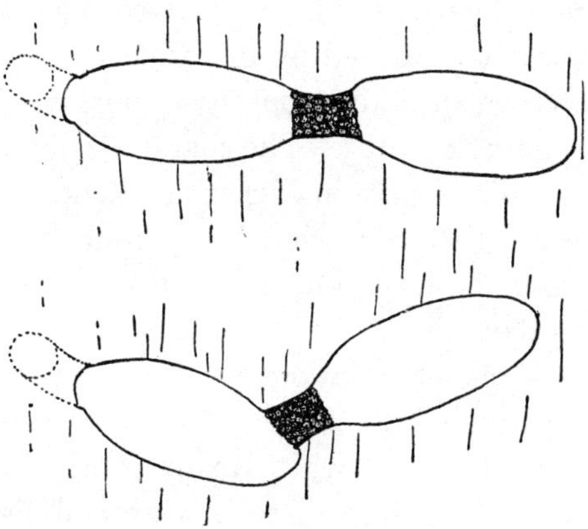

FIG. 44. The twin-celled nests of an unknown wasp. Exact size.

A few feet distant we found another pellet-pile similar to the first. Only by the same method of search, scooping off the surface earth, did we discover a second nest almost identical in form with the first: two cells lying horizontally with a constricted part between them filled with dirt (fig.

44), and in each cell a hopper bearing an egg in precisely the same position as before. One of these eggs hatched two days later, September 17; by the next day it was developing rapidly. The other egg was probably injured by the crowding of too many hoppers in a small tin box. Two of the hoppers died three days later, and one died after six days. The larva which hatched devoured its food speedily, leaving only the hardest parts of legs and integument, and it grew with astonishing rapidity. Just nine days after the discovery of the egg, the larva began to spin. It made a small area of brown silken carpet under itself, but had difficulty in forming a cocoon in the small tin box, which was quite different from its natural earthen cell. We tried to shape a little nest of cotton around it on which it might get a hold, but it could not adapt itself to its strange surroundings and died in the attempt at cocoon-making.

Although we had learned by this time just what to look for, we succeeded in finding only one more of these nests, during the summer of 1915. The characteristics of this nest and its surroundings were in every way identical with those just described. It was discovered only four days later than the others, and the larva on one of the hoppers appeared to be about a day old.

Another season's observations were unsuccessful in clearing up the mystery of the maker of these nests, so we give forth this meager record which really is no more than to make known the fact that there is a ground-digger, probably a wasp, which makes horizontal twin cells and stores them with one locust each.

*Chlorion cyaneum* Dahlb. [S. A. Rohwer].

We hereby enter our protest against *Chlorion cyaneum:* we spent over fifty hours during one summer intently watching and following members of this species foraging, without once seeing them do anything more than hunt. One could seldom spend even a little while in the field adjoining the brick-yard without seeing one or more of these blue *Chlorions* foraging among the cinders, but without getting anything. It seems probable that they detect their prey only by the sense of sight, that they prowl about, in their characteristic manner, entering holes and crevices for the purpose of finding prey, and that they are not attracted to certain holes by other powers, such as scent, hearing, etc.; else they would not waste such a vast amount of time on hopelessly fruitless areas. The prey of these wasps is crickets, and the habitat of crickets is never in beds of cinders, some of them freshly dumped and still hot. Yet these wasps go on prowling about every accessible crevice and continue searching long after one's patience and endurance have been exhausted. Sometimes they enter the same hole many times without finding anything. This would lead one to conclude that they hunt more or less stupidly and that each detail of their actions is devoid of psychological significance; possibly they are attracted to the cinders by the large number of inviting crannies, and not by any indication of the presence of crickets.

Two years ago an entire afternoon was spent in watching the similar behavior of these wasps at the foot of a straw-stack. Although they did not, to our knowledge, have the good fortune to capture any crickets, they were more justified in seeking them under wheat straw than in dry cinders.

One warm morning in Kansas we found a *C. cyaneum* in a sandy plowed field, hurrying homeward with her cricket, probably a *Gryllus abbreviatus* Serv. [A. N. Caudell]. She travelled briskly, her cricket apparently no burden, and laid it down only once for a moment. She carried it, head forward, under her body, and at one time flew with it for about three inches. She moved in a manner that indicated that she knew where she was going, and yet we are not certain that she was going anywhere in particular. She went straight across the field for thirty feet until she arrived at a deep furrow down the side; then she turned at a right angle and followed directly down this for twenty feet more and plunged into a mole-hole. She may have used it without hesitation simply because it happened to be in her path, but she travelled with all the precision and familiarity of a man walking home from his office and turning in at his own door. She remained in the hole nine minutes, then emerged hastily and soared off to the woods again. We tried to dig out the burrow, but our searches in the loose sand were all in vain.

While, in this instance, we found *C. cyaneum* dragging her cricket across the field, this method seems not to be constant. Hungerford and Williams[16] write that in Greely County, Kansas, one was observed climbing a clay bank, carrying a mature female of *Centhophilus,* evidently striving to reach an altitude sufficient to enable her to fly to her nest, and the Peckhams find that one, after running a little way, arose and flew lightly, for about eighteen feet, to a hole on the bare hillside. Here, too, Peckham's wasp differed from ours in that it had its hole in readiness on the surface, while ours, if she had a hole, had it concealed in a rodent burrow. The Peckhams illustrate a very pretty burrow of this wasp in which one egg was deposited amid seven crickets, *Gryllus abbreviatus* Linn. From their later observations, they find she does not make a new nest for each egg, but she provisions a number of cells leading from one gallery. They record[17] a very interesting incident which gives one the im-

[16] Ent. News **23**: 247. 1912.
[17] Bull. Wis. Nat. Hist. Soc. **1**: 85. 1900.

pression that she is attracted to a favorable spot for prey by her auditory sense. She "stood in the doorway, turning her head now to this side, and now to that, as though listening, and now we became conscious of the fact that a cricket was chirping loudly nearby. Perhaps she was getting the direction from which the sound came, for, after a little, she flew to the top of a tall weed, then dropped and entered a hole below, from which she issued a moment later, with a very limp specimen of *Gryllus abbreviatus*." Of course it remains entirely possible that this wasp, which seems to be possessed of a mania for peeping into all holes and crevices anyway, was not attracted at all by the cricket's song. Furthermore, this implies that she has auditory organs on the head just because "she turned her head now to this side and now to that." In fact, it has never yet been positively demonstrated that they have auditory organs anywhere.

*Chlorion* (*Isodontia*) *auripes* Fern. [S. A. Rohwer].

We have never yet seen this wasp catch its prey, but we place this account of certain aspects of its behavior in the chapter, "The Hunters of Large Orthoptera," for two reasons: first, that Fernald[18] places this, as well as the two preceding species, in the sub-family Chlorionini; and second, that Davidson[19] finds that a sister species under the name *Sphex elegans,* now called by Fernald *Chlorion* (*Isodontia*) *elegans,* uses tree crickets for the nests containing young.

One July morning we saw on the barn door a wasp carrying a piece of excelsior about three inches long. It was such an unusual sight that we ran to observe it, but, without warn-

[18] Proc. U. S. Nat. Mus. **31**: 356. 1907.

[19] Ent. News **10**: 179-180. 1899.

ing, the wasp quickly flew out the door and escaped. A few nights later, at twilight, one of this species, possibly the same individual, but without her burden, was flying about the inside wall of the barn. Eventually, she settled in one of the holes in the wall. Thinking that this was her nest and hoping to get more of her story, we did not take her then. But on the morrow, we sorrowfully learned that this was only her sleeping-quarters and not her nest at all. One more fleeting glimpse of her some days later carrying a large wheat straw only tantalized us and whetted our curiosity. So when, many days after, the twins came running to the house shouting, "It's there! It's there! the wasp with a stick in its mouth!," the family broke in disorder and ran to the spot. Like the populace rushing forth, craning their necks skyward, to view the first modern aircraft to appear above a village, so we ran hither and thither watching the maneuvres overhead of our grass carrier wasp. She wheeled and circled about, and finally landed at her burrow in a log in the corncrib. It was an old carpenter-bee hole, completely stuffed with grass. It seemed that the straws had all been drawn in by their middle, so the ends protruded from the orifice in a broom-like tuft. We removed this material, and found nothing but grass. However, we could not reach to the bottom of the burrow with the forceps.

This nest was the counterpart of several which we had seen about that time. All of them seemed to be old bee or beetle burrows in logs or timbers, and all were similarly filled with this material, tightly crammed into the hole. These nests did not appear until near the end of our sojourn in the country, so we did not learn, first-hand, the use or purpose of these straw structures, so like a bird's nest.

On the morning of our last day with them, we saw one out gathering her grasses. She alighted on a leafless branch of a plant and tried her jaws on it, but apparently it was too tough. She turned to a blade of green grass, which bent and swayed under her weight when she alighted on it. As she bit the blade off with her jaws, I expected to see her tumble when it severed, since she was sawing the branch on which she was sitting. But while the cut portion was hanging by a mere thread, she spread her wings and flew away, breaking it off as she flew. On her next trip, she flew far away and returned after four minutes with a long timothy stem protruding four inches from her body. These wasps always carry their grasses under their bodies, grasping the anterior end in their mandibles, and alight and enter the hole without shifting their burden. When we visited them on October 3, three were at work all the forenoon, busily carrying dry grass into their chosen bee-holes, and even at 4:45 p. m., when it was quite cloudy and dismal, one was still faithful to her task. Thus the season ended without our having ascertained whether they use this material for bedding, for food or as a plug to close the orifice.

We are not alone in this observation, for Packard[20] finds the same insect, under the name *Sphex tibialis* St. Fargeau, behaving somewhat similarly. He says Mr. J. Angus, who reared this species, sent him a larva in a cavity previously tunnelled by *Xylocopa virginica* in a pine board. The hole was six inches long, and the oval, cylindrical cocoons were packed loosely side by side where there was room, or one a little in advance of the other. The interstices were filled with bits of rope, which had perhaps been bitten up by the wasp itself. The end of the cell was filled for a distance of two inches with a coarse sedge arranged in layers, as if rammed in like gun-wadding. The cocoons are 80 to 90 hundredths of an inch long, oval, lanceolate, somewhat like

[20] Guide to the Study of Insects, p. 168. 1889.

those of *Pompilus.* They consist of two layers, the outer very thin and the inner, parchment-like. The larvae hibernate and turn to pupae in the spring, appearing in summer and autumn.

A similar type of behavior has been reported by Davidson for a sister species, under the name of *Sphex elegans:* "For nesting sites they prefer the larger stems, first gnawing through the thin partitions opposite the leaf insertions which naturally divide an otherwise hollow stem. The parent wasp first packs the bottom of this tube with very fine grass-like fibers, which on investigation prove to be fine strips of the loosely fibrous bark of *Audibertia polystacha,* from one-fourth inch to one and one-fourth inches in length. On this is laid the larval food supply, which consists, on an average, of from seven to eight tree crickets. The egg is laid on the breast of one of the crickets, a wad of bark fiber is placed on the top which forms the base of the next cell, etc. A copious wad, sometimes three or four inches in depth, protects the topmost cell."

The prey of *Ammobia bridwelli* Fernald. [S. A. Rohwer].

Late one August afternoon, at Meramec Highlands, Missouri, this wasp was seen entering her burrow in the soft, loose earth, under an open shed. Since it was impossible for us to remain there, we captured the wasp and dug up the nest. It was well provisioned with the long-antennaed Orthoptera, *Camptonotus carolinensis* Gerst. [A. N. Caudell]. They were eight in number, three males and five females. The earth was so loose that we could get no idea of the shape of the burrow.

# CHAPTER XI

## THE SAND-LOVING AMMOPHILA

*Sphex* (*Ammophila*) *pictipennis* Walsh. [S. A. Rohwer].

When the time comes for *Sphex pictipennis* to respond to the impulse for nidification, she proceeds about her important business quietly and without much commotion. She appears not to be especially exacting in the choice of a location, as do some species of wasps, although occasionally she is seen to abandon a place where she has begun a hole, and seek another. Usually, however, she alights upon a suitable spot, a bare area in a sunny, open field, and begins her excavation in a matter-of-course way. With the mandibles she cuts out the firm soil in the form of little chips, walks to a chosen spot about four inches away, and piles these chips up, load by load, in a nice heap. So faithful is she to this habit of piling her fresh dirt at a precise distance from her hole that often only that has served as our clue in locating a completed nest. These characteristic piles of chips are easily recognized, even when the holes are perfectly concealed. By scooping off the surface soil in a circle of about four inches radius around this pile, the burrow is almost invariably brought to light. Only once have we seen an exception to this habit of carrying the dirt to some selected spot: in that case the ground was so dry that it was easily pulverized, and as the wasp bit out each load of dirt, she stepped back an inch or so from the hole, in this direction or that, and threw it into the air, where it made a little puff of dust as it blew away in the breeze.

She digs her hole straight down for an inch or an inch and a half, then fashions an oval, horizontal pocket or chamber about three-fourths inch long and one-half inch high (fig. 45). She works without either haste or hesitation, but with precision. When at length the last mouthful of dirt has been carried out and she feels that the burrow is ready for use, she comes out and hunts for a little clod. She usually finds something suitable within a few inches of the hole, but she is very exacting in her selection and will not be satisfied with anything which falls short of her specified requirements, even though she must seek for some time. This clod must be just large enough barely to cover the mouth of

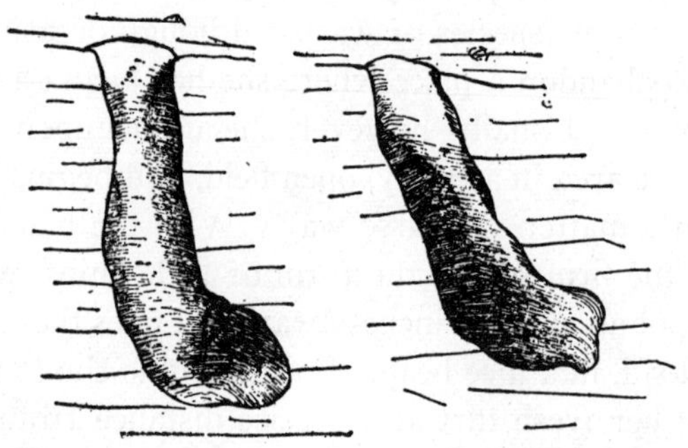

FIG. 45. The burrows of *Sphex pictipennis.* Natural size.

the hole, or to fit into it like a plug, but it must not fall into the burrow. We have seen her use a bit of stem of just the right size. This she places carefully over the entrance, to close it to intruders during her absence. Sometimes she throws one or two kicks of loose dirt over and around the spot, more completely to disguise the place. Then she goes off on the wing in low flight over the grass and weeds in quest of prey.

The duration of her absence varies. Sometimes she meets with early success in her foraging and returns with her caterpillar in an hour; sometimes she is out as long as six or eight hours, presumably in her search for prey. We have never been so fortunate as to witness this part of her work. We have seen her out foraging in the field, to be sure, hopping from leaf to leaf or flying over the grass, scanning the weeds as she lightly passes over them, but we have never seen her at the critical moment of the capture of her prey. But, sooner or later, she comes trudging home with her burden, which often is a grey cut-worm. At this part of her task she is, naturally, more conspicuous and more easily discovered than at any other time. We must not be surprised that she sometimes has some difficulty in progressing with her load; rather we must be astonished that she can move with it at all. The caterpillar is very often four times her own weight, or more, yet she brings it through grass and roots, clods and gutters. We have never seen an *Ammophila* give up a caterpillar because it was too heavy for her. Sometimes, however, the prey is so small that she can drag it with ease or even lift it clear of the ground and make rapid progress. She practically always carries it in the same manner; she turns it on its back so the smooth, rounded back will slide on the ground like a sled-runner; then she stands astride it, grasps the skin at the sides of its throat until it is drawn to look like a tight collar around the caterpillar's neck, lifts the anterior end a little so only the rounded dorsum will touch the ground or obstacles, and away she goes on all six feet. Once or twice we have seen her grasp it by the middle segment instead of by the throat, and lift it clear of the ground (fig. 46). On one occasion, when a wasp was in grave difficulties in getting her caterpillar through a tangle of grass, she managed it very ingeniously by lifting one end of the burden and propping it, almost vertically, in the fork of the grass, then lifting the other end to a slightly higher point. Thus, lifting

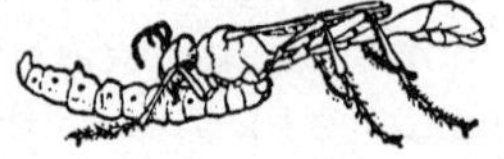

FIG. 46. *Sphex pictipennis* carrying a small caterpillar. Natural size.

the ends of the caterpillar alternately, she hoisted it out of the chasm in the grass-thicket into which it had fallen, exactly as a man, working alone, would hoist a heavy timber little by little. Our *A. pictipennis* always walks forward with her prey beneath her, as did the *Ammophilas* observed by the Peckhams, in contradiction to Westwood who says that *Ammophila,* when she has captured her prey, walks backward.

In this point of her behavior we see the grossest error in economy committed by *Ammophila.* She spends an enormous amount of energy and time in trundling her heavy caterpillar from a considerable distance, we know not how far, and then dragging it all over the region in the vicinity of her hole while locating the burrow. Since she uses but one caterpillar, she might save all this needless waste of time and energy by doing as *Priononyx* does, digging the hole conveniently near to the prey after it has been captured. The topography about the nest is usually very similar in nature to the environment of the prey and she seems not to be very particular about the location. To be sure she has a preference for beaten paths and sunny bald areas, but she as often uses any little bare spot between the weeds and grasses for her nesting-place. So why should such a stupid habit persist, entailing frequent loss, danger and expenditure of effort, while all of her other methods of work have become so refined and highly developed? The only explanation that we have to offer is that many other members of this genus use more than one caterpillar, and naturally have to return to the hole repeatedly. Perhaps in *pictipennis* this habit is a vestige of the time when she too used more than one caterpillar and must therefore have an established nesting-site.

After she arrives in the general region of her nest, there often ensues a long search for the exact location. She wanders here, there and yonder, dragging her booty with her. She seldom lays it down or leaves it; perhaps this is to guard it the more constantly from the parasites which are usually following. But occasionally, when her search has gone on in vain for a discouragingly long time, she will leave it while she hunts for the burrow, after which she usually searches as clumsily again for her caterpillar. Sometimes she hunts for an hour or more for her burrow, and occasionally she is utterly unable to find it and gives up, abandoning both prey and nest.

When finally she arrives at the nest all in readiness and waiting, it takes her only a moment to remove the plug and enter backwards, dragging the caterpillar after her. There is none of the monotonous performance we see in some species of wasps of digging at the hole a few minutes, then going and examining the prey, then digging more, etc. Many times it appeared to us that the hole was surely too small to receive so large an object; but the wasp judged better than we, for in every case it was large enough, with only one exception. This case of abnormal behavior is perhaps interesting enough to warrant narration.

We came upon the scene of an unusual performance in the life of *Ammophila*—the wasp had left the caterpillar lying beside the hole while she was digging the burrow deeper. It was a large caterpillar, and very fat. At length she essayed to take it in, but it was too large for the opening. She tried various ways, and yanked it this way and that, but each time when it would not go in she would lay it aside and dig the hole deeper, or at least enlarge the chamber at the bottom. At last, in another attempt, she dragged it in after her, but it became lodged when only one-eighth of it was protruding—hence she could neither push it out nor herself escape. We waited for a time and saw that the situation only meant death to her, so we came to her assistance. (Thus our humanity! If she had been alone with Nature she would not have left any posterity perhaps to perpetuate her stupidity!) We pulled it out with forceps—but already the Dipterous parasites which had been lurking nearby had done their deadly work, for a half-dozen squirming larvae were at the neck of the caterpillar. As it was pulled out, some of these were brushed off and fell down into the hole. She showed neither anger nor surprise at the assistance that had been rendered to her, but she appeared satisfied with the disposition of her property. She came out and picked up a large, firm pellet, took it down into the hole with her and remained quite a while, brought it up for a moment, then returned with it and remained inside for another period. Then she came out once more, threw this pellet aside and gathered a half-dozen other smaller ones, which she took down into the burrow. Oh, if we but could have seen what she was doing with them down there in her dark chamber! Did she use the first large one to kill the parasites which infested her nest? Or did she instinctively feel that it was now time to bring in material for the partition or plug at the entrance to the chamber? Hardly the latter, because when she emerged, she promptly dragged her caterpillar in again as if nothing had happened. This time she succeeded in getting it a trifle lower, so the rear end was level with the surface of the earth; then she seemed to encounter the same difficulty as before. Five minutes elapsed, and she could move it neither down nor up.

Unfortunately, we had to go then, so we dug up the nest. We watched carefully for the tiny Diptera larvae, but if they were there they were lost in the digging.

Two minutes is all the time the wasp requires for adjusting her prey and ovipositing, and sometimes she is through in less time. (Figure 47 shows the position of the egg on the caterpillar.) Then begins the task of filling the hole, and in this she works in a most calm and purposeful manner, disturbed of course if one crowds too near, but with no silly

FIG. 47. Position of egg on caterpillar. Natural size.

nervousness. She emerges head first and immediately gets some small clods, usually about three, and takes them down to the bottom. We suspect that she arranges these to serve as a partition between the chamber and the burrow, to prevent the loose soil from being packed down around the caterpillar or crowded upon the delicate egg. Then she jumps out nimbly and scratches and kicks the loose dirt nearby into the hole, goes in and stands on her head, pounding and packing it down. With each ram of the head, she emits a shrill buzzing sound. How this buzz is made we do not know, nor do we know whether it is an expression of pleasure, or of labor, or a mechanical part of the effort. Thus she brushes in and packs down several layers of loose dirt, until the hole is filled almost to the top. If she uses all the loose dirt lying nearby, she is not in the least disconcerted, but simply bites some more loose, with her mandibles, from the surface of the ground and uses that. When the depression is yet about one-fourth inch deep, she fetches a large, firm clod, sometimes as much as five times as large as her own head, and throws it into the hole. At first it appears that she is using this method as a quick way to fill up her hole. But no, she settles herself for work again, grasps the clod firmly in her mandibles and, for a minute or so, she rubs and grinds it fiercely against the bottom of the depression, with a rotary or side-to-side motion, until, under the pressure and wear, the clod crumbles and is worn to dust and becomes part of the compact filling. She then turns round and round on top of the hole, sweeping to the center the dirt which has been pushed out at the edges of the saucer-shaped depression, fetches another clod from somewhere within a distance of two or three feet from the hole and repeats the performance. Thus she uses sometimes as many as ten or twelve clods, grinding, beating and biting them to pieces, until the top of the fill is level with the ground. In this way she works the fill down much tighter, for we have often seen her use several pellets and pound them in after the hole appeared level full.

In her next selection she seems to be more particular. She goes here and yonder, pausing at clods and tiny pebbles, sometimes lifting them or turning them over. When finally she finds one which suits her fancy, usually a pebble a little larger than her head, but sometimes an unusually hard clod or bit of wood, she brings it in her mandibles and, grasping it firmly, she rubs, pounds and hammers down the dirt on the top of the hole until all traces of the fill are obliterated. When she has finished, we ourselves cannot discern the spot. Her task, so skillfully done, is now at an end; she throws her tool aside a few inches and flits away with an utterly careless air, as if she had forgotten all interest whatsoever in this place—and quite probably she has. It is interesting to note that she cannot be persuaded to use this tool before the precise time for it. Once we tossed her a tiny pebble while she was yet busy grinding to pieces her clods with a pestle-and-mortar motion, but she only took it, without ado, and laid it back on her rubbish-heap, where an annoying bit of stick and a troublesome cinder had already been placed. Later on, when she was ready for her hammer, she went directly and, to our great delight, got our pebble which she had so stolidly spurned only a few minutes before. If, in grinding up the clods for filling, one does not readily go to pieces, she does not leave it in the hole for filling but takes it out and throws it away.

Thus she finishes her task with characteristic precision, and leaves it beautifully done. In accomplishing the closing, she devotes about forty minutes of careful attention to a task which wasps of many other species finish in a few minutes.

Here we have not only the record of a tool-using habit of an insect, but also, what is equally rare and valuable, a possible clue to the probable origin of this habit or instinct. We see her using first the loose earth, then clods with which to pack the earth tighter and more tight, and finally using some object one degree harder which will pack down the remaining dust on top of the hole, but will not go to pieces and leave more litter of its own on the site.

This is not the first record of the tool-using behavior of *Ammophila*. The Peckhams have observed one instance in *A. urnaria,* and Williston[1] records the same for *A. yarrowi,* while Hungerford and Williams[2] found an *Ammophila sp.* that used an Acridiid leg for a tool in pounding down the soil. Hartman[3] finds that with *A. procera,* at the end of the operation of closing the nest, it sometimes happens "that a piece of wood is pressed down tightly, then pulled out and pressed down again, and this repeated several times,

[1] Ent. News **3**: 85. 1892.

[2] Ent. News **23**: 244-246.

[3] Bull. Univ. Tex. **66**: 17. 1905.

so that one might suspect that the wasp were here improvising a tool with which to tamp down the sand."

Considering that our tool-using insect described above would have nothing to do with the pebble until a time when it was needed for tamping, and in view of what is to follow as the result of very close observation by the two of us on another *pictipennis* mother closing her nest, we do think that they actually have highly plastic intellectual powers. Morgan says,[4] in speaking of the interesting observation of the tool-using *Ammophila* of the Peckhams: "Here we have intelligent behavior rising to a level to which some would apply the term rational, for the act may be held to afford evidence of the perception of the relation of the means employed to an end to be attained, and some general conception of purpose." But Holmes takes exception to this interpretation of Morgan by saying: "But in estimating the psychic aspect of the performance we must bear in mind that the act is one which borders closely upon the normal instinctive behavior of the insect. The seizure of pebbles in the mandibles and the packing in of dirt are parts of the instinctive process of filling the hole. The wasp combines two features of its hole-filling instinct in a rather unusual way. Does she really perceive the relation of means to end? I am not sure that she does." Whether Morgan's or Holmes' interpretation is the correct one we hope the details given below will convince the reader. In this connection it may not be amiss to relate exactly the conduct of another of these wasps, through this part of her task.

The wasp, when discovered, was carrying her caterpillar. It was a smaller worm than usual—so small that she carried it in her mandibles by grasping it in its middle, and lifting it clear off the ground, so she could use all her legs freely for progression. She made a pretty sight carrying

[4] Holmes, The Evolution of Animal Intelligence, p. 204. 1911.

her prey in this new-fashioned way. After carrying it for ten feet she dropped it and started to remove the lid off her nest. In our eagerness to see all, one of us pressed too close and she flew away a short distance in alarm. In a moment she walked back to the cut-worm, examined it and gave it a reproving sting on its under side near the pro-legs, but we could not distinguish which pair. She then straddled and seized it in the manner already described, and carried it off, making a very perfect circle about three feet in diameter, and dropped it at the identical spot from where a moment before she had indignantly taken it. A strange way, this, of responding to disturbance! She then gave it two impressions about the head with the mandibles, then passed the tip of her abdomen on its under side as it lay, ventral downward, and felt—or rather probed—in a half-dozen places, sliding her abdomen continuously backward until she reached a spot just in the rear of the last pair of pro-legs; there she thrust in her sting and let it remain for several seconds. We had thought at first, when she felt the integument with her abdomen at a number of places, that she was stinging the caterpillar, but when we saw the way she deliberately thrust in her sting and let it quietly remain there for some time, we decided that these former touches had been only of a testing or probing nature. She then resumed her work where she had left off, and opened her hole by removing one mouthful of clods. She darted in and reappeared almost instanter, carried in her cherished prey, remained inside two minutes, came out again and immediately began to fill the hole. While she was inside, we took the opportunity of observing the site closely. There was very little loose dirt or dust about the hole; all that had been taken from the hole had been carried five inches away, across a tuft of grass, and piled up neatly—in spite of the difficulties of always clambering through the tangle of grass-stems. She came out head first and carried in, one at a time, three clods of earth; these we suppose she arranged to form a plug in the angle of the "L"-shaped nest. After that, for a few seconds, she kicked loose dust into the burrow. She also kicked a straw, six inches in length, over the hole; this she carried a few inches away, and later, when it got in her way a second time, she carried it in her mandibles and flew with it for some distance and cast it away. She kicked in more loose earth, and after each portion, went in to ram or pack it down, humming in a discontinuous way—that is, it sounded as if with each ram of her head she notified us with a sharp buzz of like duration.

Thus she used all the loose dirt that lay near at hand; the region was hard and clean. There was yet about one-fourth inch of the burrow to be filled, when she came with a hard clod about five times as large as her own head, threw it into the hole and went in herself as far as possible. We thought this would be an easy way to fill up the burrow, and were surprised to see her grasp it in her mandibles and continuously, for three minutes, press down the earth in the depression with this tool, rubbing with it in a circular motion. But our surprise was greater when we saw her throw out this hard clod when she had tamped the dirt down sufficiently; the easy way of filling a hole was not her way. A much smaller clod was then thrown in and beaten to dust with her head and face. This was plainly to be seen, and this later clod must have been intended for this purpose since the mandibles and head were used to break it up, and no attempt was made to swing it in a circular motion. It is quite likely that this small one could also have served as a tool if she had wanted to use it to that purpose, and we feel sure also that the former one could have been bitten and pounded to pieces with her stout mandibles, had she wished to do so. But she had done the necessary pounding; filler was now needed and she made it. The question confronted us of how she would get dust to fill in the rest of the hole. That troubled her not at all; with her strong mandibles she dug up the hard earth nearby and kicked it in until the depression was full, and packed it again with her head. To accomplish this she almost stood on her head, bracing herself with her hind legs. In our eagerness we crowded too near again, whereupon she flew off and walked around for three minutes; then she returned and resumed the work, exactly where she had left off under disturbance, and finished the pounding with her head. She next found a hard piece of clay a few inches away and, using it as before, packed down the loose earth. After rubbing with this for five minutes she left it in the hole, dug up some more earth and kicked it over the site, quite covering this last tool, so she went back to the hole and with her mandibles fished out this same clod and again used it for one minute to pack down the last layer perfectly smooth and level with the surrounding earth. Then she laid the useful clod to one side. The interesting fact is that she should have remembered just where her tool was last left. After an additional few seconds of dust-kicking, to make the spot look exactly like the rest of the field, she flew carelessly away, her task done.

This is the method of work generally followed fairly uniformly, by *Ammophila,* in her nidification. However, the members of this species show much individuality in their behavior, and meet emergencies in such varied and interesting ways that it will be of interest to note some of their digressions from the usual method.

In the manner of departing from the finished burrow when starting out on a foraging trip, these wasps show so much variation that it has been quite impossible for us to ascertain which is the normal and which the abnormal conduct. We are inclined to believe that, if they are frightened

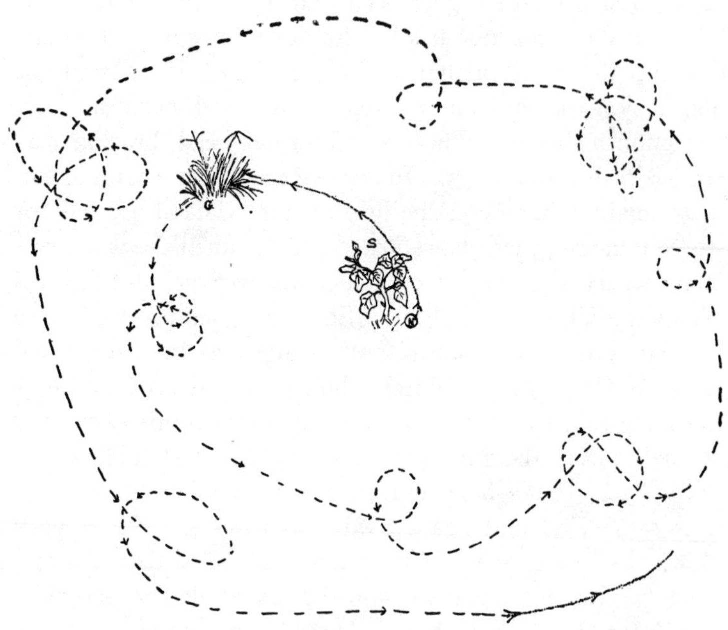

FIG. 48. Diagram to show the way one mother *S. pictipennis* studied the landmarks about her nest.

away from their burrows, leaving suddenly without getting any landmarks, they have grave difficulties in returning to their nests. Occasionally one departs on the wing from her incompleted burrow, without any appearance of examining the region. More commonly, however, they go around the covered nest in widening circles, first walking near the hole, then running, hopping and at last flying in larger circles, and finally soaring off to the fields in quest of prey. One wasp which we stealthily watched seemed unusually precise in her manner of examining the location before departing for the hunting-grounds. The hole was finished, and she had brought three pieces of dirt and carefully covered it. She flew to a leaf a few inches away. From this perch she descended three times to do some unnecessary scratching over the hole. By these maneuvers she may have been getting her landmarks (see fig. 48)—in fact, we suspect that she was, for she walked all over this small *Solanum* (*S* in the figure) which overhung her burrow (*N*), examining it all the while, and as she came to the leaf directly above her nest she usually peered down and sometimes descended to do some scratching, then returned to continue her examination of the weed. Then she turned her attention to a small tuft of grass (*G*), the object next in nearness to her nest, and scrutinized it. After this minute examination, she dropped down upon the earth and walked in an almost perfect circle around the nest, not all at once, but in arcs, and at the termination of each arc she would waltz about in tiny circles, sometimes one whirl, and sometimes two or even three times around, and then proceed with the next arc, without once becoming confused in her directions or missing the lines of her well-defined circle. The little waltzing whirls were almost always from left to right, but once she circled from right to left. The accompanying crude diagram (fig. 48) will aid in making clear this remarkable performance. While we had no measure of the length of the arcs, it seemed to us they were wonderfully uniform in size. This precision is only in harmony with the other instances of fine physical judgment which we so often see in the conduct of this wasp. At the conclusion of the first circle, she commenced a second of increasing radius, but as she progressed she got to running and hopping, and soon flew away to the vegetation beyond. A moment later we saw her climbing up a ragweed in the rôle of a forager.

She left at 10 o'clock and we could not wait for her return, but at 4: 30 p. m. we examined the nest and were surprised to find it just as we had left it. We removed the little lumps of clay with which she had covered it, but the hole was empty, so we replaced them; no prey after six and one-half hours! We began to wonder if she had gotten lost in spite of her accurate orientation.

Early the next morning, we again examined the spot and found it tightly filled in. A little careful digging soon revealed the cut-worm, with the delicate egg on its side. Hence she must have returned to the nest with the prey some time between 4: 30 and sunset, after an absence and a search of six hours or more. Her locality study served the purpose of her accurate return, although many marks were required to guide our return.

In another case, the burrow was ready for use and the wasp proceeded to close it temporarily, as described elsewhere, while she went foraging. Here her judgment must somehow have been amiss, for the first two pellets which she brought were so small that they fell down into the hole; but the third was large enough to rest on top nicely like a lid. Then she concealed the spot deftly by adding some other bits of earth and a kick or two of dust, and departed for green fields. She did not take the usual flight of orientation, but began by searching in the weeds nearby. She flitted or hopped from plant to plant, but while doing this her path described a circle around the hole. Suddenly she flew directly away out of our sight. Five minutes later, she returned and continued scanning the weeds in this region, and at one time even walked over her own nest and stopped short on her pile of pellets for a moment, then flew away.

In observing *pictipennis,* the fact is demonstrated again and again, that the insects, when returning to the object of their search, are not guided by any special sense, but in all probability, as the Peckhams, Turner and others have shown for seemed to be in a state of torpor, and would move only when prodded. They were divided and part placed in a box of excelsior out-of-doors under the south porch, part in the laboratory, and part back under the eaves in the attic where the temperature was intermediate between the other two places. But one by one all died; it could not be ascertained among these limited numbers that any one location was more favorable to them than the others. The *P. annularis* survived for less than two days, but the last of the *rubiginosus* females did not die until December 20.

One June morning, a *P. rubiginosus* alighted on a potato plant in the garden and immediately pounced upon a large larva of a striped potato beetle, mumbled it in her jaws and seemed to try to turn it over. After about forty seconds, she suddenly dashed away, perhaps alarmed at our intrusion. The larva was apparently uninjured, and remained on the leaf.

They also feed upon flower heads, and are known to cut open the fruits of Opuntia and other cacti and feed upon the juices.[11]

*Polistes annularis* Linn. [S. A. Rohwer].

When, on April 7, 1915, we found *P. annularis* out in great numbers, we were both astonished and delighted at the propitious opening of the wasp season. They were queens that had wintered over, and were taking advantage of the first warmth of spring.

The site of this first appearance of the wasps was the east face of the high, rocky bluff overhanging the Mississippi River at Cliff Cave, near St. Louis. Along this bluff, in the warm morning sunshine, were hundreds of queen

[11] Bull. U. S. Dept. Agr. No. 113: 36, 45. 1912.

wasps. They were resting or flying idly around among the rocks and along the sunny railroad track below; by far the greatest numbers were to be seen in the sheltering crevices of rocks in the cliff. Careful examination of the swarms proved that the wasps were all of the one species, all queens, and—most interesting of all points—that they were all gregarious. We did not on that day find a single solitary individual. Many of the groups were small, from three to ten queens, and others were larger; we estimated three colonies to contain from twenty-five to fifty wasps each, and one about a hundred resting quietly together, while a fourth colony was enormous—we do not think an estimate of a thousand would be excessive. Even the members of this large group were so docile that we could easily approach near enough to them to ascertain the sex. At the side of the stream below, many were drinking water. It was, of course, too early in the season for nest-building, but we were elated with the thought that a little later in the season we should find a wonderful supply of material for observing how they begin to build their nests.

A few dead wasps were found scattered about the ledges, and frequently, when we chipped off a piece of loose rock, a dead queen was to be found in the cranny behind it. In two spots there was evidence that this elimination had been particularly heavy. On the ledge behind two colonies of mason-bees were a great many wings of these insects, but no bodies. These two sites were probably good places for *annularis* to spend the winter, and also good places for a lizard, a mole or a bat to come and feed. It was evident that the wasps had not died a natural death, since only the wings remained. Whatever may have been their fate, it seems that their severe sting has availed nothing in giving them protection.

Later in the season, June 25, we returned to this place

with visions of wondrous wasp activities. Imagine our surprise when not one *P. annularis* was to be seen, and no nests on the rocks, as we had expected. Only two *Polistes* were seen that day, and they were *P. pallipes*. We cannot account for this strange disappearance, unless they had dispersed or migrated. Several lizards were seen along the railroad track at the foot of the bluff, but we cannot believe that they could annihilate so large a population of insects which are so well equipped for flight and defense. Yet again on this date, in one crevice in the bluff which seemed an ideal hibernating-nook, we found upwards of fifty queens of *P. annularis,* dead. This shows that we must count upon heavy elimination.

The interest of this April congregation of *P. annularis* was only increased when, on October 25, 1916, we found an assemblage of one hundred or more queens behind a closed shutter of an old abandoned building at Clifton Terrace, Illinois. This particular window was the most sheltered nook on the building, sunny and well protected from the raw winds. We searched at all the other shutters, but no wasps were behind them. Whether the love of companionship, or the mere attraction of physical comfort had drawn them thus together cannot be declared; we only know that they all had the ability to congregate in the warmest spot, and not one was to be found elsewhere in that vicinity. The group comprised three species of *Polistes;* perhaps seventy-five per cent of them were *pallipes,* twenty per cent *annularis* and five per cent *bellicosus*. It appeared that the entire population of the neighborhood was here assembled, yet there was not a male among them.

At Raleigh, North Carolina, Brimley[12] has taken males all winter, from the end of November to the end of March; but, while we have looked for males during the winter, we

[12] Ent. News **19**: 107. 1908.

have never succeeded in finding them. It seems as though it is normal for the males to die of exhaustion after fertilizing the queens, but it might be possible for some unfortunate ones, with no opportunity to function sexually, to retain sufficient vitality to prolong their longevity.

While all species of *Polistes* customarily place their nests in buildings, we found several very large last-year's nests on shrubs in a small, uncultivated patch of ground, about fifty by one hundred feet, in the Illinois valley. (See fig. 51.) Wheat-fields surrounded it on all sides. The nests were attached to the bushes about four or five feet from the ground. The striking feature was that several of these old nests had a number of queens of *P. annularis* clustering upon them. It was April 24, 1914, just the time in the spring when the wasp queens would be likely to go house-hunting. They may have been only resting on these old nests, but we have long had a notion, and so have other writers, that they sometimes use old nests, and that more than one queen sometimes finds a home on such a nest; hence we accepted this evidence in partial confirmation of our impressions. The following table shows the number of queens that were at rest on each nest:

| No. nests | No. queens on each |
|---|---|
| 1 | 0 |
| 3 | 1 |
| 3 | 5 |
| 1 | 6 |
| 1 | 16 |

Besides this, we found several new nests in the making, of three or four cells each, some containing eggs, and presided over by queens as follows:

FIG. 51. Nest of *Polistes sp.* Slightly reduced.

| | |
|---|---|
| Nests with 1 queen, | 1 nest |
| Nests with 2 queens, | 1 nest |
| Nests with 4 queens, | 2 nests |

There were also some queens in clusters, without any evidence whatever of nests being built.

That old nests are sometimes used, but usually not the old cells, is evidenced by the fact that flourishing *Polistes* nests are often found with bright, clean cells along the periphery and a center of soiled, partly disintegrated cells. However, one should not attach to this fact too much assumption of intelligent choice, for we often find nests in strange situations which are probably accidental, as, for instance, the mud nests of *Chalybion* and *Pelopoeus* often found plastered upon *Polistes* nests, or, like one curiosity which we saw, a pipe-organ nest and two mud nests all subjoining a large paper nest. Whether the queen falls upon old nests as accidentally as she does upon the rafters of a barn or other site, is a problem worth study; but, whether through luck or foresight, we must admit that the queen enlarging an old nest, with the stem and foundation already built and the material at hand which may be again used, has much of her work already done at a time of year when she is without assistants.

We usually think of *Polistes* as inhabitants of sheds, and in such places they are most abundant, but their nests are built in trees as well, where there is no shelter whatever from wind and rain. Judging by the large size of these nests, which of course denotes strong colonies, we see that they are little affected by the elements.

They seem, moreover, to be able to adapt their nesting habits to unusual conditions. We once found a nest in a rusty tomato can in a city rubbish heap. *Polistes variatus*[13]

[13] Hungerford and Williams, Ent. News **23**: 255. 1912.

in Kansas, when without trees and buildings, suspend their nests in the tunnels of rodents.

The nests of *P. annularis* sometimes attain great size. The following data recorded by Pierce[14] are of interest: Of two nests taken in Texas, one had 1575 cells, and the

FIG. 52. A nest of *Polistes annularis* among the branches.

other had 1212 cells. These 2787 cells gave forth 1553 wasps of which 1311 were males and 242 were females. Two hundred sixty-six wasps were stylopized by *Acroschismus pallidus* Brues. He says further that stylopized *P. annularis* are not so active as normal individuals, but are often seen feeding on flowers, and some lived from 13 to

[14] Bull. U. S. Nat. Mus. No. 66: 17. 1909.

16 days after the exit of the male parasites from their bodies. Some were even found hibernating thus. Fox[15] found, at Denison, Texas, a nest of *P. annularis* which measured eleven by sixteen inches.

The large nest of *P. annularis* illustrated in figure 52 was found overhanging a dry creek-bed near St. Louis. It was almost on edge among the branches, eight feet from the ground, and bore about twenty queens. They were all frightened away by the removal of some of the leaves in order that the nest might be photographed. The nest had probably been built elsewhere, and either the wind or high water had lodged it here in an unusual position apparently without having caused any change in the life of the progeny.

In one case we noticed a strange phenomenon: one cell in a *P. annularis* nest contained two eggs. The second egg was additional—not merely a misplaced one—for the 28 cells of the nest contained 29 eggs. Ten days later we noticed, however, that only one egg in this cell was developing; the other seemed not to have hatched.

One *P. annularis* returned several times to our out-door dinner table in the country, to eat the juice from a bowl of apple-sauce. It drank long and steadily, standing knee-deep in the juice.

Miss Murtfelt records the fact that these wasps removed strips of paper from the bags that were used to protect clusters of grapes. After chewing the material into pulp, they carried it away for the building of the nest. Pierce (loc. cit. p. 22) finds that this wasp is the host of three species of stylops. Robertson mentions it as feeding upon various flower-heads, and we have observed it feeding upon flowers of the madeira vine and goldenrod.

[15] Ent. News **7**: 57. 1896.

*Polistes pallipes* Lepel.

We had long been possessed of an idle curiosity to know how *Polistes* would behave if their nests were turned upside down, so the experiment was tried of inverting several of the nests of *P. pallipes*. This was done by taking down the nest, passing a long hat-pin through the center and stem of the nest, and thus pinning it back in its place upside down, with ample space allowed above for the easy entrance and exit of the wasps to the cells.

After one of the *Polistes* nests had been inverted, the inmates removed much of the material from the nest and commenced to build another nest on the ceiling at the identical spot where this one had been. At last only one wasp at a time was to be seen working at this spot, while the others remained below and cared for the inverted nestlings. In time, the wasps abandoned this new project and all worked on the inverted nest, carrying on the household affairs in the usual way, excepting that they removed the material from the middle of the nest and from it this time built other normal cells beneath, using the roof of the old nest, now inverted, for the ceiling of the new cells.

In another colony, the duties went on normally, and none of the new cells were placed vertically on the old roof (now ceiling), but the new cells around the periphery were so built as to be almost horizontal, radiating from the stem of the nest.

In two other inverted colonies, the affairs of the household went on normally, but no attempt was made to add new cells.

A year later, in June, when turning over a large stone, we found a queen of *P. variatus* Cress. with her nest of a dozen cells, two of which were sealed and the others with wasplings in various stages of development. We inverted this stone, to observe the behavior of the queen, taking precautions, however, to lay another broad stone of the same color above it, in order to give her the roof and the shelter from the light and weather to which she was accustomed. She remained on the upturned nest until 3 p. m.. about five hours, and then deserted it. The next day the little black ants were stealing the goodies from the exposed nest. Watch was kept at frequent intervals for the next two days, but the queen never returned.

Another small nest of *P. pallipes,* built on the sheltered side of a loose door which leaned against the side of a barn, was exposed, by turning the door, to the direct rays of the August sun. The nest was soon deserted by the owners. Shortly afterward we found that the larvae, too, had been torn out, probably by birds.

All wasps are usually so diligent about their domestic duties that we seldom catch them doing so commonplace a thing as eating—in fact, we are almost surprised when we find them pausing to take nourishment for themselves.

Early one August morning, we found a *P. pallipes* visiting a small wound in a willow tree. It remained for perhaps a half-hour, with its head buried in the soft, moist tissues, but when it left we could see that it carried away no wood-pulp. Hence we concluded it was only breakfasting off the juice and pulp.

A cottonwood tree bore a decayed spot on the top of a projecting root. Two *P. pallipes* were busying themselves about it when we discovered it at 9:40 a. m. Thinking it would be a good chance to see them gather pulp for nidification, we watched their every movement. A few minutes later a black and yellow Eumenid came to the same place as if returning to a familiar spot. During the next hour while we remained, they came and went at intervals, often pausing on the rotted wood for ten minutes or more,

When they departed, we could see clearly that they never carried away any pulp. They spent their time with their heads buried in the rotted wood, with their abdomens pulsating in and out, which movement in the wasp generally denotes contentment. We thought that they might be merely seeking moisture, so we placed near them a piece of juicy peach, from our lunch. This they stolidly ignored, however, although they seemed to be aware of it and even climbed over it on their way to the much preferred rotten pulp. Hence we again concluded that instead of gathering the wood-pulp for the construction of their nests, they were merely enjoying their own repast.

They are not always vegetable-feeders, however. On a nest hung above the laboratory door, one worker brought in a caterpillar. A second immediately cooperated with the first, and together they soon divided it into two equal parts; then each took his portion and complacently chewed it to pulp.

We have previously recorded[16] how, when one comes upon a *Polistes* nest at night, one finds the inhabitants quietly at rest, their bodies and legs spread flat against the under surface of the nest. They seem to be fully asleep, for one may hold a strong light near them for several minutes before they show the slightest response. Early last year, when the queens were nesting alone, we wondered what became of them at night. It seemed that they went elsewhere to sleep, until a careful examination of fifteen nests of *P. pallipes* revealed them in hiding during the night on top of the nest, and completely invisible from below. There they clung to the stem of the nest, between their roof and the ceiling of the barn. This condition was constant for all the queens at that stage of nidification, and

[16] Ann. Ent. Soc. Amer. 9: 241. 1916.

brings to light the interesting variation of position in sleep when the queen is alone and when the numbers are great.

Dr. C. H. Turner[17] has published a very interesting and detailed account of the feeding, homing and hunting behavior of an orphan colony of *P. pallipes*. Tower[18] has done some work on the ontogeny of the color pattern in this wasp. Pierce finds *P. pallipes* stylopized by the twisted-wing parasite, *Acroschismus bowdichi,* and says that a female was taken by Mr. Dury "so laden with parasites that it could not move." It contained nine male pupae. Robertson finds them feeding on various flower heads. Packard[19] says says that a male with the abdomen removed lived for five and one-half hours, while a female with the head removed lived actively for forty-one hours. Snyder[20] says that, in the Bermuda Islands, *P. pallipes* is of a lighter shade than in the United States. Bermuda has coral roads and white calsomined roofs, and he suggests that selective elimination has been a factor in causing the survival of the light colored individual.

*Polistes bellicosus* Cress. [S. A. Rohwer].

Two specimens of *Polistes bellicosus,* a yellow-striped wasp, and also another Hymenopteron often came down to the water to drink. Occasionally they stopped at the water's edge, but more often they would fly to the middle of the puddle of still water and there alight upon the surface, spread their legs in the fashion of the water strider and drink long and deep, apparently in full enjoyment. They

[17] Psyche **19**: 184-190. 1912.

[18] Decen. Publ. Univ. Chicago **10**: 21. Fig. 72-74. 1903.

[19] Psyche **2**: 17. 1877.

[20] Ent. News **19**: 147. 1908.

did not swim nor spin about, as do the water striders, but rested calmly on the water with legs spread; and when they had finished they arose lightly on the wing and flew off. Sometimes they spent a long time there, probably for the purpose of cooling off.

On one occasion, a *Pelopoeus* was lying on its side, motionless and partly submerged. At first we suspected a tragedy—that the insect had come to the water exhausted or had made a false step in alighting and had been drowned—but when we approached and essayed to pick it up, it darted away. However, two *Ammophila sp.* were taken from the pond drowned. We do not know whether the water really has its dangers for them, or whether these had merely come to this spot when already injured or exhausted and ready to drop.

*Vespula germanica* Fabr. [S. A. Rohwer].

We hesitate to call this little wasp a scavenger, and yet we have seen it enjoying discarded fragments of our food so often that we have grown to expect to see it on the deserted picnic ground, feasting on the remains left from the lunch-baskets. On one day, August 21, we captured twenty workers, and many more were present, feeding on grape-jelly, greasy chicken-bones and other fragments left by the picnickers of the previous day. While feeding, they are as intent as bees on a water-melon rind, and may be captured with ease. They seem practically omnivorous. We have seen them eating of an astonishing variety, including grapes, pears, apple-sauce, paw-paw, dead roach, juice in salmon can, cold broth, flowers of buck-brush, madeira vine, banana, eyes of a dead rat. Several were seen sipping water at the spring. A few hours after a young rooster had lost his head at the chopping-block, the head was found teeming with these greedy scavengers. They jostled and swarmed over the tongue, eyes and all exposed moist surfaces (fig. 53).

In early spring, the queens always keep close to the ground in flight, and often enter openings like mole-holes or crevices in the rocks. We could easily understand their low flight and hunting behavior, since it is well known that this species builds paper nests underground; they were probably not foraging but nest-seeking or site-hunting. On May 11, 1915, we saw many in the fields at Meramec Highlands conducting themselves in this manner.

FIG. 53. *Vespula germanica* were as thick as flies on a freshly removed rooster's head.

While they usually build their nests underground, we once found one in a hollow log lying on the ground. It was discovered early in June, and then comprised three empty cells, six covered ones and about a dozen with larvae. From the covered cells, four adults emerged on June 28 and 29 and July 3. The nest was small and had four layers of covering over the top and partly overlapping on the sides.

*Vespa maculata*

A pair of insects, tumbling violently about on the door-step, attracted our attention. Closer observation revealed *Vespa maculata* in deadly combat with a large gray fly. Soon one wing of the fly flew off; then the head popped off. Even then, more tumbling ensued, until presently the wasp triumphantly adjusted the fly under her body and flew to the grape-arbor nearby. Here she paused to complete the preparation of her prey, which consisted of much malaxation of the fly and biting off its other wing; then she flew away with it.

For days thereafter she chased flies at the kitchen door and at our out-door dinner table. Other wasps were often there, too, sharing our food—drinking our fruit-juice, stealing our cake, even pillaging our sausage—but *Vespa maculata* never bothered anything but the flies which congregated there. With a swiftness exceeding that of a chicken-hawk in its onset upon a barn-yard, she would appear above the table, pounce upon an unsuspecting fly either on the wing or resting on the table, and carry it up to the grape-arbor overhead. There she would either snip off its wings and head preparatory to carrying it away, or, as is her custom, hang herself up by one hind leg and swing to and fro up-side-down while devouring the prey.

They are large, boisterous and decidedly terrifying in their manner. However, they themselves do not always escape, for we once found one dead, ensnared in a spider's web.

Wasps of all kinds are almost always a hot-weather population; hence we were much surprised, on November 16, to find a *V. maculata,* very active, upon the window-pane. It was left there, that its voluntary course of action might be observed. That day was unusually warm; on the cooler days, the wasp was only slightly active. On November 28, it was placed in a jelly-glass containing cotton, but either the confinement did not suit it, or its days were near an end, for it survived less than two days more.

In January, 1910, a large nest was taken at Kimmswick, Missouri, having several dead wasps lying between the tiers of the paper.

# CHAPTER XIII

## THE MINING AND OTHER WASPS OF THE FAMILY EUMENIDAE

*Odynerus geminus* Cress. [S. A. Rohwer].

Certainly one of the daintiest pieces of work executed by the solitary wasps is the little turret built by *Odynerus geminus*. This is a neat little chimney, built of pellets of mud plastered one upon another, surmounting the wasp's burrow in the ground. It is a little less than three-eighths inch in diameter, outside measurement, very thin and delicate, rough on the outside, showing the delineation of each pellet of mud as it was superimposed upon the other, but smooth on the inside; the interior diameter of one-fourth inch is just the same as the hole in the earth beneath it—in fact, it is merely a built-up continuation of this hole. The turret rises to a height of about three-fourths inch above the surface of the ground, then turns at a right angle and extends in a horizontal course for the same length. The completed turret looks just like a miniature "elbow" of a stovepipe (see fig. 54).

The wasp has a pretty way of entering this novel tunnel; she stands beneath the turret, gently lifts the front part of her body until the first pair of legs can reach the edges of the chimney, and thus holding on she deftly raises the body and climbs in.

The gallery beneath this quaint architecture is clear-cut,

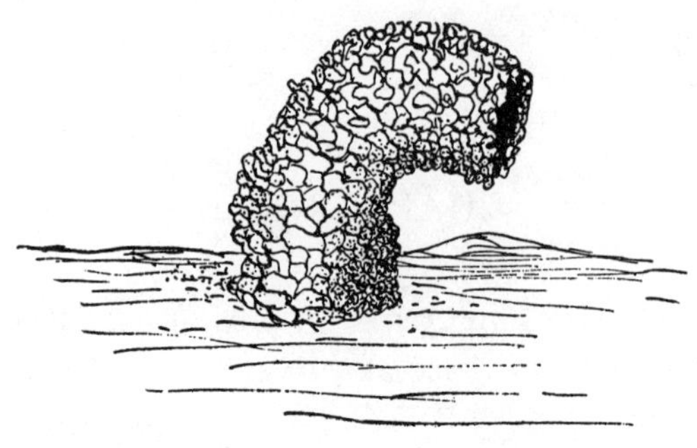

FIG. 54. The turret over the burrow of *Odynerus geminus.* Twice natural size.

about one-fourth inch in diameter and two inches in total length. It goes straight downward for half its length, then turns abruptly, usually forming an angle of approximately 60° with the perpendicular, although occasionally this angle approaches a right angle. The end of this channel is very slightly wider than the upper portion, and forms one of the "pockets" which make up the nest (see fig. 55). Other channels, with a similar pocket, may branch off from the main burrow at the point of the sharp bend. We have found from one to four pockets to a single nest, but we do not know whether the wasps vary so in their habits of nest-building, or whether the smaller nests were only incomplete. We suspect that the construction of a single cluster of cells extends over a considerable length of time, because, in one nest of four pockets which we excavated, one cell contained a larva of considerable size, while the others contained smaller larvae or egg and caterpillars.

Hungerford and Williams[1] find no mud tubes over the tunnels of *O. geminus,* and a part if not all of the pellets of earth are deposited within two or three inches of the entrance to the hole. We find that *O. geminus* drops her

[1] Ent. News **23**: 253. 1912.

pellets nearer to the entrance than does *O. dorsalis,* the latter scattering them over a much larger area. We too have seen an occasional nest of *geminus* without the turret, but we attributed these cases to some accident, the intrusion of man or beast. We watched three such nests, whose turrets had been destroyed, to see whether they would be reconstructed, but no attempt was ever made by the wasps to repair them.

FIG. 55. Photograph of the nest of *O. geminus,* showing the mandible-marks on the wall of the vertical channel. Natural size.

Of course such a piece of work as this perfect little chimney would be impossible without mud, whereas they are usually built in dry, barren places. Hence this wasp, like her sister *O. dorsalis,* carries water and disgorges it a little at a time, to wet the soil, making just enough mud at a time for one pellet.

We have never been so fortunate as to witness the beginning of this pretty tower, but we have seen the builder carrying out the pellets of mud through the chimney and dropping them a few inches from the burrow. The accompanying figure (fig. 56) illustrates a number of these pellets, which nicely show the marks left by the manipulation of the mandibles.

We suspected that the dirt taken out of the hole was applied to the chimney, but we were perplexed that the wasp should apply part of her excavated clay to the turret, and, with the same careful precision, carry out and discard other pellets. Finally, near the end of the season, on September 16, we got a clue to the answer to the question. We found a turret which seemed incomplete; it went straight up for one-third inch and had no curve or horizontal portion. The wasp was carrying out moist pellets but instead of applying them to the turret she was taking them out a few inches from the hole and discarding them. When we returned the next afternoon the turret stood at precisely the height at which we had left it. The wasp was no longer carrying out pellets, but she emerged every few minutes and played about the mouth of the chimney. Imagine our surprise when closer scrutiny revealed to us that she was at these times biting off a mouthful of clay from the margin of the chimney, after having moistened the spot with water just as she does in digging her hole, and carrying it down into the burrow! Her work was methodical and accurate—really charming to see. She would come up to the top of the turret, spread a drop of water, bite off and knead together a large mouthful and carry it down, head first, into the hole, and come up in a moment to repeat the performance precisely. The fact that she moistened only enough clay at each trip to make the desired chunk indicates again that she must carry the supply of water in some other way than in the mouth; perhaps deep down in her throat. When her supply of water was exhausted, she flew away for more. Returning after a few moments, she first went down into her hole to see if all was well, then came up and promptly resumed her work of breaking down the little wall, mouthful by mouthful, and carrying it down into the cell. The supply of water

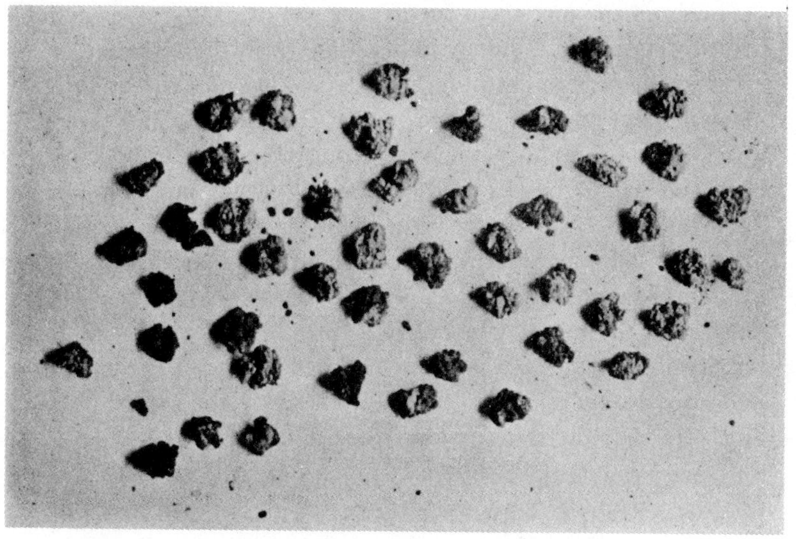

FIG. 56. A collection of mud pellets carried out in the mouth by *Odynerus geminus* and dropped near the nest. Natural size.

sufficed for eight loads of mud. When it was gone, she came out and paused on the brink for a moment to clean herself and then flew away, in the same direction as before, for water. This quantity was disposed of in precisely the same manner as before; she first went down to examine the cell immediately after her return, then came out on top and paused to clean herself before going for more water.

Now the turret was almost gone, and as the work progressed the rear portion of her body protruded more and more. This gave us a direct clue to what was happening down below. Sure enough, when all the turret was gone, it was proved that the material in the chimney was exactly the amount required to fill and seal up the burrow flush with the surface of the ground. Here then was our explanation: the wasp digs her burrow and carries out the earth in moist pellets; all the dirt from the gallery she carefully saves and constructs into a chimney, while that from the chamber or pocket she carries out and discards. When the nest is provisioned she plugs up the mouth of the chamber and packs back into the gallery the very same clay which she took out and has at hand exactly the required amount of filler, and also material of the right color to render the plug in her hole indistinguishable from the surrounding earth. By this method the security of the young is well safeguarded also, for the entire channel is so firmly packed that it is impossible to probe it or even to trace it when digging, as one can often easily do with the nests of the wasps that kick the dry dirt loosely into their burrows.

This wasp worked arduously in packing down the last dirt on the top of the hole, moistening it with the remainder of her load of water. After she had finished applying more earth, she fetched one more load of water and applied it to the plug, presumably to make it more firm and compact. She stood pounding and smoothing the seal down with her head, her body curled almost in a circle so her abdomen nearly touched her head, and her folded wings sticking up vertically.

Thus, it seems, wasps vie with one another in wonderful ways of effecting the security of their young, and each new method seems more marvellous than the last.

Another turret-building Eumenid and its little chimney came under our notice at about 2 p. m. The nest underground could not have been an extensive one, as could be seen by the paucity of the pellets strewn nearby, so when we saw the wasp carrying in caterpillars, we suspected that it was her first cell that she was provisioning.

The top soil in that place was black loam to a depth of one-fourth inch, while the subsoil was of red clay. The basal half of the turret was made of black earth and the upper half of red clay, and all of the pellets strewn about were of red clay. This color-arrangement proves that the wasp begins, immediately upon commencing her burrow, to construct her turret out of the first soil excavated, and adds the deeper mouthfuls of clay, in their turn, higher on the turret until the required size is attained (or the required amount of material reserved), and throws away the remaining pellets taken out of the chamber or such portions of the nest as will not need to be refilled with earth. This chimney was of the standard form and dimensions.

The proprietress was carrying in caterpillars. The first one was procured in five minutes, and the second one in twenty-five minutes. While she was gone we made a scratch on the surface of the ground to help us to locate the nest. This confused or alarmed her so that she flew about for several minutes before entering. Finally she ventured into the nest but flew out again and away, carrying her caterpillar with her. Not until a half-hour had elapsed did she return, and then she came empty-handed. Once more she entered her hole and flew out again uneasily, and began to dismember the turret, pellet by pellet, and carry the clay into the hole. We have noted previously how they plug up their holes by removing all of the turret and carrying it in for filler, so we thought that she was now doing the same, although we were surprised that she should finally seal up the tunnel, when apparently only one cell was finished below. When about one-fourth of her chimney had been taken down we caught her to make sure of her identity and proceeded to open the burrow. Great was our surprise upon finding that she had placed a plug of mud in the mouth of the cell that she had filled with caterpillars, and another thin layer over the top of the hole flush with the surface of the ground, while the tunnel, which for permanent sealing is always completely filled, was empty. Here we see that when danger threatened, and insufficient time was at hand to seal the burrow normally, she did the best thing possible to safeguard the young in the shortest possible time. Since we often find from two to four cells emanating in all directions from the central tunnel, it might be that in this case, since this nest had only one cell, her intentions were to return and construct other branch galleries and cells from the bottom of this empty main channel, when she felt that an intruder was not lurking near. Such behavior ought to make man feel like a vain pretender when he presumes to lay an exclusive claim to intelligence.

The burrow was the regular vertical tunnel with the chamber at the bottom turning to one side, as we have already photographed (see fig. 55). There were seven caterpillars in the chamber, of the species of *Loxostege,* discussed fully elsewhere. They were all actively moving, and could even walk about.

The egg was hanging by a tiny thread from the wall. It had been deposited at 3 p. m. on September 10, and it hatched at 7:30 a. m. on September 13, thus having a period of incubation of about two and one-half days. The miniature larva wriggled out through one end of its shell and fell right down among the squirming caterpillars. Their activity seemed to do it no harm, however, for it thrived for ten days and became large and husky, until one morning it was found dead. Fabre thinks that the egg would be injured by the wriggling mass of caterpillars, if it were not hung up out of their reach, but here we think, as with *O. dorsalis,* the egg might be placed among the caterpillars with safety. In this instance we dug up the whole nest in a lump of earth, leaving the arrangement intact, so the fragile larva dropped to the food-mass below.

An interesting little experiment on the homing of *O. geminus* was carried on. We had thought that the little chimney might be of service to the wasp by aiding her to locate her hole upon her return to the nest. One turret was kicked away by an animal, but she showed no more confusion in locating her nest when the chimney was gone than when it stood at its full height.

For our own convenience, on the first day we marked one turret with a piece of paper an inch square pinned to the earth beside the hole. This was of course very conspicuous on the bare ground, and we wondered if it might have anything to do with the perfect ease with which, for three days, the mother wasp unfailingly came straight to her nest. So, while she was away for water, we moved the paper to a point three inches away from the nest, in the direction from which she always came with water. When she returned, she alighted very near to the paper, paused, walked around it, took a short flight and again alighted *on the paper* and for five minutes seemed interested solely in the paper. Then she arose for another brief flight, during which we hastened to replace the paper in its original position beside the burrow, and stepped back; she immediately alighted on the spot and continued her work, as if nothing had happened. Whether she found her nest by aid of the short flight or by the guidance of the paper cannot be determined positively, but this much is certain: that she returned to the paper twice, and then gave it five minutes of her attention because it was associated with her nest, and, even though her home was only three inches away, she was compelled to take a second flight of orientation in order to locate it.

In the vicinity of the turret just described, we found in the bare ground some plugs of mud sealing former holes. These were no longer a mystery to us after we had seen *O. geminus* break down her chimney, make mud of it and

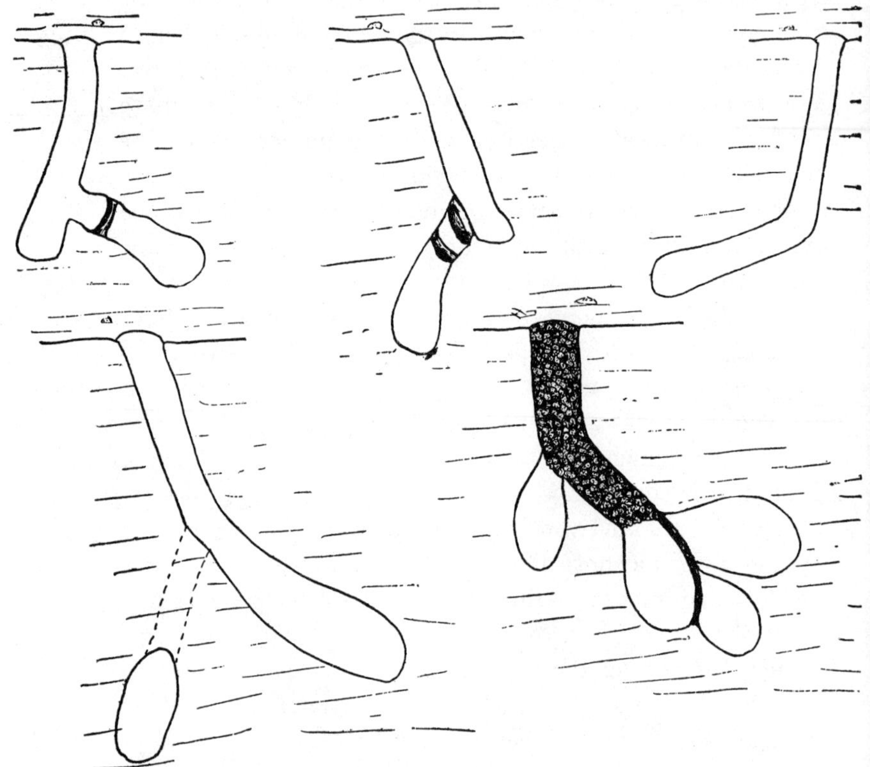

FIG. 57. Burrows of *Odynerus geminus* in various stages of construction. Natural size.

close the hole flush with the surface. Near each of these were strewn twelve or fifteen old pellets of mud of the type which *geminus* always throws away when excavating her chamber. The first nest which we dug out seemed a perfect piece of work. Clustered around the base of the vertical channel were four pockets, all alike and all containing caterpillars of the species used exclusively by *O. geminus.* (See figure in lower right-hand corner of fig. 57). There were fifty-two caterpillars in all, or an average of thirteen to a cell. They were writhing briskly and seemed very much alive, but they were unable to walk. The larvae were small but apparently healthy. Another of the sealed burrows near by had precisely the same external appearance, but had only one cell below ground (upper right-hand figure). This contained eleven caterpillars of the same species of *Loxostege* as the others, and the egg was hanging from the wall by a short but strong silken thread.

One certain incomplete turret surmounting an open hole was watched for three days, but it neither increased nor decreased in height, and since we saw no signs of activity about it, we dug it up. The main channel went down as usual for an inch, where it branched and terminated in two pockets (see fig. 57, lower left figure). One of these contained a large *O. geminus* larva and was well sealed with a plug of mud in the mouth of the chamber, while the second was open and contained only four caterpillars, and apparently was unfinished. Probably the mother wasp had met with an accident which had prevented her from finishing the nest, but the incomplete nest gives us the evidence that the turret is left standing until the pockets below are all finished.

Hungerford and Williams have some evidence that the cells are often used more than once as brood chambers. They also illustrate many galleries and cells to one nest, apparently made by one mother. The most complex nest in our experience is that shown in figure 57, in which the cells diverge from the central gallery in a shower.

When we opened one new nest, we were surprised to find in its single cell one lone caterpillar and the mother wasp

This burrow was dug out at about 5 p. m.; perhaps the little owner had merely gone into her burrow for a night's lodging, or it may be that we had only caught her there when busy with nidification. While we suspect that *O. geminus* sleeps in her hole the same as does *O. dorsalis,* we found one insect asleep on *Melilotus,* clinging to the stalk. However the sex of this individual was not noted.

The very first *O. geminus* worker of the year was seen in the field on June 5, but they were not at all common until August, and most of the above notes were made in the first half of September. Some which we reared at home emerged as adults in June. On September 24, we noted that during that week the turrets of *geminus* had been scarce. This disappearance of wasps was probably due to the increasing coolness and the fact that their normal season was over; but it may also have been due to the fact that all the puddles of water in the vicinity had dried up in the long-continued drought.

Of the hundreds of caterpillars exhumed from the nests of *O. geminus,* every one was of the same species. They were identified by Dr. S. B. Fracker as belonging to the genus *Loxostege,* of the family *Pyraustidae.* Dr. Fracker writes further that it was difficult to be sure of the species since the alcohol had taken out all the color, but in all probability they were *L. similalis.* Thus the two species of *Odynerus, O. geminus* and *O. dorsalis,* dwelt together in this field (fig. 2) and found plentiful food for their young, yet each adhered strictly to her own choice of prey, the one using only *Loxostege* and the other taking exclusively *Pholisora catullus.* Since the two species are so similar, it seems to us surprising that they should be so strict in their choice of prey as never to accept what is entirely pleasing to the other. Hungerford and Williams[2] note a similar

[2] Ent. News **23**: 254.

behavior. They find that "*Odynerus annulatus* and *O. geminus* occur in the same locality, but differ widely in habits. *Annulatus* provisions its nest with the larva of *Loxostege sticticalis* (*Pyralidina*), *geminus* with the larva of *Pholisora catullus* (Hesperidae) although the larva of *L. sticticalis* was common for *geminus*."

We have found wide variation in the number of these caterpillars used by *O. geminus;* all the way from four to fourteen in the cells. This difference must be due to faulty instinct on the part of the mother wasps. We do not see how the larvae could thrive equally well on such varied provision. In rearing some larvae from egg to adulthood, we offered them additional caterpillars when they had eaten all that their mothers had provided for them, and they gladly accepted and devoured many more.

A study of the longevity of a large number of these caterpillars which had been entombed in the cells showed great variation.

| | |
|---|---|
| Died after 7½ months ........ | 1 |
| Died after 54 days ........... | 2 |
| Died after 18 days ........... | 5 |
| Died after 12 days ........... | 1 |
| Died after 9 days ........... | 4 |
| Died after 8 days ........... | 2 |
| Died after 7 days ........... | 2 |
| Died after 5 days ........... | 5 |

The great majority of them lived from five to eighteen days after having been exhumed; this is not of course exactly the same as the length of time they survived the stinging, but corresponds roughly to it. They were for the most part very active when the space permitted it, squirming and writhing vigorously and doing everything but walking away. One seeing this activity could understand at once why it might be safer for the delicate egg to be fastened up to the wall by a strong thread than to be dropped ruthlessly into a writhing mass like this, although we suspect that in most cases it would survive.

A few of the caterpillars showed exceptional longevity. Two remained active for fifty-four days, and one astonished us by continuing to live from September to the following April, or seven and a half months. After the first three months, it ceased spontaneous writhing and moved only upon stimulation, but remained plump and healthy-looking until the last. Does the poison of the sting act as a preservative? It must have some such potency, for without it under natural conditions these caterpillars, imprisoned without food, would have died and decayed in a day or two, or pupated, but it seems that after the wasps have finished with them, they can do neither.

*Odynerus dorsalis* Fab. [S. A. Rohwer].

Each species of wasp has its own highly specialized method of building its nest. Some bite out the earth in chunks, some dig it to pieces and carry it out in armfuls, others scratch and kick it out according to various fixed habits. So *O. dorsalis,* too, has her own peculiar method which differs from the others. She carries water, mouthful by mouthful, and moistens the spot of hard, dry earth, so converting it into mud which she carries out in pellets. We have never chanced to see her working, except when the earth was dry and hard; we should like much to know whether she continues to carry water when she digs her nest after a rain. Perhaps their method of work may well be gleaned from the detailed description of the behavior of a single individual which seemed to us typical in practically all points.

Fig. 58. *Odynerus dorsalis;* her burrow with the mud pellets strewn about, and her method of lowering the caterpillar into the burrow. Natural size.

When we discovered this wasp at work at 8:50 on the morning of July 31, her hole was already begun and about one-half the length of her body in depth. She would stand on her head in the hole and bite out a little clod, at the same time turning around, screw-like, about one-quarter or one-half a revolution, in order to work from all directions alike. Then she would back out of the hole with her round, well-formed pellet of mud in her mandibles, always fly from two to fifteen inches with it, and drop it. These mud-balls were fairly uniform in size, and round—not mere clods of dirt bitten out. (See the pellets strewn about in fig. 58).

After working thus for about ten minutes, she went away, probably for a fresh supply of water. We waited so long for her return that we began to think that she had abandoned the enterprise; but, after fifteen minutes, she reappeared and began her work afresh. She worked almost incessantly, and took out 15 pellets in 8 minutes. When she emerged from the hole with the last pellet and flew away a few inches to drop it, she did not return immediately to continue her burrowing, but continued her flight at a high speed and in a direct line toward the northwest. She was gone from our sight just one and a half minutes, when we saw her returning, straight from the same direction. Iseley[3] says that when they return from their watering-places he can see their mouth-parts glistening; we were unable to see so much, but she resumed her work as before, so we suppose she carried the water in her gullet. This time she worked 8 minutes, the same as before, and in that period took out 12 pellets; upon emerging to cast away the last she flew straight and swiftly off to the northwest, just as before, and returned in 1¼ minutes. Thus she seemed to work with pretty precision and accuracy, yet we doubt

[3] Kan. Univ. Sci. Bull. **8**: 287. 1913.

the economy of this elaborate method of work. In a half-hour she had deepened her hole just the length of her own body; other wasps, such as *Priononyx* or *Sphex,* digging and kicking out the dirt, would have progressed much faster.

With this supply of water, she worked 7 minutes and took out 11 loads of earth, after which she surprised us by flying off toward the northeast. A quarter of an hour elapsed before she returned. She must have found a supply of water somewhere in that direction, however, for she resumed work normally, taking out 12 mud-balls in just eight minutes. On the next two journeys, she resumed her northwesterly course; the first time she made the trip in one minute and the next time in only one-half minute. Can it be that she was learning by experience to make her trips more quickly or directly?

By this time we were sufficiently familiar with her usual course to make it comparatively easy to follow her in her flight to her watering-place, except that it required such sprinting as was neither becoming to our mature figures nor befitting to a July day. The pond, a mere puddle of rain-water which remained in a small depression, was some 200 feet distant. When she arrived she went direct to the edge of the clearest part of the puddle, took a long drink, and when she arose in flight she seemed very heavy on the wing, probably because of being gorged with water. We were surprised to find that even after she had made so many trips to the pond, her course was not quite direct. Instead, her going out and her return to the nest followed the course indicated in the little diagram, the left in figure 59. She flew west-by-northwest to the railroad track, down the track to a point even with her tiny pond, then to the pond and home again, with only a minor detour in her return route, as indicated.

This time she worked only 5 minutes and removed 7

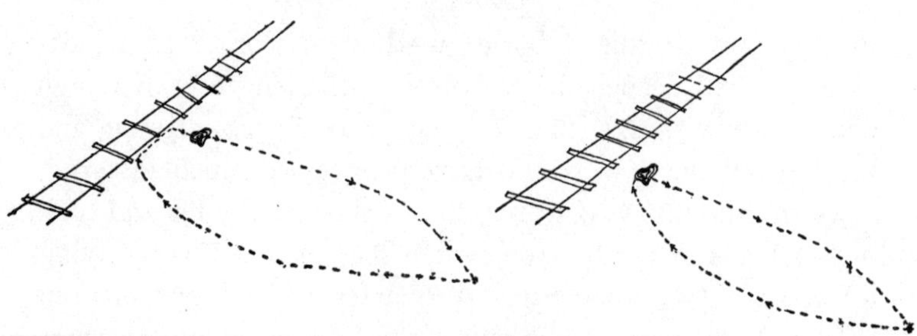

FIG. 59. The course of flight of *Odynerus dorsalis* to the puddle of water.

pellets, when she soared off to the northeast. We waited for her at her old pond, and, although she had flown in the opposite direction, she eventually appeared there, paused a moment for a load of water and hurried on back to her hole, following her habitual route precisely, and arriving after an absence of just 6½ minutes. Why these roundabout courses? We do not know, but this shows that, even though these wasps are familiar with the direct route, they do not always adhere to it. The hole was now about two inches deep; the pellets were larger and fewer to each mouthful of water. Either the work was becoming more arduous or it was telling on her strength, for she moved more heavily and occasionally staggered when she dropped a ball. The next three working periods were 8, 6 and 5 minutes, and in them she took out only 8, 9 and 9 pellets. Our St. Louis wasps generally worked at a different pace from Iseley's Kansas *O. dorsalis;* the latter made the trip for water in less than a minute, but with each load of water they removed only 5 or 6 pellets of earth, while ours always took out from 7 to 15 pellets.

In making her trip toward the northwest she now simplified her course somewhat to a more nearly direct route, similar to the right-hand diagram in figure 59. Once more she went off on her northeasterly tour and was gone 15 minutes—in fact, so long that she had trouble in locating her burrow. Previously she had come to it directly every time without a moment's confusion, but as unhesitatingly as a man returns to his own home. She flew about, as if confused, within twelve or eighteen inches of the burrow for over a minute; then she gave up the search, went back to the weeds about twenty-five feet away in the direction from which she usually came, and from there came back to it directly, showing again the necessity of going back to her starting-point for her bearings. It was then necessary for us to go. When we left her, she was continuing her northwest trips by the oval route last described. In deserting this wasp, we probably missed a most excellent opportunity of seeing the complete nidification, for this nest was probably nearing completion.

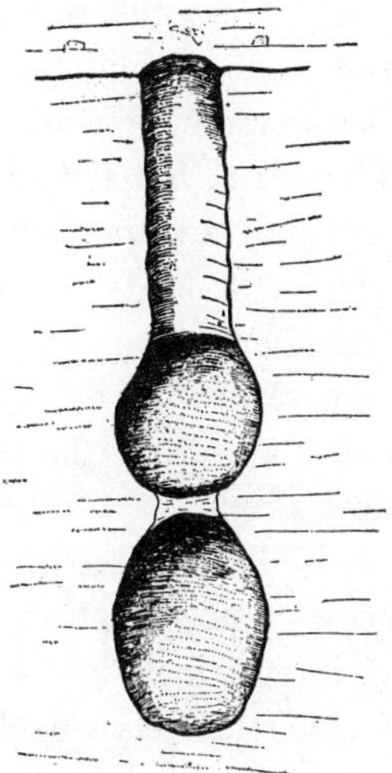

FIG. 60. The burrow of *Odynerus dorsalis.* Natural size.

The nests are always about two or two and one-half inches in depth, and a quarter to three-eighths inch in diameter at the top. The hole goes straight down for one-quarter to one-half an inch and then widens to form a spherical chamber a half-inch in diameter (see figs. 60, 61). From the bottom of this the gallery continues, the same diameter as before, for a short distance and expands into a second chamber similar to the one above. The lower cell is filled with caterpillars, the egg is left swinging by a delicate thread from the wall of the cell, and the mouth of the compartment is sealed up with a plug of mud; then the upper cell is similarly filled and sealed with a mud plug in the neck of the cell. Finally a closure of mud is inserted in the top of the hole flush with the surface, sometimes artfully constructed so as to be indistinguishable from the surrounding earth, but more often there is the saucer-like depression, caused by biting out earth to fill the hole, which Iseley has so well described. But right here is a very interesting and curious point: the entire gallery from the top of the upper cell to the surface plug is not filled in solid for its entire length, as are the holes of other burrowing wasps, although often it is a short channel (fig. 61); but it has only the firm plug at the top and bottom and an air-chamber between. The purpose of this arrangement leads one into pretty speculation. Does the air-chamber in the channel help to maintain a more uniform temperature in the cells beneath? The depth is sometimes so slight that the difference could not amount to much at any event.

Iseley, too, finds that the nests are vertical with one or two cells. He describes one exception, however, which is very surprising and interesting: a colony of eight nests built in the face of a vertical clay bank, with from three to seven cells to each burrow. We have never yet found more than two cells—except in one nest which was apparently abnormal, which had an extra (small) cell between the two normal ones (figure 62); neither have we found these insects building in the face of clay banks. It is surprising indeed to find one small group of individuals digressing so far from the established custom of the species, yet adhering

Fig. 61. Two burrows of *Odynerus dorsalis*. Natural size.

to a more or less uniform scheme of their own among themselves. As he suggests, these excavated burrows show a sharp contrast to the earthen cells under a tuft of grass, described by Hartman.[4] Mr. Hartman tells us, however, in a letter, that he suspects that probably his species was erroneously identified for him.

[4] Bull. Univ. Texas, No. 66.

In all of the channels and nests may be seen, on the side-walls, the mandible-marks, in lateral strokes, or half-rings, where bites were taken out horizontally, not up and down. (See fig. 63.) The figure also betrays the method of procedure in nest-digging: as the length of the burrow increases, the width also increases, so that at the bottom there is a start on the first globular cell. When this has been completed and provisioned and the egg deposited, undoubtedly the widening of the second cell occurs, and perhaps the soil removed in this widening goes to form the plug for the lower cell.

When the home is at last in order and Madam *Odynerus* goes a-marketing, she does precisely what most other wasps scrupulously avoid: she leaves her nest wide open. To be sure, there is yet nothing in it to attract or reward marauders, but neither is there in the newly-finished burrows of other species, so one is again left wondering what may have been the origin of such an instinct—what condition can have brought such pressure upon the species as to establish in them so fixed a habit.

Iseley (*loc. cit.* p. 289) was very fortunate to observe her hunting in a patch of mallow. When *O. dorsalis* comes upon a crumpled leaf containing the larva of the spotted skipper, she commences tearing energetically at the silken nest, first at one end and then at the other. Sometimes more than five minutes is required to dislodge a caterpillar, but more often the victim is jerked from its cover in less than a minute, seized by the neck and stung two or three times under the thorax. Vigorous malaxation follows the stinging, after which the caterpillar is carried to the nest without delay.

These wasps, when returning from the field, seem to experience no difficulty whatever in locating their burrows. They carry their prey on the wing, usually with com-

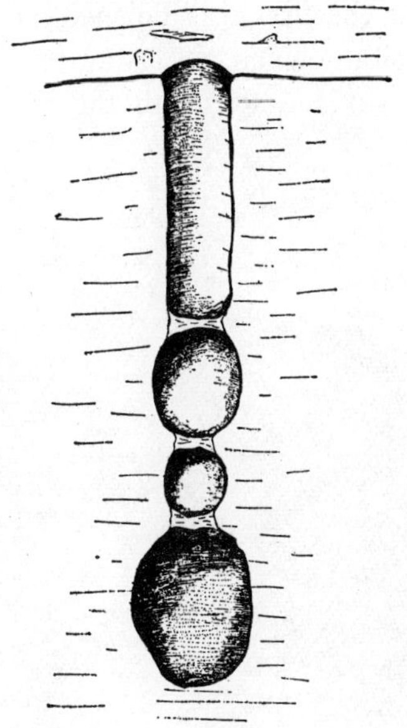

FIG. 62. An unusual burrow of *Odynerus dorsalis.* Natural size.

parative ease, hugging it tightly all the while, alight at the brink of the hole and push it in ahead of them, holding to it as they lower it (see fig. 58); then they follow it into the hole, remain inside for a few seconds—perhaps a half-minute—and then come backing out. Sometimes the wasp soars away directly in quest of other game; at other times she sits down and washes her face for a moment, then rises and poises on vibrating wings an inch or two above the hole, turns around on the wing as if inspecting the site, then circles about and flies away. She is calm, gentle and composed in all the maneuvers, betrays no nervousness and wastes no time in blustering.

We had long suspected that this wasp builds not one burrow but a group of burrows, and were glad to read Iseley's statement of having seen one begin a second hole immedately after the first was finished, and close beside it. On several occasions, when we began to dig up a nest and scooped off the surface soil with the trowel, the removal

FIG. 63. The mandible-marks on the tunnel of *Odynerus dorsalis*. Natural size.

of the thin layer revealed three or four nests near together. We have only occasionally noticed, in our St. Louis wasp-field, the pretty saucer-like depressions which betray the location of the closed nests.

One such group of nests particularly impressed us. For a week at least we had been watching a certain *O. dorsalis* as we crossed the field each morning. On every occasion she was busily engaged in digging her burrow, yet day after day the hole seemed ever unfinished. One evening we determined to open it to see if the wasp used it for sleeping-quarters. The first stroke of the trowel revealed three similar nests, all close together in a row. It has always been our custom to place our little markers one inch west of the burrow. A closer examination showed the marker to be just one inch west of the first covered one, while it was three inches west of the open or unfinished one. Hence we have every reason to believe that the one mother had really dug all three, and we had been too dull to perceive that she was not working on the same one all the time. These three nests had but one cell or chamber each. One-celled nests were rare in the previous year as well as this year, in our vicinity. Can it be that this trait of habit or instinct is heritable, that this individual should show a rare trait so persistently in her work?

Incidentally, we found the wasp sleeping in the upper part of the unfinished burrow. The sealed chamber beneath her and the cell of the middle nest contained eggs and green Hesperid caterpillars, sixteen in all, while the oldest and original hole had a full-grown larva together with the remains of one-third of a caterpillar and some excrement. With it in the cell were fifteen white pupal cases of an Hymenopterous parasite, clustered in one corner. Since the larva was full-grown and healthy, and apparently had not been disturbed by them, one can only suspect that the Hymenoptera had been parasitic upon the caterpillars before their capture, instead of upon the wasp larva.

The number of caterpillars used by these wasps varies greatly; occasionally as few as three are tossing about in the compartment, and in other cases the cell is crammed full with eight or ten. We, too, have found that the wasp does not oviposit at the conclusion of the provisioning, as do other species, but whenever it suits her fancy—or physiology. We sometimes find the little egg swinging from the wall on its thread when the provisioning is only begun or half done.

Among the St. Louis population of *dorsalis* we have found only the one species of caterpillar used as prey, *viz.*, the Hesperid larva, *Pholisora catullus* [Drs. Barnes and McDunnough], while Iseley has found two species of Lepidopterous larvae used by the Kansas *O. dorsalis*, the species mentioned above and *Pyrgus tesselata*.[5]

We are not positive that *O. dorsalis* always sleeps in her burrows, but we have found her in the unfinished holes at twilight and on dark, cloudy days a sufficient number of times to make us certain that at least the females do so frequently while the digging is in progress. Of course the problems remain of where the males sleep, and where the females find shelter when they have not open holes at their disposal.

It has always seemed to us remarkable that the nests of *O. dorsalis* are not more often ravaged by parasites or enemies, since the owner always leaves the burrows wide open during her long absences. Yet we believe she suffers less at the hands of such impostors (at least in the nests which have come under our notice) than do some of her sister species which always close their burrows behind them with such exacting care.

From one open hole we saw an *O. dorsalis* emerging and watched her closely to ascertain her method of egress. Imagine our surprise when we saw her carry out a *P. catullus* caterpillar in her front and middle pairs of legs, pause at the brink of the hole for several seconds to adjust the

[5] We have observed *O. dorsalis* in three widely separated areas but never yet have we found her using caterpillars other than *Pholisora catullus.*

caterpillar properly between forelegs and mandibles, and fly away with it. Was she a deliberate robber, or was she only a home-seeker who had by error entered the wrong nest and was removing only that which she had brought with her and which was rightfully hers? These wasps are usually very careful in finding their nests, and while they sometimes peep into two or three others before arriving at their own, we have seen only this one go so far as to enter the hole of another.

One day we saw a black wasp running and hopping about in the region of the holes of *O. dorsalis* for about five minutes; finally it entered one of the holes, and we captured it, as it emerged, to ascertain its identity. It was a *Notogonidea argentata* Bve. [S. A. Rohwer]. In this case, too, we were uncertain whether *Notogonidea* was invading the nest of *Odynerus* through a blunder or through mal-intent. This wasp hunts crickets, and she probably entered this hole in search of them.

Certain Diptera sometimes pester *Odynerus*. One two-celled nest, which we found apparently securely sealed, contained eight Diptera pupae.

On the same day on which we made the above discovery, September 18, we watched a small gray Dipteron, *Hilarella n. sp.* [C. H. T. Townsend], following an *O. dorsalis* which was homeward bound with her green caterpillar. The little fly tagged behind her most persistently, keeping just at a safe distance, a few inches to the rear of the wasp. It followed and poised in the air with all the skill which insects of their profession usually display. Both flew near to the ground, and if *O. dorsalis* rested for an instant, the fly would hover or poise on vibrating wings a few inches away; if the rest was prolonged, the fly would rest on the ground or a grass-blade nearby. It was pretty to see the shadow on the whitened earth of the two insects in the bright sunlight, moving in unison as if they were invisibly united. The wasp flew hither and thither in an evasive way in the region of her nest for fully twenty minutes before finally entering her hole. We have never seen another of these wasps experience such difficulty in locating her nest; can it be that this one spent this time and effort flying to and fro in an effort to evade her pursuer?

We have never witnessed the attack of the wasp upon the caterpillar, but, as Iseley says, they are stung and paralyzed. They keep fresh, plump and green, and usually respond to stimulus, writhe and void excrement for from three days to a week after their entombment; and we have had some which continued to live and remain plump for two or three weeks or even more. Following are some typical records which show the longevity of the prey (all caterpillars moving actively about when taken from the nest):

| | | | |
|---|---|---|---|
| Nest A. | 1 died after 8 days[6] | Nest *D.* | 1 died after 25 days |
| | 3 died after 15 days | | 1 died after 27 days |
| | 1 died after 25 days | Nest *E.* | 1 died after 6 days |
| Nest *B.* | 1 died after 12 days | | 1 died after 8 days |
| | 1 died after 14 days | | 1 died after 14 days |
| | 1 died after 19 days | Nest *F.* | 1 died after 3 days |
| | 1 died after 20 days | | 1 died after 5 days |
| Nest *C.* | 1 died after 3 days | | 1 died after 6 days |
| | 2 died after 6 days | | 1 died after 9 days |
| | 2 died after 9 days | | 1 died after 12 days |
| | 2 died after 10 days | | 1 died after 15 days |
| | 1 died after 14 days | | 1 died after 18 days |
| | 1 died after 22 days | | |
| | 1 died after 26 days | | |
| | 1 died after 29 days | | |

[6] The number of days after the nests were exhumed. Of course the number of days since their capture somewhat exceeds this.

The question arises apropos of this: does the acid of the sting serve in any way as a preserving fluid to keep the flesh in good condition? For certainly if we were to gather these caterpillars and shut them up without food they would starve to death and putrefy long before the length of time noted above had elapsed.

The delicate little egg is suspended by a short silken thread from the top or wall of the cell. Fabre would have us believe that this ingenious contrivance saves the egg from being crushed among the mass of heavy, writhing caterpillars in the lower part of the nest. This explanation appears very plausible, but we have found repeatedly that this protection is not absolutely necessary, for we have recklessly removed the egg from the cell and dropped it into a mass of squirming caterpillars in a vial; these eggs have always hatched and made thrifty larvae, often growing to adulthood. Although the tiny thread appears very delicate, it is astonishingly strong.

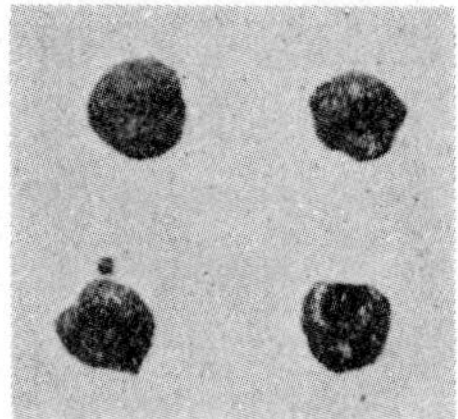

FIG. 64. After the feast. Empty heads of *Pholisora catullus* caterpillars—all that the *Odynerus* infant leaves.

By the day following oviposition, the egg has enlarged to twice its size and is of a golden yellow color, and usually it hatches on the second day. The little larva is then about 10 mm. in length, with transparent body walls and clear pale green contents, a very pretty little organism. It drops down upon the caterpillars and greedily devours them, one after another, not only sucking out the juices, but consuming the entire carcass, excepting the dry shell of the little black heads (see fig. 64, the remains of a feast). The supply of food provided by the mother for the growing infant varies greatly, but we have never ascertained whether that supply is sometimes actually inadequate or excessive, or whether the young merely accepts whatever is given it and gets through somehow. In our eagerness to keep alive all that we had at home for observation, we gave all of them additional food and it was almost always accepted greedily. Once we were so daring as to offer a fat, prosperous larva a small brown caterpillar instead of the customary green ones. The larva turned at once to this new fresh food, but mumbled about it mincingly for only a minute and then went back to resume chewing at its old half-eaten green carcass. We suspect that some of them are in real need of more food before they pupate, especially since some have as few as three little caterpillars upon which to subsist. We chanced to find one good-sized larva which must have been eating dirt, for the abdomen was full of earth. Yet overfeeding probably tends to make them overfat and delicate. We had one which was a thriving infant and promised to be a fine adult. After it had sucked dry seven caterpillars it was enormously large and fat. As we transferred it to a clean bottle, in the hope of seeing it spin its cocoon, we let the vial fall to the table, and the jar caused the body walls of the fatling to burst. Of course, in nature the larva runs no risk of such a catastrophe, and yet the circumstance suggests that overfeeding may make them, as well as other organisms, soft.

There is an astonishing degree of variation in the duration of the different periods of development in this species. There seems to be no fixed time for hatching, spinning or any of the functions. Moreover, we have not yet ascertained any causes, climatic, environmental or hereditary, to account for such variations. This variability will be easily noted from the tabulaton of a few typical cases, as follows:

| *Date of oviposition* | *Hatched* | *Finished feeding* | *Spun* |
|---|---|---|---|
| 9-10 | 5th day | | 14th day |
| 9-11 | 2d day | 8th day | 15th day |
| 9- 1 | 5th day | (injured | |
| 8-31 | 3d day | 10th day | 14th day |
| 9-11 | 3d day | | 15th day |
| 9- 1 | | 14th day | 18th day |
| 9- 1 | 6th day | | 15th day |
| 9- 1 | 6th day | 14th day | 15th day |
| 9-10 | 5th day | 14th day | |

On August 2 we exhumed a three-fourths grown larva, with its last caterpillar. We gave it three more, which it eagerly devoured. After five days more it began to spin. It was unable to construct its cocoon normally in the tin box; so we made in the box a nest of tiny bits of soft paper. After that it succeeded better in covering itself, but we could still see the insect within. Not until August 19, or twelve days after first spinning, did it transform into a mummy-like pupa within the web. On September 12, after a pupal period of thirty-six days, an adult female emerged. There is a possibility that the transformation of this individual may have been delayed by the impeded construction of the cocoon. This adult was kept in a cage and lived on sugar-water for eight days. This, too, would indicate that at least two generations emerge each year.

One of the perplexing problems is the question of how the wasp in the lower cell, when adult, can emerge without injuring its younger brother in the cell above. To be sure, they probably lie dormant all winter and are ready for emergence at approximately the same time in the following spring; and yet we cannot see how even then they could make their way out without often coming into disastrous collision. This may account, in part, for the large number of dead adults of this species more than of *B. nubilipennis,* which we have dug out in the spring. We have never ascertained whether these dead wasps are the young adults which never found their way out to the light of day, or wasps of the parent generation which may have died while sleeping in their burrows or may have been entombed by the mud of heavy rains.

The variation in the periods of development mentioned above may help to clear up this conflict of the emerging wasps, or again it may only add to the confusion. This point was suggested to us by a certain burrow, an exceptional nest in this vicinity in that it had three cells (fig. 62). We dug it up just after the top cell had been closed. One would logically expect to find the occupant of the lowermost cell of the tier the largest, but we were surprised to find the larva in the middle cell large, the bottom one small and the uppermost still of course in the egg stage. How this state of affairs could have come about remains a mystery.[7] We wanted to follow up this development, but the lowest larva died. However, when they arrived at the stage of pupation, the middle or largest one spun its cocoon only three days earlier than the smallest one (which was still in the egg stage when we found it). Hence we may believe that the difference in the date of maturation of these and the intermediate one would have been even less.

Fabre finds that, in certain bees, one sex hatches earlier than the other, and the mother can control the sex of the

[7] The fact that the foregoing table shows the incubation of the egg to vary from 2 to 6 days may mean a correlation of the period to the sex of the developing larva.

eggs so that the one to emerge first is deposited in the uppermost cell; thus it can emerge first and leave the way clear for the second inmate of the nest. We have as yet no intimation as to whether or not such a condition may hold in *Odynerus*.

The season for *O. dorsalis* seems to be from about the middle of July or the first of August to the middle of September, but stragglers are occasionally seen outside the limits of those dates. The earliest individual seen was out on July 2.

*Odynerus anormis* Say [S. A. Rohwer].

On July 22, we carried home a hollow stem which bore evidence of being occupied. Mud partitions divided the pith-chamber in the stem into five cells. From these cells, five *Odynerus anormis* emerged, from July 24 to 26. The top of the cavity was not sealed, but was open for about an inch; in this space we found Diptera puparia, which on the next day gave forth adults of *Sarcomacronychia trivittata* Townsend [C .H. T. Townsend]. We could not tell whether these were there accidentally or whether the life history of this fly is interlinked with that of *O. anormis*.

At Lake View, Kansas, a little later in the season, we saw two specimens of this wasp, and watched them for over a half-hour, as they ran about constantly prying into holes in the sand and often entering them. They showed no discrimination regarding the size of the hole; sometimes the holes were those of very small bees, and sometimes quite large like *Bembix* burrows. We suspect that they were foraging.

The Peckhams[8] find this species making nests in stalks and using caterpillars for provisions, although the species

[8] Wasps, Social and Solitary, p. 91. 1905.

of the prey is not mentioned; it might be that she uses subterranean caterpillars, since our notes show that she enters numerous holes in a foraging manner.

Robertson finds the adults frequenting many species of flowers.

*Odynerus designatus* Cress. [S. A. Rohwer].

Two of these Eumenid wasps were found fast asleep on a pig-weed at 4:30 p. m. on August 28. Both were curled around leaf petioles. At 4 a. m. the following day, it rained, and rain continued to fall until 10 o'clock. At 9:30 in the morning, they were in the identical places and positions, and dripping wet. The rain had not aroused them to activity in the least; on the contrary, they were in a kind of stupor which rendered them very easy to pick up. They were not alone in their misery. Nearby were found a number of other insects, *Pelopoeus caementarium,* May beetles and others, behaving similarly.

*Odynerus pedestris* Sauss. [S. A. Rohwer].

On a clay bank (see fig. 27), rising about six feet above the level of the ground, we saw, on October 3, this Eumenid entering and leaving an open hole at intervals. After catching her, we dug up the nest; this was of the exact size of the drawing in figure 65.

This wasp makes a gallery and, from time to time, constructs chambers beneath it, as they are needed, similar to the manner of *Philanthus sp.,* except that the latter usually builds them from the sides of the gallery, whereas this one builds the gallery, drops a branch of it to a chamber, continues the gallery and makes another chamber therefrom, and so on.

The first cell that this one had made, the one nearest the orifice, contained a half-grown larva and four greenish-blue caterpillars, all of one species of Gelechiidae [S. B. Fracker], (the larva was too immature to determine the species). The next cell contained six specimens of the same Lepidopterous larva, and hanging by a tiny thread from

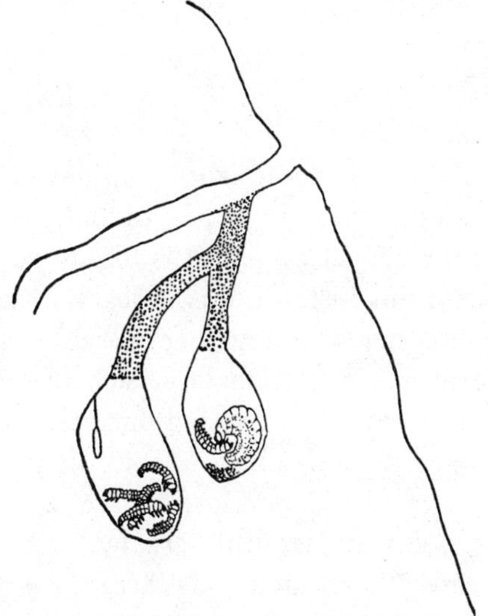

FIG. 65. The nest of *Odynerus pedestris,* in a clay bank. Natural size.

the wall was the egg. The small, petiole-like gallery that led from the main gallery to this was tightly packed with soil, and the continuation of the main channel in a parallel direction led us to think that a third cell was about to be hollowed out of the end of this gallery. One has not far to seek to suspect that the earth that is removed in the digging of the new gallery and cell is used for the filling of the short neck of the cell just provisioned.

The fat larva which we captured in the first cell ate all it could find, and also two caterpillars that we gave it from the other cell. The next day, when we introduced a large one we found in the field, it made a brave effort to eat this; but its strength proved unequal to coping with its tough skin and its wriggling activity. Two days later the larva died.

No details of biological significance could be found in the literature on this wasp.

*Odynerus foraminatus* Sauss. [S. A. Rohwer].

The first *Odynerus foraminatus* with which we became acquainted were nesting in a pile of old, weathered logs. They are solitary dwellers, and it is highly doubtful if they live in colonies; this instance was probably a case of a number of them nesting near together merely because the site afforded the proper conditions for each one.

One wasp in particular attracted our attention. She had her burrow in a log twelve inches from the ground. Twice she entered; then we crept close to see what she was so mysteriously doing in her little cranny. She had about a half-dozen caterpillars, and was arranging and packing them close together, until they were forced so deep into the hole that they were out of sight. Then she left, and soon returned with a moist pellet of gray fire-clay and used it inside the hole, probably for a partition. She brought a second load; then we took her, to ascertain her identity.

Nearby were other nests of this kind (see fig. 66), which were similarly situated. As we watched one, the wasp's behavior took a most remarkable form. We are certain that our presence did not cause it, for we were careful not to intrude. Without apparent cause, she carried out four caterpillars, one at a time, and dropped them in the road six feet away. We followed and found one of them; it was *Enarmonia sp.*, of the family Tortricidae [S. B.

Fracker]. In bringing out the last caterpillar, another, the fifth, was dislodged and jostled to the opening of the hole. When she returned, she carefully took this back into the

FIG. 66. *Odynerus foraminatus* and her home in the log. Insect and opening to burrow exact size.

THE PRINCIPLES OF PSYCHOLOGY,
*William James*
The full long-course, unabridged, of one of the great classics of Western literature and science. Wonderfully lucid descriptions of human mental activity, the stream of thought, consciousness, time perception, memory, imagination, emotions, reason, abnormal phenomena, and similar topics. Original contributions are integrated with the work of such men as Berkeley, Binet, Mills, Darwin, Hume, Kant, Royce, Schopenhauer, Spinoza, Locke, Descartes, Galton, Wundt, Lotze, Herbart, Fechner, and scores of others. All contrasting interpretations of mental phenomena are examined in detail—introspective analysis, philosophical interpretation, and experimental research. "A classic," *Journal of Consulting Psychology*. "The main lines are as valid as ever," *Psychoanalytical Quarterly*. "Standard reading . . . a classic of interpretation," *Psychiatric Quarterly*. 94 illustrations. 1408pp. 5⅜ x 8.
20381-6, 20382-4 Two volume set, paperbound $6.00

VISUAL ILLUSIONS: THEIR CAUSES, CHARACTERISTICS AND APPLICATIONS,
*M. Luckiesh*
"Seeing is deceiving," asserts the author of this introduction to virtually every type of optical illusion known. The text both describes and explains the principles involved in color illusions, figure-ground, distance illusions, etc. 100 photographs, drawings and diagrams prove how easy it is to fool the sense: circles that aren't round, parallel lines that seem to bend, stationary figures that seem to move as you stare at them – illustration after illustration strains our credulity at what we see. Fascinating book from many points of view, from applications for artists, in camouflage, etc. to the psychology of vision. New introduction by William Ittleson, Dept. of Psychology, Queens College. Index. Bibliography. xxi + 252pp. 5⅜ x 8½. 21530-X Paperbound $1.50

FADS AND FALLACIES IN THE NAME OF SCIENCE,
*Martin Gardner*
This is the standard account of various cults, quack systems, and delusions which have masqueraded as science: hollow earth fanatics. Reich and orgone sex energy, dianetics, Atlantis, multiple moons, Forteanism, flying saucers, medical fallacies like iridiagnosis, zone therapy, etc. A new chapter has been added on Bridey Murphy, psionics, and other recent manifestations in this field. This is a fair, reasoned appraisal of eccentric theory which provides excellent inoculation against cleverly masked nonsense. "Should be read by everyone, scientist and non-scientist alike," R. T. Birge, Prof. Emeritus of Physics, Univ. of California; Former President, American Physical Society. Index. x + 365pp. 5⅜ x 8. 20394-8 Paperbound $2.00

ILLUSIONS AND DELUSIONS OF THE SUPERNATURAL AND THE OCCULT,
*D. H. Rawcliffe*
Holds up to rational examination hundreds of persistent delusions including crystal gazing, automatic writing, table turning, mediumistic trances, mental healing, stigmata, lycanthropy, live burial, the Indian Rope Trick, spiritualism, dowsing, telepathy, clairvoyance, ghosts, ESP, etc. The author explains and exposes the mental and physical deceptions involved, making this not only an exposé of supernatural phenomena, but a valuable exposition of characteristic types of abnormal psychology. Originally titled "The Psychology of the Occult." 14 illustrations. Index. 551pp. 5⅜ x 8. 20503-7 Paperbound $3.50

FAIRY TALE COLLECTIONS, *edited by Andrew Lang*
Andrew Lang's fairy tale collections make up the richest shelf-full of traditional children's stories anywhere available. Lang supervised the translation of stories from all over the world—familiar European tales collected by Grimm, animal stories from Negro Africa, myths of primitive Australia, stories from Russia, Hungary, Iceland, Japan, and many other countries. Lang's selection of translations are unusually high; many authorities consider that the most familiar tales find their best versions in these volumes. All collections are richly decorated and illustrated by H. J. Ford and other artists.

THE BLUE FAIRY BOOK. 37 stories. 138 illustrations. ix + 390pp. 5⅜ x 8½.
21437-0 Paperbound $1.95

THE GREEN FAIRY BOOK. 42 stories. 100 illustrations. xiii + 366pp. 5⅜ x 8½.
21439-7 Paperbound $1.75

THE BROWN FAIRY BOOK. 32 stories. 50 illustrations, 8 in color. xii + 350pp. 5⅜ x 8½.
21438-9 Paperbound $1.95

THE BEST TALES OF HOFFMANN, *edited by E. F. Bleiler*
10 stories by E. T. A. Hoffmann, one of the greatest of all writers of fantasy. The tales include "The Golden Flower Pot," "Automata," "A New Year's Eve Adventure," "Nutcracker and the King of Mice," "Sand-Man," and others. Vigorous characterizations of highly eccentric personalities, remarkably imaginative situations, and intensely fast pacing has made these tales popular all over the world for 150 years. Editor's introduction. 7 drawings by Hoffmann. xxxiii + 419pp. 5⅜ x 8½.
21793-0 Paperbound $2.25

GHOST AND HORROR STORIES OF AMBROSE BIERCE, *edited by E. F. Bleiler*
Morbid, eerie, horrifying tales of possessed poets, shabby aristocrats, revived corpses, and haunted malefactors. Widely acknowledged as the best of their kind between Poe and the moderns, reflecting their author's inner torment and bitter view of life. Includes "Damned Thing," "The Middle Toe of the Right Foot," "The Eyes of the Panther," "Visions of the Night," "Moxon's Master," and over a dozen others. Editor's introduction. xxii + 199pp. 5⅜ x 8½.
20767-6 Paperbound $1.50

THREE GOTHIC NOVELS, *edited by E. F. Bleiler*
Originators of the still popular Gothic novel form, influential in ushering in early 19th-century Romanticism. Horace Walpole's *Castle of Otranto*, William Beckford's *Vathek*, John Polidori's *The Vampyre*, and a *Fragment* by Lord Byron are enjoyable as exciting reading or as documents in the history of English literature. Editor's introduction. xi + 291pp. 5⅜ x 8½.
21232-7 Paperbound $2.00

BEST GHOST STORIES OF LEFANU, *edited by E. F. Bleiler*
Though admired by such critics as V. S. Pritchett, Charles Dickens and Henry James, ghost stories by the Irish novelist Joseph Sheridan LeFanu have never become as widely known as his detective fiction. About half of the 16 stories in this collection have never before been available in America. Collection includes "Carmilla" (perhaps the best vampire story ever written), "The Haunted Baronet," "The Fortunes of Sir Robert Ardagh," and the classic "Green Tea." Editor's introduction. 7 contemporary illustrations. Portrait of LeFanu. xii + 467pp. 5⅜ x 8.
20415-4 Paperbound $2.50

EASY-TO-DO ENTERTAINMENTS AND DIVERSIONS WITH COINS, CARDS, STRING, PAPER AND MATCHES, *R. M. Abraham*

Over 300 tricks, games and puzzles will provide young readers with absorbing fun. Sections on card games; paper-folding; tricks with coins, matches and pieces of string; games for the agile; toy-making from common household objects; mathematical recreations; and 50 miscellaneous pastimes. Anyone in charge of groups of youngsters, including hard-pressed parents, and in need of suggestions on how to keep children sensibly amused and quietly content will find this book indispensable. Clear, simple text, copious number of delightful line drawings and illustrative diagrams. Originally titled "Winter Nights' Entertainments." Introduction by Lord Baden Powell. 329 illustrations. v + 186pp. 5⅜ x 8½. 20921-0 Paperbound $1.00

AN INTRODUCTION TO CHESS MOVES AND TACTICS SIMPLY EXPLAINED, *Leonard Barden*

Beginner's introduction to the royal game. Names, possible moves of the pieces, definitions of essential terms, how games are won, etc. explained in 30-odd pages. With this background you'll be able to sit right down and play. Balance of book teaches strategy — openings, middle game, typical endgame play, and suggestions for improving your game. A sample game is fully analyzed. True middle-level introduction, teaching you all the essentials without oversimplifying or losing you in a maze of detail. 58 figures. 102pp. 5⅜ x 8½. 21210-6 Paperbound $1.25

LASKER'S MANUAL OF CHESS, *Dr. Emanuel Lasker*

Probably the greatest chess player of modern times, Dr. Emanuel Lasker held the world championship 28 years, independent of passing schools or fashions. This unmatched study of the game, chiefly for intermediate to skilled players, analyzes basic methods, combinations, position play, the aesthetics of chess, dozens of different openings, etc., with constant reference to great modern games. Contains a brilliant exposition of Steinitz's important theories. Introduction by Fred Reinfeld. Tables of Lasker's tournament record. 3 indices. 308 diagrams. 1 photograph. xxx + 349pp. 5⅜ x 8.20640-8Paperbound $2.50

COMBINATIONS: THE HEART OF CHESS, *Irving Chernev*

Step-by-step from simple combinations to complex, this book, by a well-known chess writer, shows you the intricacies of pins, counter-pins, knight forks, and smothered mates. Other chapters show alternate lines of play to those taken in actual championship games; boomerang combinations; classic examples of brilliant combination play by Nimzovich, Rubinstein, Tarrasch, Botvinnik, Alekhine and Capablanca. Index. 356 diagrams. ix + 245pp. 5⅜ x 8½. 21744-2 Paperbound $2.00

HOW TO SOLVE CHESS PROBLEMS, *K. S. Howard*

Full of practical suggestions for the fan or the beginner — who knows only the moves of the chessmen. Contains preliminary section and 58 two-move, 46 three-move, and 8 four-move problems composed by 27 outstanding American problem creators in the last 30 years. Explanation of all terms and exhaustive index. "Just what is wanted for the student," Brian Harley. 112 problems, solutions. vi + 171pp. 5⅜ x 8. 20748-X Paperbound $1.50

SOCIAL THOUGHT FROM LORE TO SCIENCE,
*H. E. Barnes and H. Becker*
An immense survey of sociological thought and ways of viewing, studying, planning, and reforming society from earliest times to the present. Includes thought on society of preliterate peoples, ancient non-Western cultures, and every great movement in Europe, America, and modern Japan. Analyzes hundreds of great thinkers: Plato, Augustine, Bodin, Vico, Montesquieu, Herder, Comte, Marx, etc. Weighs the contributions of utopians, sophists, fascists and communists; economists, jurists, philosophers, ecclesiastics, and every 19th and 20th century school of scientific sociology, anthropology, and social psychology throughout the world. Combines topical, chronological, and regional approaches, treating the evolution of social thought as a process rather than as a series of mere topics. "Impressive accuracy, competence, and discrimination . . . easily the best single survey," *Nation*. Thoroughly revised, with new material up to 1960. 2 indexes. Over 2200 bibliographical notes. Three volume set. Total of 1586pp. 5⅜ x 8.
20901-6, 20902-4, 20903-2 Three volume set, paperbound $9.00

A HISTORY OF HISTORICAL WRITING, *Harry Elmer Barnes*
Virtually the only adequate survey of the whole course of historical writing in a single volume. Surveys developments from the beginnings of historiography in the ancient Near East and the Classical World, up through the Cold War. Covers major historians in detail, shows interrelationship with cultural background, makes clear individual contributions, evaluates and estimates importance; also enormously rich upon minor authors and thinkers who are usually passed over. Packed with scholarship and learning, clear, easily written. Indispensable to every student of history. Revised and enlarged up to 1961. Index and bibliography. xv + 442pp. 5⅜ x 8½.
20104-X Paperbound $2.75

JOHANN SEBASTIAN BACH, *Philipp Spitta*
The complete and unabridged text of the definitive study of Bach. Written some 70 years ago, it is still unsurpassed for its coverage of nearly all aspects of Bach's life and work. There could hardly be a finer non-technical introduction to Bach's music than the detailed, lucid analyses which Spitta provides for hundreds of individual pieces. 26 solid pages are devoted to the B minor mass, for example, and 30 pages to the glorious St. Matthew Passion. This monumental set also includes a major analysis of the music of the 18th century: Buxtehude, Pachelbel, etc. "Unchallenged as the last word on one of the supreme geniuses of music," John Barkham, *Saturday Review Syndicate*. Total of 1819pp. Heavy cloth binding. 5⅜ x 8.
22278-0, 22279-9 Two volume set, clothbound $15.00

BEETHOVEN AND HIS NINE SYMPHONIES, *George Grove*
In this modern middle-level classic of musicology Grove not only analyzes all nine of Beethoven's symphonies very thoroughly in terms of their musical structure, but also discusses the circumstances under which they were written, Beethoven's stylistic development, and much other background material. This is an extremely rich book, yet very easily followed; it is highly recommended to anyone seriously interested in music. Over 250 musical passages. Index. viii + 407pp. 5⅜ x 8.
20334-4 Paperbound $2.25

THREE SCIENCE FICTION NOVELS,
*John Taine*

Acknowledged by many as the best SF writer of the 1920's, Taine (under the name Eric Temple Bell) was also a Professor of Mathematics of considerable renown. Reprinted here are *The Time Stream,* generally considered Taine's best, *The Greatest Game,* a biological-fiction novel, and *The Purple Sapphire,* involving a supercivilization of the past. Taine's stories tie fantastic narratives to frameworks of original and logical scientific concepts. Speculation is often profound on such questions as the nature of time, concept of entropy, cyclical universes, etc. 4 contemporary illustrations. v + 532pp. 5⅜ x 8⅜.
21180-0 Paperbound $2.50

SEVEN SCIENCE FICTION NOVELS,
*H. G. Wells*

Full unabridged texts of 7 science-fiction novels of the master. Ranging from biology, physics, chemistry, astronomy, to sociology and other studies, Mr. Wells extrapolates whole worlds of strange and intriguing character. "One will have to go far to match this for entertainment, excitement, and sheer pleasure . . ."*New York Times.* Contents: The Time Machine, The Island of Dr. Moreau, The First Men in the Moon, The Invisible Man, The War of the Worlds, The Food of the Gods, In The Days of the Comet. 1015pp. 5⅜ x 8.
20264-X Clothbound $5.00

28 SCIENCE FICTION STORIES OF H. G. WELLS.

Two full, unabridged novels, *Men Like Gods* and *Star Begotten,* plus 26 short stories by the master science-fiction writer of all time! Stories of space, time, invention, exploration, futuristic adventure. Partial contents: *The Country of the Blind, In the Abyss, The Crystal Egg, The Man Who Could Work Miracles, A Story of Days to Come, The Empire of the Ants, The Magic Shop, The Valley of the Spiders, A Story of the Stone Age, Under the Knife, Sea Raiders,* etc. An indispensable collection for the library of anyone interested in science fiction adventure. 928pp. 5⅜ x 8. 20265-8 Clothbound $5.00

THREE MARTIAN NOVELS,
*Edgar Rice Burroughs*

Complete, unabridged reprinting, in one volume, of Thuvia, Maid of Mars; Chessmen of Mars; The Master Mind of Mars. Hours of science-fiction adventure by a modern master storyteller. Reset in large clear type for easy reading. 16 illustrations by J. Allen St. John. vi + 490pp. 5⅜ x 8½.
20039-6 Paperbound $2.50

AN INTELLECTUAL AND CULTURAL HISTORY OF THE WESTERN WORLD,
*Harry Elmer Barnes*

Monumental 3-volume survey of intellectual development of Europe from primitive cultures to the present day. Every significant product of human intellect traced through history: art, literature, mathematics, physical sciences, medicine, music, technology, social sciences, religions, jurisprudence, education, etc. Presentation is lucid and specific, analyzing in detail specific discoveries, theories, literary works, and so on. Revised (1965) by recognized scholars in specialized fields under the direction of Prof. Barnes. Revised bibliography. Indexes. 24 illustrations. Total of xxix + 1318pp.
21275-0, 21276-9, 21277-7 Three volume set, paperbound $8.25

HEAR ME TALKIN' TO YA, *edited by Nat Shapiro and Nat Hentoff* In their own words, Louis Armstrong, King Oliver, Fletcher Henderson, Bunk Johnson, Bix Beiderbecke, Billy Holiday, Fats Waller, Jelly Roll Morton, Duke Ellington, and many others comment on the origins of jazz in New Orleans and its growth in Chicago's South Side, Kansas City's jam sessions, Depression Harlem, and the modernism of the West Coast schools. Taken from taped conversations, letters, magazine articles, other first-hand sources. Editors' introduction. xvi + 429pp. 5⅜ x 8½. 21726-4 Paperbound $2.00

THE JOURNAL OF HENRY D. THOREAU
A 25-year record by the great American observer and critic, as complete a record of a great man's inner life as is anywhere available. Thoreau's Journals served him as raw material for his formal pieces, as a place where he could develop his ideas, as an outlet for his interests in wild life and plants, in writing as an art, in classics of literature, Walt Whitman and other contemporaries, in politics, slavery, individual's relation to the State, etc. The Journals present a portrait of a remarkable man, and are an observant social history. Unabridged republication of 1906 edition, Bradford Torrey and Francis H. Allen, editors. Illustrations. Total of 1888pp. 8⅜ x 12¼.
20312-3, 20313-1 Two volume set, clothbound $30.00

A SHAKESPEARIAN GRAMMAR, *E. A. Abbott*
Basic reference to Shakespeare and his contemporaries, explaining through thousands of quotations from Shakespeare, Jonson, Beaumont and Fletcher, North's *Plutarch* and other sources the grammatical usage differing from the modern. First published in 1870 and written by a scholar who spent much of his life isolating principles of Elizabethan language, the book is unlikely ever to be superseded. Indexes. xxiv + 511pp. 5⅜ x 8½. 21582-2 Paperbound $3.00

FOLK-LORE OF SHAKESPEARE, *T. F. Thistelton Dyer*
Classic study, drawing from Shakespeare a large body of references to supernatural beliefs, terminology of falconry and hunting, games and sports, good luck charms, marriage customs, folk medicines, superstitions about plants, animals, birds, argot of the underworld, sexual slang of London, proverbs, drinking customs, weather lore, and much else. From full compilation comes a mirror of the 17th-century popular mind. Index. ix + 526pp. 5⅜ x 8½.
21614-4 Paperbound $2.75

THE NEW VARIORUM SHAKESPEARE, *edited by H. H. Furness*
By far the richest editions of the plays ever produced in any country or language. Each volume contains complete text (usually First Folio) of the play, all variants in Quarto and other Folio texts, editorial changes by every major editor to Furness's own time (1900), footnotes to obscure references or language, extensive quotes from literature of Shakespearian criticism, essays on plot sources (often reprinting sources in full), and much more.

HAMLET, *edited by H. H. Furness*
Total of xxvi + 905pp. 5⅜ x 8½.
21004-9, 21005-7 Two volume set, paperbound $5.25

TWELFTH NIGHT, *edited by H. H. Furness*
Index. xxii + 434pp. 5⅜ x 8½. 21189-4 Paperbound $2.75

LA BOHEME BY GIACOMO PUCCINI,
*translated and introduced by Ellen H. Bleiler*

Complete handbook for the operagoer, with everything needed for full enjoyment except the musical score itself. Complete Italian libretto, with new, modern English line-by-line translation—the only libretto printing all repeats; biography of Puccini; the librettists; background to the opera, Murger's La Boheme, etc.; circumstances of composition and performances; plot summary; and pictorial section of 73 illustrations showing Puccini, famous singers and performances, etc. Large clear type for easy reading. 124pp. 5⅜ x 8½.
20404-9 Paperbound $1.25

ANTONIO STRADIVARI: HIS LIFE AND WORK (1644-1737),
*W. Henry Hill, Arthur F. Hill, and Alfred E. Hill*

Still the only book that really delves into life and art of the incomparable Italian craftsman, maker of the finest musical instruments in the world today. The authors, expert violin-makers themselves, discuss Stradivari's ancestry, his construction and finishing techniques, distinguished characteristics of many of his instruments and their locations. Included, too, is story of introduction of his instruments into France, England, first revelation of their supreme merit, and information on his labels, number of instruments made, prices, mystery of ingredients of his varnish, tone of pre-1684 Stradivari violin and changes between 1684 and 1690. An extremely interesting, informative account for all music lovers, from craftsman to concert-goer. Republication of original (1902) edition. New introduction by Sydney Beck, Head of Rare Book and Manuscript Collections, Music Division, New York Public Library. Analytical index by Rembert Wurlitzer. Appendixes. 68 illustrations. 30 full-page plates. 4 in color. xxvi + 315pp. 5⅜ x 8½. 20425-1 Paperbound $2.25

MUSICAL AUTOGRAPHS FROM MONTEVERDI TO HINDEMITH,
*Emanuel Winternitz*

For beauty, for intrinsic interest, for perspective on the composer's personality, for subtleties of phrasing, shading, emphasis indicated in the autograph but suppressed in the printed score, the mss. of musical composition are fascinating documents which repay close study in many different ways. This 2-volume work reprints facsimiles of mss. by virtually every major composer, and many minor figures—196 examples in all. A full text points out what can be learned from mss., analyzes each sample. Index. Bibliography. 18 figures. 196 plates. Total of 170pp. of text. 7⅞ x 10¾.
21312-9, 21313-7 Two volume set, paperbound $5.00

J. S. BACH,
*Albert Schweitzer*

One of the few great full-length studies of Bach's life and work, and the study upon which Schweitzer's renown as a musicologist rests. On first appearance (1911), revolutionized Bach performance. The only writer on Bach to be musicologist, performing musician, and student of history, theology and philosophy, Schweitzer contributes particularly full sections on history of German Protestant church music, theories on motivic pictorial representations in vocal music, and practical suggestions for performance. Translated by Ernest Newman. Indexes. 5 illustrations. 650 musical examples. Total of xix + 928pp. 5⅜ x 8½. 21631-4, 21632-2 Two volume set, paperbound $4.50

THE METHODS OF ETHICS, *Henry Sidgwick*
Propounding no organized system of its own, study subjects every major methodological approach to ethics to rigorous, objective analysis. Study discusses and relates ethical thought of Plato, Aristotle, Bentham, Clarke, Butler, Hobbes, Hume, Mill, Spencer, Kant, and dozens of others. Sidgwick retains conclusions from each system which follow from ethical premises, rejecting the faulty. Considered by many in the field to be among the most important treatises on ethical philosophy. Appendix. Index. xlvii + 528pp. 5⅜ x 8½.
21608-X Paperbound $2.50

TEUTONIC MYTHOLOGY, *Jakob Grimm*
A milestone in Western culture; the work which established on a modern basis the study of history of religions and comparative religions. 4-volume work assembles and interprets everything available on religious and folkloristic beliefs of Germanic people (including Scandinavians, Anglo-Saxons, etc.). Assembling material from such sources as Tacitus, surviving Old Norse and Icelandic texts, archeological remains, folktales, surviving superstitions, comparative traditions, linguistic analysis, etc. Grimm explores pagan deities, heroes, folklore of nature, religious practices, and every other area of pagan German belief. To this day, the unrivaled, definitive, exhaustive study. Translated by J. S. Stallybrass from 4th (1883) German edition. Indexes. Total of lxxvii + 1887pp. 5⅜ x 8½.
21602-0, 21603-9, 21604-7, 21605-5 Four volume set, paperbound $11.00

THE I CHING, *translated by James Legge*
Called "The Book of Changes" in English, this is one of the Five Classics edited by Confucius, basic and central to Chinese thought. Explains perhaps the most complex system of divination known, founded on the theory that all things happening at any one time have characteristic features which can be isolated and related. Significant in Oriental studies, in history of religions and philosophy, and also to Jungian psychoanalysis and other areas of modern European thought. Index. Appendixes. 6 plates. xxi + 448pp. 5⅜ x 8½.
21062-6 Paperbound $2.75

HISTORY OF ANCIENT PHILOSOPHY, *W. Windelband*
One of the clearest, most accurate comprehensive surveys of Greek and Roman philosophy. Discusses ancient philosophy in general, intellectual life in Greece in the 7th and 6th centuries B.C., Thales, Anaximander, Anaximenes, Heraclitus, the Eleatics, Empedocles, Anaxagoras, Leucippus, the Pythagoreans, the Sophists, Socrates, Democritus (20 pages), Plato (50 pages), Aristotle (70 pages), the Peripatetics, Stoics, Epicureans, Sceptics, Neo-platonists, Christian Apologists, etc. 2nd German edition translated by H. E. Cushman. xv + 393pp. 5⅜ x 8.
20357-3 Paperbound $2.25

THE PALACE OF PLEASURE, *William Painter*
Elizabethan versions of Italian and French novels from *The Decameron*, Cinthio, Straparola, Queen Margaret of Navarre, and other continental sources — the very work that provided Shakespeare and dozens of his contemporaries with many of their plots and sub-plots and, therefore, justly considered one of the most influential books in all English literature. It is also a book that any reader will still enjoy. Total of cviii + 1,224pp.
21691-8, 21692-6, 21693-4 Three volume set, paperbound $6.75

THE WONDERFUL WIZARD OF OZ, *L. F. Baum*
All the original W. W. Denslow illustrations in full color—as much a part of "The Wizard" as Tenniel's drawings are of "Alice in Wonderland." "The Wizard" is still America's best-loved fairy tale, in which, as the author expresses it, "The wonderment and joy are retained and the heartaches and nightmares left out." Now today's young readers can enjoy every word and wonderful picture of the original book. New introduction by Martin Gardner. A Baum bibliography. 23 full-page color plates. viii + 268pp. 5⅜ x 8.
20691-2 Paperbound $1.95

THE MARVELOUS LAND OF OZ, *L. F. Baum*
This is the equally enchanting sequel to the "Wizard," continuing the adventures of the Scarecrow and the Tin Woodman. The hero this time is a little boy named Tip, and all the delightful Oz magic is still present. This is the Oz book with the Animated Saw-Horse, the Woggle-Bug, and Jack Pumpkinhead. All the original John R. Neill illustrations, 10 in full color. 287pp. 5⅜ x 8.
20692-0 Paperbound $1.75

ALICE'S ADVENTURES UNDER GROUND, *Lewis Carroll*
The original *Alice in Wonderland*, hand-lettered and illustrated by Carroll himself, and originally presented as a Christmas gift to a child-friend. Adults as well as children will enjoy this charming volume, reproduced faithfully in this Dover edition. While the story is essentially the same, there are slight changes, and Carroll's spritely drawings present an intriguing alternative to the famous Tenniel illustrations. One of the most popular books in Dover's catalogue. Introduction by Martin Gardner. 38 illustrations. 128pp. 5⅜ x 8½.
21482-6 Paperbound $1.00

THE NURSERY "ALICE," *Lewis Carroll*
While most of us consider *Alice in Wonderland* a story for children of all ages, Carroll himself felt it was beyond younger children. He therefore provided this simplified version, illustrated with the famous Tenniel drawings enlarged and colored in delicate tints, for children aged "from Nought to Five." Dover's edition of this now rare classic is a faithful copy of the 1889 printing, including 20 illustrations by Tenniel, and front and back covers reproduced in full color. Introduction by Martin Gardner. xxiii + 67pp. 6⅛ x 9¼.
21610-1 Paperbound $1.75

THE STORY OF KING ARTHUR AND HIS KNIGHTS, *Howard Pyle*
A fast-paced, exciting retelling of the best known Arthurian legends for young readers by one of America's best story tellers and illustrators. The sword Excalibur, wooing of Guinevere, Merlin and his downfall, adventures of Sir Pellias and Gawaine, and others. The pen and ink illustrations are vividly imagined and wonderfully drawn. 41 illustrations. xviii + 313pp. 6⅛ x 9¼.
21445-1 Paperbound $2.00

*Prices subject to change without notice.*

Available at your book dealer or write for free catalogue to Dept. Adsci, Dover Publications, Inc., 180 Varick St., N.Y., N.Y. 10014. Dover publishes more than 150 books each year on science, elementary and advanced mathematics, biology, music, art, literary history, social sciences and other areas.